AN ENGLISH CANADIAN POETICS

VOLUME I: THE CONFEDERATION POETS

EDITED BY ROBERT HOGG

Talonbooks

Talonbooks
P.O. Box 2076, Vancouver, British Columbia, Canada V6B 3S3
www.talonbooks.com

Typeset in Scala and printed and bound in Canada.
Printed on 100% post-consumer recycled paper.

First Printing: 2009

The publisher gratefully acknowledges the financial support of the Canada Council
for the Arts; the Government of Canada through the Book Publishing Industry
Development Program; and the Province of British Columbia through the British
Columbia Arts Council and the Book Publishing Tax Credit for our publishing
activities.

LIBRARY AND ARCHIVES CANADA CATALOGUING IN PUBLICATION

 An English Canadian poetics / edited by Robert Hogg ; with an
introduction by D.M.R. Bentley.

Includes bibliographical references.
Contents: v. 1. The Confederation poets.
ISBN 978-0-88922-613-5 (v. 1)

 1. Canadian poetry (English)—History and criticism. 2. Poetics.
I. Hogg, Robert, 1942-

PS8143.E54 2009   C811.009   C2008-906407-0

Contents

difficult to access texts. Aalya Ahmad provided an invaluable service in the former, and Chris Turnbull did much to help organize the long list of authors, titles, dates and places of first publication for the entire project. Thanks to you both for doing the tedious background work with such good will, and for the accuracy and care you took in providing me with workable materials.

Needless to say, no project of this order could be accomplished without the many authors, editors and publishers who initially or secondarily brought the materials to print. In the case of the Confederation Poets, all materials are now in the public domain and permissions for the original work were therefore unnecessary. However, I have drawn several pieces from two compilations from the 1970s for this first volume, and have relied on the expertise of their editors whose comments greatly clarified the texts. Permissions are gratefully acknowledged to University of Toronto Press and their editors for material drawn from Barrie Davies, ed., *At the Mermaid Inn: Wilfred Campbell, Archibald Lampman, Duncan Campbell Scott in The Globe 1892–93*, 1979. These include short essays by Wilfred Campbell: 90–92, 185–86, 263–64, 277–79, 331–34 and 341–43; short essays by Archibald Lampman: 10, 44–45, 97–98, 125–26, 152–53 and 180–82; and one essay by Duncan Campbell Scott: 182–83. Permissions are also acknowledged for reprinting essays from: W.J. Keith, ed., *Selected Poetry and Critical Prose—Charles G.D. Roberts*, University of Toronto Press, 1974. These include the following essays by Roberts: "The Outlook for Literature: Acadia's Field for Poetry, History and Romance," 260–64; "Pastoral Elegies or Shelley's 'Adonais,'"282–95; "The Poetry of Nature," 276–81; "A Note on Modernism," 296–301; and "From the Prefatory Note to *Selected Poems*, 1936," 302–03. I would also like to thank Wilfrid Laurier Press and Laurel Boone for permission to reprint the short introduction by Wilfred Campbell found in Laurel Boone, ed., *William Wilfred Campbell: Selected Poetry and Essays*, Wilfred Laurier University Press, 1987, 179–80. Marian (Bourinot) Dickie, a distant cousin and possibly the last living relative of Arthur S. Bourinot, has granted permission to reprint Lampman's essay, "Happiness," which Bourinot reprinted in his privately published *Archibald Lampman's Letters to Edward William Thomson*, 1956, 48–52. Permission from McClelland and Stewart to reprint Duncan Campbell Scott's "Poetry and Progress" from his *The Circle of Affection and Other Pieces in Prose and Verse*, 1947, 123–47 is also deeply appreciated. D.M.R. Bentley has generously offered primary materials from his invaluable website for the study of the Confederation Poets. The prose portion of this site can be found at: http://www.uwo.ca/english/canadianpoetry/confederation/roberts/non-fictional_prose /index.htm.

Photographs of the authors found in this text are reprinted from two early texts. Duncan Campbell Scott's photo is from the frontispiece of his *Lundy's Lane and Other Poems*, New York: George H. Horan Company, 1916. Photos of W.W. Campbell, Bliss Carman, Archibald Lampman and Charles G.D. Roberts are found in J.E. Weatherall, ed., *Later Canadian Poems*, Toronto: Copp Clark Co., 1893.

Acknowledgements

Numerous people have supported this project, from its inception several years ago to the publication of this first volume, and I am certain to forget to credit some. First, I would like to thank Mike Smith, who was Dean of Arts and Social Sciences at Carleton University in Ottawa when I applied for the Marston LaFrance Leave Fellowship in 2003. It was his belief in me and in this project that caused him to approve the fellowship and thus provide the freedom from my normal teaching duties to bring it to fruition. Many others associated with his office were highly supportive; these include John Shepherd, Associate Dean at the time, who gave me the confidence to apply, and the previous Dean, Aviva Freedman, who supported earlier applications for research grants. Working in their office was Wendy Wynne-Jones who was a tower of moral support and encouragement during the application process. No one's application for undertaking such a project comes without the solid backing of their own department, and here I'd like to thank Larry McDonald and Rob Holton, two Chairs of Carleton's English Department whose letters on my behalf I can credit for convincing the Dean this project and my purported abilities were deserving of support. Karl Siegler, editor and publisher of Talonbooks, also supported this project with the concrete assessment of a publisher looking to do a book; again, his faith in my abilities and in the worth of the project did much to make it a reality.

Over the course of the production, several people have provided invaluable help and advice. A number of years ago, my colleague Michael Gnarowski encouraged me to begin this project, and recommended me for an Ontario Arts Council grant which I received. Another colleague, Barbara Carman Garner, kindly leant me several rare volumes of essays by her distant relative Bliss Carman. The eminent poet and critic Frank Davey, a friend for over fifty years, gave me sound advice as to the organization of the three volumes, and suggested I look for specialists to introduce each volume. It was he who recommended David Bentley, who in turn provided an excellent critique of my original selection of texts for this first volume, and who noted a few omissions. I am of course grateful for Dr. Bentley's knowledgeable and apt introduction to this first collection: I could not have hoped for better.

Since the inception of the project I received several research grants from Carleton University which made much of the laborious copying work possible, and provided equipment and software to accomplish the task of scanning material from photocopies into electronic text for editing. Some of these funds went to graduate students who skillfully prepared these transcriptions and helped locate some of the more

A Note on the Bibliographies

A short bibliography follows each biographical introduction in the text; these are by no means meant to be definitive, but rather an indication of the range of work done by the authors and the critical attention they have received. Since these texts generally refer to individual writers, a few words should be said regarding the Confederation Poets as a group. Only a few years ago, a comprehensive bibliography on the Confederation Poets and their contemporaries was included in D.M.R. Bentley's *The Confederation Group of Canadian Poets, 1880–1897* (Toronto: U of Toronto P, 2004). Since an electronic version of this book is also available through ebrary.com, interested parties can readily access this database. Furthermore, Bentley's Introduction to the same text provides a comprehensive treatment of the conditions which gave rise to this literary movement, and how the name came to be applied to only four or five of the poets who emerged onto the literary scene during the 1880s and 1890s in Canada.

Malcolm Ross did more than anyone else to establish four of these authors as central to the movement and to Canadian letters when he edited his much read and taught poetry anthology, *Poets of the Confederation: Charles G.D. Roberts; Bliss Carman; Archibald Lampman; Duncan Campbell Scott* (Toronto: McClelland and Stewart, 1960). Two further book-length treatments of this period include an appraisal done in 1974 by George Woodcock, *Colony and Confederation: Early Canadian Poets and their Background* (Vancouver: U of British Columbia P [Electronic resource available through ebrary.com]); and the recent collection, edited by Tracy Ware, titled *A Northern Romanticism: Poets of the Confederation* (Ottawa: Tecumseh, 2000).

Preface

When, in 1968, as a young Canadian poet, I was hired by the English Department of Carleton University to teach Literature with a specialization in Modern American Poetry, there were as yet no courses offered in Canadian Literature—a situation common throughout the country until the late 1960s. Given Canada's colonial history, "great literature in English" was considered to be British, and since WWII increasingly American. Any literary work written by Canadians was thought by definition therefore to be no more than a pale colonial imitation, or a poor and distant cousin of works written by Canada's imperial betters, and "Canadian literature" was thought by the academic establishment to be too peripheral, in both quality and quantity, to warrant specific, dedicated courses of study.

By the early 1970s, after a decade of a populist global cultural revolution that ushered in what is now considered the post-colonial age, Canadian literature was finally becoming a credible subject of respect in Canadian English departments, and Carleton University set out to make it a newly prominent element of its curriculum. I was offered a seminar in Contemporary Canadian Poetry, which gave me free rein to teach the work of my immediate mentors and contemporaries whose work I was reading assiduously, and many of whom I knew personally.

Poetry anthologies in those early years were inadequate, so I taught the work of my contemporaries using a selection of individual books, chapbooks and texts, often by poets who had not yet published a collection of selected poems. But whereas in my seminars in Contemporary American Poetry I was able to complement the study of the poetry with a recently published text titled *The Poetics of the New American Poetry*, which had come out in 1972, I was forced to search far and wide, and in the most diverse places for any articles on poetics by contemporary

Canadian poets. These precious articles I would photocopy, and then duplicate for my students on a replicating device using a chemically coated paper that produced a pinkish-purple offprint, which perversely began fading into eventual oblivion the moment it met with daylight. Later, of course, we came upon better days, but still, over many years, no other anthologies were published that collected such poetics.

Over the decades since the 1960s, I amassed more than two hundred such essays by Canadian poets, and began to consider the value of editing an anthology of them. In the course of my deliberations, I became obsessed—and I think that is clearly the word—with the idea of collecting as completely as possible every article on poetics by a published Canadian poet and, wish beyond dream, trying to find a publisher reckless and magnanimous enough to consider publishing such a collection in several volumes. During the summer of 2000, while visiting Talonbooks at their location which was then in Burnaby, I mentioned the idea to publisher Karl Siegler. To my astonishment, he immediately embraced it as a great Millennium Project. I don't think he meant by that that it should take me a millennium to complete it! But, thanks to a leave of absence funded by the Marston LaFrance Leave Fellowship during 2004–05, I was given time to bring my random collection into clearer focus, and begin the process of deciding how the various volumes would be differentiated, and above all, what would be included, and what left out.

Because I believe Canadians will always be interested in the history and development of ideas in their literature, and because these ideas inevitably have an influence on those of younger poets who read their forebears, I decided that the volumes should be structured in chronological order, while the articles in each volume might be grouped typically by author and then by first publication date, while allowing for exceptions where this makes sense.

Thus the series begins with a volume of articles by members of a group that has become known as the Confederation Poets, who were the first Canadian poets to publish their ideas on poetics; with the second to include their successors, the Early Modernists; and so on. After discussions with a growing number of colleagues now able to work in the relatively new field of Canadian literary theory, I decided to invite specialists in each period to write an introduction to the volume for which they are best suited. This, in turn, has increased the complexity of the organization of individual volumes, but will have the effect of giving each a more distinct quality through a thoroughly informed, particular and cohesive point of view. As general editor of the series, I have retained full control over the selection process, but opened the door to the grouping together of articles representing specific literary periods, movements or "schools." Since I anticipate this project will result in the publication of several volumes, inviting a specialist in each of these periods to introduce their poets' critical voices and vocabularies will bring a refreshingly different perspective to bear on each volume. D.M.R. Bentley, an authority on the Confederation Poets, has agreed to provide an introduction to *An English Canadian Poetics, Volume I: The Confederation Poets*, and I am currently in negotiations with other prominent scholars regarding each of the subsequent volumes.

Disconcertingly, people are often wont to ask me what, after all, is meant by the term "poetics"? What does it mean, and how does one decide what should be included by this term and what excluded? In the broadest sense of the word, "poetics" is a term which is more or less synonymous with "literary criticism," and I think maintaining and foregrounding this link with respect to the specific literary genre of poetry has significant historical value. Some of the most classic examples of poetics in this tradition of literary criticism can be found in the frequently assigned anthology by W.J. Bate: *Criticism: The Major Texts*. Most of the familiar titles of the essays it contains are by poets, with the notable exceptions early on of Aristotle's *Poetics* and certain passages from Plato. Thus we have: Horace's *The Art of Poetry*; Sidney's *An Apology for Poetry*; Milton's Prefaces to *Paradise Lost* and to *Samson Agonistes*; Wordsworth's Preface to the second edition of the *Lyrical Ballads*; Poe's *The Poetic Principle*; Shelley's *A Defense of Poetry*; Yeats's *The Symbolism of Poetry*; and Eliot's *Tradition and the Individual Talent*.

Many such statements on poetics are also to be found in various collections of American poetry, such as the *Norton Anthology of American Literature* in two volumes, and the remarkable collection edited by Donald Allen and Warren Tallman titled *A Poetics of the New American Poetry*. Within these volumes we find: Emerson's *The Poet* and his famous essay *Nature*; Whitman's prefaces and afterwords to several editions of *Leaves of Grass*; and a host of essays concerning the nature and craft of writing by American poets such as Ezra Pound, Hart Crane, William Carlos Williams, Charles Olson, Robert Creeley, Robert Duncan; and among the Beats, Allen Ginsberg, Gary Snyder and Michael McClure.

All of the above are also readily found in American anthologies of literature, often alongside the poetry. This is not the case with statements or essays on Canadian poetics. A random sampling of disparate and uncontextualized articles by Canadian poets not included in any anthologies of Canadian poetry includes, among a great many others: W. Wilfred Campbell's "Literature, Music and the Arts ... "; Charles G.D. Roberts's "The Poetry of Nature"; Archibald Lampman's "Style" and "Poetic Interpretation"; Bliss Carman's "The Poet in Modern Life"; D.C. Scott's "Poetry and Progress"; A.J.M. Smith's "The Refining Fire: The Meaning and Use of Poetry"; Earle Birney's "Madness and Exorcism of Poetry"; Irving Layton's "Politics and Poetry"; Miriam Waddington's "Women and Writing"; Louis Dudek's "Functional Poetry: A Proposal"; Phyllis Webb's "Polishing up the View"; Robert Kroetsch's "For Play and Entrance: The Contemporary Long Poem"; George Bowering's "The End of the Line"; Fred Wah's "Making Strange Poetics"; Daphne Marlatt's "musing with mothertongue"; and Erin Mouré's "Poetry, Memory, and the Polis." All of these Canadian articles are either included in this volume, or are projected to be collected in subsequent volumes of *An English Canadian Poetics*.

Essays on poetics such as the above constitute an attempt by the poets, for the most part, to address the writing process itself; but they also discuss, either directly or indirectly, a number of other concerns intimately associated with the arts, culture and politics of their time. Thus Wordsworth, Emerson and Carman are all preoccupied with the idea of Nature which they conceive as integral to the human psyche and the creative temperament. Modernist Realism on the other hand largely differentiates itself from Romanticism in the way in which "nature" is perceived in and configured by the writing as an objective "outside" or "other." So an essay concerning "nature" may well be as much about the creative imagination for the Romantics as it is about the poetic process by the Early Modernists.

In the main, I have tried to consider how such articles directly advance our understanding of the poetry by each particular author, or by that of the group or school to which he or she may be said to belong. Understandably, ideas considered central to one generation may be ignored, critiqued or taken up in quite another fashion by the next. In some measure, a chronological reading of poetics is akin to a cultural history or a sociological survey of attitudes prevalent at a particular time and place, albeit often from a self-consciously elite perspective that so often colours the critical discourse of writers and artists. In particular, we can see how such intellectuals view their place in society and posit the value of their craft to that society. For example, Emerson's glorification of the poet in 1840s America is sharply different from Louis Dudek's lament for the lost significance of poetry in his 1981 Canadian article "Whatever Happened to Poetry?" Both poets provide a critique of culture and its failure to exercise imagination; but, whereas Emerson is eternally hopeful of the "advent of the great poet," Dudek expresses disappointment that his contemporary Canadian citizens pay only lip service to high culture, and would therefore find even the notion of "the great poet" rather irrelevant.

So it is readily apparent that while such essays are invariably about "writing," they also address a variety of concerns that are often seen to be central to the process of composition, and therefore deemed suitable for publication or public reception at a certain period in history, whereas they might not be deemed suitable for such purposes at some other date. Thus, in each historical time and place, some topics are more frequently touched upon, while others are discussed less. Any attempt at constructing a list of topics relevant to a discussion of poetics removed from it historical context is bound to prove scandalously short-sighted, or non-inclusive, but I have followed some rules which, over many years of teaching, and thinking about poetics, have proved useful.

The most general and important of these is that each article under consideration should advance our understanding of the poet's work. To this end it may discuss: COMPOSITION: which includes Language, Diction, Rhetoric and Prosody; GENRE: specifically, types of poetry, such as Satire, War Poems, Lyric, Epic, Documentary, Long Poem, etc.; HISTORY AND BIOGRAPHY where these directly inform the writing and publishing; ARTS AND CULTURE generally, which include notions of Tradition and Anti-tradition; STYLE AND TECHNIQUE, here differentiated from Composition above to include the various literary "isms" such as uses of Symbolism, Imagism, Cubism, Realism, etc.; HUMAN GEOGRAPHY, which includes particular concepts of Nature, Landscape, Ecology, Regionalism, Urban Reality, Patriotism or one's sense of belonging to a particular country or region; POLITICS AND SOCIAL ISSUES, including Nationalism, Capitalism, Marxism, Democracy, Ethnicity, Feminism and a host of other public issues; and PHILOSOPHY/RELIGION, which ranges from the Christian status quo of the Confederation Poets to the Existential questioning of religious belief by Irving Layton, and the semi-canonization of Marxist theory in many poets in the latter part of the twentieth century.

From these criteria, it would seem that any discursive article discussing such topics would qualify for inclusion in the anthology, but I have set some fairly strict secondary parameters for inclusion as well. First, if the anthology is to be representative of a truly public discourse, every article must have been written by a published poet. Second, the article itself must have been previously published or at least delivered as an address in a public venue. As an obvious corollary to this, no articles have been, nor will be, solicited for the project from living poets who, although they might contribute something of merit to the discourse, this would also compromise the spirit in which an historical document should be collected, and there is much to mistrust in such an endeavour, not the least of which is the propensity for revisionist history.

Some principles of exclusion have also been adopted. Extracts from letters have been avoided with a very few exceptions—I am reminded of their occasionally pivotal importance, one of the most well-known of which is the famous letter by Keats to his brother on "Negative Capability." Interviews and fragments from interviews have been excluded, since these are constructed in a different spirit, are frequently less deeply considered, and their direction is often influenced by the person conducting the interview whose own role is thereby also valorized, distracting us from our focus on poetics per se. Besides, since collections of interviews with poets abound, and while they clearly offer other kinds of insights into their work, their inclusion would make this set of volumes an endless project. There will be no translations into English, since this is expressly a collection of English Canadian poetics. Book reviews, with very few exceptions, have been omitted, because they are typically less about the poet's own work than about that of another, and because they are again so abundant as to make inclusion impossible. While arguments can be made for anthologizing all of the above, they should form a separate set of volumes which I heartily invite a subsequent editor to undertake. Lastly, most poets have traditionally written on all manner of subjects unrelated to their craft, and Canadian poets are no exception. Such writings often have social, political or historical interest, yet they are not germane to a discussion of poetry or poetics, and so these necessarily have been excluded. Finally, there are no essays on poetics by some poets because, geniuses though they be, they simply had neither the inclination nor the interest to publish their ideas on writing in prose form. None of the precursors to the Confederation Poets wrote articles on poetics, for example, and I have searched in vain for pieces by some of our finest and most published writers in the twentieth century. Just as an example, Raymond Souster wrote the barest introduction (unsigned) to one collection of three poets titled *Cerberus*, while his contemporary Louis Dudek wrote far more on poetics than we will be able in fairness to include. There is a paucity of poetics by either Margaret Atwood (*Survival* notwithstanding) or by Michael Ondaatje, two of the most-read Canadian poets of the twentieth century. So we must not judge the calibre of the poet or their poetry by the presence or absence of their published poetic theory.

As in all teaching, perhaps the best way to introduce the reader to the subject of poetic theory as expressed by poets is to provide a few excerpts from the overall project along with some contextual commentary. Since I envision poetics primarily as a companion to the understanding of poetry—without which "poetics" (or literary theory written by non-practitioners of the art) would have a dubious existence—I have here taken the liberty of quoting several poems which are the subject of their authors' related critical discourse in prose.

Because the ideas of the Confederation Poets are immediately available in the first volume, with its informative introduction by D.M.R. Bentley, I will begin by making only an oblique reference to this first group of writers by one of their successors—surely the kind of poet Bliss Carman had in mind when he observed in a letter on 5 April 1917: "Perhaps when the war is over, and we begin to arrange our ideals of life on a new basis, we shall have some fine poetry again, [b]ut I feel that when that time arrives, only new men, young men, or those who have taken part in the struggle will be entitled to take part in the parliament of art. The Victorian days belong to history. I believe the new days will be better, but I doubt if any of the men who came to maturity before the great war will be able to find the new key, the new mode, the new tune." It speaks volumes that one of the poets to whom Carman seeks to pass the torch of Canadian poetry in this letter, "to find the new key, the new mode, the new tune," was not a man, as all the Confederation Poets were, but a woman: the argumentative young socialist poet, Dorothy Livesay.

Livesay's short piece is both a plea for recognition, and a battle cry for substantive and objective criticism of Canadian poetry at the outset of

WWII. An "Open Letter to Sir Charles G.D. Roberts" (whose work can be read in the first volume) appeared in the April 1939 edition of *New Frontier*. It has little to do with Roberts's poetry (except to praise a recent poem of his) and instead calls upon him as an established literary voice in Canada to encourage a level of criticism of poetry, which Livesay finds sadly lacking. The passages in quotations suggest the vacuous hyperbole which typified the journalistic boosterism that passed for criticism in the populist press of the day.

> For ten years, to my knowledge, Canadian poetry has been "on the upsurge," "in the throes of spiritual re-birth," "comparable to the Irish renaissance." And for ten years not a critic outside Canada has taken note of this remarkable development or seen fit to compare Canadian poetry with contemporary movements in England or the United States. Rather have the few critics who have noticed us, commented only on the puerility and the lack of originality of our poets, on their outstanding self-satisfaction. Who is right? The Canadian poet (and that tripping bridegroom, the Canadian critic)? Or the disinterested outsider? ...
>
> In my opinion [she continues] there will be no young poets in Canada until we have mopped up every critic who has yet ventured to speak in the respectable journals. For to call their namby-pamby back-patting, criticism, is to defile that word beyond recognition. Their argument is, presumably, that if anyone is found with even a glimmer of poetic expression, that glimmer must be nurtured long and carefully, with the utmost persuasive love. They would take Keats and smother all the freshness out of his soul, till his swelled head routed the Muse! And they do take every maiden who yearns, with her arm around a birch tree in the rain, and tell her she is a "genuine lover of beauty" who sees "a poem's living soul"—ad infinitum. Relatives then rally: fond mothers and doting fathers, overwhelmed that they have produced so rare an offspring. Such medicine can only tend to stifle real talent (which implies hard work), and so propagate bad poetry. (209)

Livesay calls for a new kind of Canadian critic who will not idolize poets but who will regard Canadian poetry from a universal (preferably socialist) perspective:

> We need a group of people [that is, critics] whose first concern is poetry itself, not poets. Who would be content to study poetry as it is being

sung all over the world, and who would not insist that their own efforts
be regarded. From such a group could come critics, Canadian critics,
who would have the necessary background and culture to be objective
when they turned to the writing of their own people. (210)

Her concluding plea to Roberts indicates the passion and serious-
ness of her call to action: "Will you help? Will you speak of it? There
must be many of us who feel this way. Or else indeed our country is
benighted" (210). The above passages address a crisis in both modern
poetry and modern criticism as felt by a young, emerging voice in
Canadian letters. It is odd, yet perhaps cunning, that the feisty young
socialist female poet would call upon one of the bastions of early Mod-
ernist poetry for help in her new enterprise. Little change is likely to
come from the old guard, and the plea is probably far more rhetorical
than literal. In fact, Roberts was seventy-nine when this piece appeared,
and would die only a few years later.

The kind of poetry Livesay was writing, and which was being ignored,
is worth looking at in order to clarify her outcry. In a moment, I'll quote
a fragment of her now well known poem "Day and Night." Written in
1935 or 1936, the poem first appeared in *Canadian Poetry Magazine* in
1940. It was reprinted in a 1968 collection titled *The Documentaries* for
which Livesay provided some useful introductory commentary, that will
also be found in a volume of our poetics anthology, but which is often
not included in anthologies of poetry. She speaks at some length of her
experiences as a social worker in New Jersey in the early thirties during
the Depression, and very particularly of the relations between blacks
and whites working side by side in the industrial centres. Then she de-
scribes how she came to write two early socialist poems, "The Outrider"
and "Day and Night." The information she provides is indispensable to
our understanding of these poems, and encourages us to view them not
only as novel Canadian poems, which they certainly were, but as part of
a larger testimony against the exploitation of the labour force in Amer-
ica and elsewhere. By accessing her prose commentary on the poems,
we come to a better understanding of the poetry itself as well as the
poet's view of her place in the international world of letters. She writes:

> During those three years as a social worker I had abandoned writing
> any poetry that was lyrical or personal. But now, so near to New York
> City, I was able to make trips to Greenwich Village and delve about in
> bookshops—perhaps seeking some relief from the Marxist literature

I had been consuming for so long. I mean *New Masses* and *The Daily Worker* and countless pamphlets and political tracts on economics and the class struggle. What was my astonishment and unbelief, to find that British poets like Auden, Spender and C. Day-Lewis were writing a poetry freed from dogmatism. It was revolutionary, true, but full of lyricism and personal passion! There was nothing like that in Canada nor even in America. Here was a movement in literature that met my own inclinations, for it discarded the pessimism of T. S. Eliot and reclaimed a brave new world—that of Blake and Whitman. This discovery moved me deeply. I could share it with no one, but from that moment on there was planted within me the desire to write poetry once more—this new sort of poetry.

Soon after that experience I returned to Canada .... During that winter I wrote "Day and Night." This documentary is dominated by themes of struggle: class against class, race against race. The sound of Negro spirituals mingled in my mind with Cole Porter's "Night and Day" and Lenin's words (I quote from memory): "To go two steps forward we may have to take one step back." That phrase captured my imagination for it seemed to me that the capitalist system was putting that concept in reverse. Although the poem was written in 1935–36 it was not published until 1940 in *Canadian Poetry Magazine*, which E.J. Pratt had launched. Pratt said that he was delighted to find a poem written by a Canadian that was not concerned with the colour of maple leaves, but with the social and industrial scene in cities. But many middle-class souls were shocked. Later it became clear that what I did for Canadian city life—a social realist portrait—Anne Marriott was doing for the prairie in her beautiful documentary, "The Wind Our Enemy." Perhaps we two *were* just isolated "bourgeois intellectuals" but the impact of the times, the crises of social life, deeply moved us. The poetry was crying out. (*The Documentaries* 16–17)

DAY AND NIGHT

I

Dawn, red and angry, whistles loud and sends
A geysered shaft of steam searching the air.
Scream after scream announces that the churn
Of life must move, the giant arm command.
Men in a stream, a moving human belt

Move into sockets, every one a bolt.
The fun begins, a humming, whirring drum—
Men do a dance in time to the machines.

III

One step forward
Two steps back
Shove the lever,
Push it back
While Arnot whirls
A roundabout
And Geoghan shuffles
Bolts about.

One step forward
Hear it crack
Smashing rhythm—
Two steps back
Your heart-beat pounds
Against your throat
The roaring voices
Drown your shout
Across the way
A writhing whack
Sets you spinning
Two steps back
One step forward
Two steps back ....

"Green of new leaf shall deck my spirit" cries the voice of the dissident worker narrating the poem in the concluding stanza in hopes of a better physical life in future, a buoyant optimism countering the anger and desperation of the working man.

Inhabiting quite a different social world is the poet A.J.M. Smith who came to prominence within the McGill circle in the 1920s and who continued to influence Canadian literature through to the 1960s when he edited an *Oxford Anthology of Canadian Poetry*. His essay "Refining Fire: The Meaning and Use of Poetry" appeared in *Queens Quarterly* LXI in the fall of 1954 (353–64) and was reprinted in (and here quoted from) in A.J.M. Smith, ed., *On Poetry and Poets* (59–69). The essay attempts a recapitulation of the early modernist belief that poetry serves the public as a kind of surrogate religious experience. "A poem is not a description of experience, it is itself an experience, and it awakens in the mind of the alert and receptive reader a new experience analogous to the one in the mind of the poet ultimately responsible for the creation of the poem" (59). "The great poets," for Smith, "are those who have dared to descend more deeply into the heart of reality" (60), and thus for him the "value of a poem lies in the intensity with which an experience has been encountered, and the accuracy with which its consequences, good or evil, delightful or painful, have been recognized and accepted" (60). Smith argues there are two kinds of poetry: that which affirms traditional values and beliefs, and is essentially optimistic; and poetry that challenges orthodoxy and "tells us unpleasant truths" (62). As readers, says Smith, we have a moral obligation to read with as much perception and accuracy as possible, in order to experience the intensity which the poet has communicated, and in turn grasp the "hidden and uncomfortable truths" (67) which the poet has unveiled. The "secrets of the heart" (67) which the poet reveals are not personal, not limited to the writer, but resonant in the reader as well, and thus the poet wakens a latency of knowing which the reader has hitherto not realized.

The usefulness of poetry then, is that it unites writer and reader, individual and community, in a commonality of spirit. Smith quotes Shelley's *A Defence of Poetry* where he writes: "A man to be greatly good, must imagine intensely and comprehensively; he must put himself in the place of another and of many others ... "(68). Smith also draws somewhat less convincingly upon Auden's succinct statement, "We must love one another or die" (68). Admittedly, these are thoughts gathered during the Cold War, and hence there is good cause for the anxiety and no little need for self scrutiny. But Smith's reliance, ultimately, is upon a power greater than the self which can, through self-denial, or a kind of artistic humiliation, bring about a spiritual enlightenment. The decay of society can be remedied through "the recovery of myth" (68) that great modernist project. Only by acknowledging and taking responsibility for our guilt and suffering will we be able to regain lost innocence, for which Smith substitutes freshness and clarity of vision. And yet, despite a rather bleak post-WWII reality, Smith affirms a positive outlook:

But the modern world is not Hell; the suffering is not eternal nor infinite nor hopeless. It is rather the refining fire into which Arnaut Daniel in the *Purgatorio* dived back, because, as he said to Virgil, "I see with joy the day for which I hope before me." (69)

There is salvation for man, through poetry; but only after the poet has awakened us to the darkness in ourselves, which is rather akin to sin, and only through the ministrations of poetry, which is rather like a sacramental practice. Like Joyce and Eliot whom he admires, Smith has a hard time divesting himself and his readership from guilt and original sin. Having dispensed with the outward trappings of organized religion, he reinvents them in the sacramental function of Art. His concluding remarks speak not just of clarification and renewal, but of redemption. The poet is the new high priest of culture.

Refreshingly, however, midway through his essay, Smith introduces and then discusses a delightful little poem titled "Flowers by the Sea" by the American poet William Carlos Williams which had appeared back in 1923, and which reflected Williams's Cubist interests at that time. Smith quotes the poem as an example of novelty of vision through "unexpected reversal of images" (61).[1] The poem, he says, is an example of that difficult kind of poetry which forces us to think about what a poem is doing, not just what it is saying. The incongruity of the image is belied by the casualness of the statement, which seems perfectly natural by contrast, and we are delighted by "the paradox that the sea and the pasture each suggests the other's basic nature rather than its own" (61). Here is Williams's poem:

FLOWERS BY THE SEA

When over the flowery sharp pasture's
edge, unseen, the salt ocean

lifts its form—chicory and daisies
tied, released, seem hardly flowers alone

but color and the movement—or the shape
perhaps—of restlessness, whereas

the sea is circled and sways
peacefully upon its plantlike stem

Smith comments:

> "Flowers by the Sea" expresses an experience, which culminates for both
> poet and reader in the intuitive flash at the close, when it is perceived
> not that the flowers and the sea are like one another ... but that the
> flowers *are* a sea and the sea *is* a flower .... [I]ntense concentration ...
> leads to a form of truth that is more limited but more precious than
> the truth of science or fact, for it is a truth perceived simultaneously
> by the heart, the imagination, and the mind. (61)

This "intuitive flash" or Joycean epiphany as he also calls it, refers to an
intense reckoning with something deeper than what we usually perceive
in the world, and which cannot altogether be described as a purely
intellectual experience, although Smith attempts to limit it as such.
Smith rests content to describe this "exhilaration" (62) of discovery in
elusive terms: "Not in metaphysical poetry only does intellectual action,
whether slowly or swiftly brought to a consummation, resolve itself in
emotion when it comes to its successful and dramatic conclusion" (62).
There are sexual and Christian implications in this statement which
Smith, unlike the metaphysical poets themselves, is unwilling or unable
to express.

Well, if sex and god are in hiding in Smith's essay, only god is in
hiding in the poetry and poetics of Irving Layton. And yet, different in
temperament as these two poets are, there are remarkable similarities
in their ideas on poetry. So, in his Preface to *The Laughing Rooster* in
1964 in which he strives to define the creative process, Layton says:

> In this business of writing, a man can only speak of what he knows,
> of what he has himself been brought face to face with. What else is
> poetry but a self-authenticated speaking, a reaching down into the
> roots of one's being. Roots, did I say? That's much too nice a word.
> Confusions, rather—doubts, perplexities, inner conflicts, joy, desire,
> chagrin—the terror and the ecstasy of living daily beyond one's
> psychic means.

He continues:

> Can anyone really explain what happens in the writing of a poem? I
> doubt it. There are those whose professional careers in the non-
> creative aspects of literature entitle them to a measure of dogmatism,
> but when I examine my own creative processes I am left wondering ....
> The major poets have large-sized, terrifying demons inside their

psyches .... If one of these demons were ever let loose in a university, the professors of literature would be out of a job.

Happily, as I write this preface, I am safely retired; woe unto those for whom it is of course intended! On the subject of inspiration, Layton avers that unlike Blake, he has never heard the voice of any angel, though it "would be great fun to casually drop such a piece of news at a cocktail party" (*Engagements* 111). On the other hand, he claims to have received most of his better poems from a source and in a fashion which are impossible to explain:

> [T]here are poems I've written for which it seems to me I can take no credit at all, their composition from beginning to end ... having proceeded without any intervention at all of my will or reason, or where the intervention has been ... negligible. And I would add, too, that I consider these poems among the best I've written.

Layton then describes the process by which an early poem, "The Swimmer," much anthologized since, had its inception. The matter of fact description of events surrounding the writing of the poem clearly belies the complex activity of the poet's inner mind during the process. Of particular interest in this passage are the careful references to mundane aspects of the morning and early afternoon preceding the time of composition; the description is completely devoid of drama, romanticism, even artistic implication, although once seized by the need to write the poem out, the poet becomes utterly absorbed by the process and inured to the world around him. Let's look at the description, and then the poem itself.

> Though I had composed a considerable quantity of verse while I was at the university, it is only with the writing of "The Swimmer" that I realized the poet's vocation might be mine. I had taken my wife to the beach at Caughnawaga where we spent the morning and the better part of the afternoon. After we had returned home I went out for a walk along St. Catherine Street and turned into a restaurant for a cup of coffee. When I was seated at the table, without warning a succession of images, induced no doubt by the day's experiences, threw my mind —there's no better way I can put it—into a lucid turmoil. The images were accompanied by an insistent rhythm that seemed to be scouring my innermost self for words and phrases to attach itself to or to lift up from my buried consciousness and carry forward in its irresistible

sweep. Perhaps that's all that rhythm really is—the sound we hear when ideas and memories are fused and the past takes on the startling immediacy of the present. Rhythm is the sound we hear when time is wiped out; when there's no past or future, but only NOW. Luckily, I had a pencil with me. I grabbed the napkin and spilled the entire poem onto it in a mood of such intense concentration, the restaurant and all its noises were completely blotted out from my awareness. Nothing existed for me at the time except the words I saw forming on the napkin: an irregular black stain whose magical growth gave me a sensation of almost unbearable ecstasy and release.

What I've just described has happened to me many times since. My shabby, everyday self seems to be flung aside and somebody bearing only the slightest resemblance to me takes over. (*Engagements* 112)

THE SWIMMER

The afternoon foreclosing, see
The swimmer plunges from his raft,
Opening the spray corollas by his act of war
The snake heads strike
Quickly and are silent.

Emerging see how for a moment
A brown weed with marvellous bulbs,
He lies imminent upon the water
While light and sound come with a sharp passion
From the gonad sea around the Poles
And break in bright cockle-shells about his ears.

He dives, floats, goes under like a thief
Where his blood sings to the tiger shadows
In the scentless greenery that leads him home,
A male salmon down fretted stairways
Through underwater slums ...

Stunned by the memory of lost gills
He frames gestures of self-absorption
Upon the skull-like beach;
Observes with instigated eyes
The sun that empties itself upon the water,

And the last wave romping in
To throw its boyhood on the marble sand.[2]

Over the years when I taught Canadian poetry I frequently included
a poem written in 1951 by Earle Birney titled "Bushed." In the course of
only thirty lines it delineates the experience of a man's becoming utterly
taken over by the fact of his own interior isolation and the impinging
and unremitting reality of the wilderness. Unable to cope with the fact
of nature without romanticizing it, he succumbs to a second delusion:
that the wilderness is savage and intent on his destruction. In the end,
it is not nature which is oppressive or that destroys him, but rather his
own predisposition to paranoia and madness. Fifteen years after writing
the poem at Wreck Beach near UBC where he was a professor, Birney
gave an illuminating talk for CBC in 1966 as one of a series of lectures
for the *Ideas* program titled "The Writing of a Poem: Compulsion and
Suppression" (subsequently published in *The Creative Writer* 24–33)
where he describes the inception of this poem in detail, and it is
fascinating to discover its roots in two seemingly unconnected episodes
in his personal life—neither of which gave rise to anything within
himself that is similar to what the figure in the poem experiences—
although I'll be forced to qualify this in a moment.

The description goes on for several pages, and is assuredly some-
what apocryphal, since the poet purports to quote from memory a
lengthy conversation between two other professors which he overheard
while showering at the gym at UBC. Ostensibly, the poet is goaded into
action by his disappointment at their unrealistic contention that they
can survive a nuclear holocaust by retreating to a cabin in the Rockies
where they plan to hole up and live out the impending disaster. Their
fatuousness drives the poet to want to respond, and in the course of the
preamble, he invents a scenario where he jocularly rejects their proposal
and interjects his own voice alongside theirs. But, he later explains, the
invented banter, and attempts through several drafts of a poem to
capture this scenario, serve only momentarily to suppress a greater,
personal urgency to reach down into himself and write about powerful
psychic events long buried in his past.

The two professors' flippant fantasy about a cabin in the Rockies
awakens memories of a childhood experience he's repressed. Though
Birney's attempts to write anecdotally about their dialogue end in
failure, unexpectedly, their fantasy serves to remind him of a real cabin
near Mystic Lake which he'd visited in his youth, and of a still earlier

memory when, aged twelve, he learned of the death of a local trapper named Old Sam whose corpse he'd seen a Mountie bring into town. The term "Bushed" that gives title to his subsequent poem, and which summarizes the real perplex which has kept it from being written, is a word that had been uttered glibly by his father four decades previously. His father had intended the word to sum up simplistically the experience Old Sam had undergone—to put to rest any further childish questioning on the subjects of the old man's madness and death by starvation. Birney's prose description of the events leading up to the writing of the poem is exacting and powerful, and it shows how the mind seeks first to suppress, and then gives in to the compulsion that motivates the artist to create:

> The cabin, that was what mysteriously bugged me. Not the unlikely cabin those two profs would have built, but the old one, already deserted, by Mystic Lake thirty-five years ago when I'd passed it by. Why, why, did I keep remembering that cabin, in which I had never stayed, about which I knew nothing then, or since? And what had all this to do with the vapid talk of two professors in a shower?
>
> I hoped, by writing a third draft, to find out. Over the next month I went through four more drafts before I really knew. Knew that my poem wasn't about the professors at all, or about atom-bomb survival, but about a cabin I had never seen, and its inhabitant, whom I had last glimpsed when he was a corpse muffled on a pack-saddle. The name Mystic Lake spoken by one of the men in the shower, had triggered first the memory of an old abandoned log cabin there, and then a far deeper more scary vision from an even earlier day, when I was perhaps twelve. It was a late spring day when, walking home from school, I saw a Mountie riding, leading behind him a packhorse on which the outline of a dead man was bundled. And the next day my father told me it was the bearded trapper, Old Sam, who used to come into town every spring from some cabin far out, beyond the Park boundaries, to stock up supplies for the year with what pelts he had caught and carried on his back over the wild mountains. Suspicious-eyed, crazyhaired Old Sam, silent even in the store, shoving his pencilled list of needs over the counter with big scaly hands. That spring he hadn't come in. The Mounties went out to his cabin. They had to break in, for it was barred on the inside. They found his half-starved corpse frozen on the bed. But there was still a store of food in the

cabin. "Bushed," my father said. "The woods got him, the loneliness." Bushed! That was my title, my theme.

I suppose the mystery of that old man's death, the awful corridors of the human mind it hinted at, had been too much for my twelve-year-old psyche to face; I had suppressed all memory of the man and his death, I had refused to let my imagination wrestle with it. And again, a few years later, when I camped with other teen-agers by Mystic Lake, the deserted cabin there had prompted a recall of the life and death of Old Sam, and again I had repressed the association. But it was there, bedded deep in me, till a professor in a shower, when I was fifty-two years of age, had said "Mystic Lake", and my unconscious stirred and bedevilled me till at last I had given it the words that left me at peace—nine drafts and two months later. ("The Writing of a Poem: Compulsion and Suppression," in *The Creative Writer* 31–32)

Just before reading the poem in the broadcast, Birney comments on the nature of the poet's mind and the similarity of its possible fate to that of the victim of the literal wilderness, Old Sam. The poem, he says, "reveals something about how my own mind would go, if I were no longer able to shape its schizophrenic moments into an amulet of words" (32). Earlier in the talk, he had spoken about obsession in Lowry and Melville, and of the prevalence of madness during the so called Age of Reason which afflicted several prominent writers. Birney evidently feared the "the natural subconscious release of the poet's psyche from his compulsion for autistic thinking, a compulsion which otherwise might build to the point where autistic thinking would take him over entirely, and the poet would no longer be a poet, but a schizophrenic lodged in an asylum ... "(28). This does not seem like the outward Earle Birney many of us knew, and it may be a fanciful ruse to add drama to the role of the creative writer. But the prospect of real insanity haunts us all at times, and Birney here gives voice to the fear of that possibility, and thus adds a personal connection to the drama which unfolds in the poem "Bushed."

BUSHED

He invented a rainbow but lightning struck it

shattered it into the lake-lap of a mountain
so big his mind slowed when he looked at it

Yet he built a shack on the shore
learned to roast porcupine belly and
wore the quills on his hatband.

At first he was out with the dawn
whether it yellowed bright as wood columbine
or was only a fuzzed moth in a flannel of storm

But he found the mountain was clearly alive
sent messages whizzing down every hot morning
boomed proclamations at noon and spread out
a white guard of goat
before falling asleep on its feet at sundown

When he tried his eyes on the lake, ospreys
would fall like valkyries
choosing the cut-throat
He took then to waiting
till the night smoke rose from the boil of the sunset

But the moon carved unknown totems
out of the lakeshore
owls in the beardusky wood derided him
moosehorned cedars circled his swamps and tossed
their antlers up to the stars
Then he knew though the mountain slept, the winds
were shaping its peak to an arrowhead
poised

But by now he could only
bar himself in and wait
for the great flint to come singing into his heart
(*The Creative Writer* 32–33)

I'd like to conclude this preface by discussing a recent piece of prose, not exactly prose either, for it has much in common with poetry, and with the book-length prose-poem to which it was appended when it was published in 1984. The piece is titled "musing with mothertongue" and it can be found at the back of *Touch to My Tongue*, an explicit rendering of a lesbian relationship between the author, Daphne Marlatt, and her lover at the time, Betsy Warland. When the richly textured beauty of the poem ends, it seems to refuse to give way to discursive prose for the "musings" which follow, and instead elides into a discussion of language in the prose narrative which is alternately ornate and stark, fluid and cryptic. As we read, we are reminded that we all speak the "mothertongue," a phrase which goes back centuries, and which relates also to the mother country of our birth, and of our heritage. But Marlatt's mothertongue draws special attention to the role of women in culture and their centrality in the transmission of language from parent to child. It is a woman's view more than a universal one, for it seeks by this to correct what had, before the advent of feminism, for so long been taken for granted by our culture, that language and literature are, in the main, the province of men:

> If we are women poets, writers, speakers, we also take issue with the given, hearing the discrepancy between what our patriarchally-loaded language bears (can bear) of our experience and the difference from it our experience bears out—how it misrepresents, even miscarries, and so leaves unsaid what we actually experience. ("musing with mothertongue" in *Touch to My Tongue* 47)

Marlatt seeks a language of poetry which avoids the trammels of male-dominated discourse, and seeks to transform usage at the level of syntax—since the lexical nature of English is largely set by tradition, although of course new terms are possible, and new coinages abound in her writing. But modern and post-modern poetics have proven themselves remarkably capable of fluidity and diversity of expression. The great strength of Marlatt's writing, whether in poetry or prose, has been her capacity to discover a rhythm which is both uniquely her own and at the same time powerfully expressive of the body, and particularly the female body. The opening passage of "musing with mothertongue" indicates this from the outset; with a clear assertiveness it speaks to a woman's experience of language, where birth, and birthing—bringing forth—are central elements of the expression. And whether consciously or otherwise the description is inclusive, invites the male reader also, for the experience of being born into the world is universal just as the acquisition of language from and through the mother occurs to every child.

Here, as in *Touch to My Tongue*, Marlatt eschews capitalizing the first words of sentences and also the first person pronoun. This serves, I feel, to indicate the cyclical rather than linear nature of experience, in which

events flow into one another, and where the self, though clearly differ-
entiated from other bodies, nonetheless takes its place among them
rather than as something or someone separate, or first place singular, as
we typically say. These are methods of avoiding priority, and advancing
equality, within the very structure of the writing and the mode of
expression rather than through didactic statement, although the latter
is not altogether absent:

> the beginning: language, a living body we enter at birth, sustains and
> contains us. it does not stand in place of anything else, it does not
> replace the bodies around us. placental, our flat land, our sea, it is both
> place (where we are situated) and body (that contains us), that body of
> language we speak, our mothertongue. it bears us as we are born into
> it, into cognition. (45)

And while it is something we acquire and whose meaning we must
learn, language, says Marlatt, is also a phenomenon which exists
primarily as sound, a "body of sound" (45) which leads us back to the
"one dominant sound" of the mother's womb. It is, in effect, our second
body, the modus by which we body forth to communicate with each
other in the fullest sense through the interplay of even, or perhaps
especially, the smallest particles of speech whose sensuousness attracts
and establishes correspondences among themselves through "asso-
nance, euphony, alliteration, rhyme" (46) and which in the same breath
draws together both speaker and hearer of the verse because our mutual
appreciation of these instances of delight make a dance in which all are
caught up.

> like the mother's body, language is larger than us and carries us along
> with it. it bears us, it births us, insofar as we bear with it. if we are
> poets we spend our lives discovering not just what we have to say but
> what language is saying as it carries us with it. (46)

Drawing on Kristeva, and feminist writers in Quebec, Marlatt
envisions a new language for women which connects them back to
primal understandings and forward to newfound sensibilities, from the
"presyntactic" to the "postlexical field" where intelligence recovers its
etymological roots in the idea of gathering with the hand, and where
usage permits many puns and figures of speech in order to rediscover
correlations lost, or to construct associations anew, which will lead to
further sensibilities and understandings.

inhabitant of language, not master, not even mistress, this new woman writer ... in having is had, is held by it, what she is given to say. in giving it away is given herself, on that double edge where she has always lived, between the already spoken and the unspeakable, sense and non-sense. only now she writes it, risking nonsense, chaotic language leafings, unspeakable breaches of usage, intuitive leaps. inside language she leaps for joy, shoving out the walls of taboo and propriety, kicking syntax, discovering life in old roots. (49)

"Kicking syntax!" We have come a long way from Dorothy Livesay's calling Charles G.D. Roberts a pioneer in Canadian poetry and asking the grand patriarch of Canadian letters for critical support. But Marlatt's plea to be heard in a new way is, of course, a desire for a fundamental change in the way society regards language and sexuality. It is a call for openness, for accommodation, for inventiveness, for freedom of expression. For as she says in her last un-sentence in the essay: "putting the living body of language together means putting the world together, the world we live in: an act of composition, an act of birthing, us, uttered and outered there in it" (49). Not so much an un-sentence since it is grammatically traditional, rather what Eli Mandel called a "life sentence"[3] referring to the poet's commitment to language and to the writing wherein we are contained.

I'll close with a section from Marlatt's *Touch to My Tongue* which begins not with a title but with the open-ended heading "climbing the canyon even as .... " The passage describes her driving up the Fraser Canyon towards Lytton where the Thompson and the Fraser rivers meet in a confluence of sensual meanings; she is driving north and then east as she leaves her lover behind in Vancouver, and the use she makes of geography and the environment are a powerful testimony to the manner in which our landscape has become not only a force which impinges on the Canadian imagination, but a fact of that imagination as it expresses a very human will to survive the rupture of parting, and to retain, over physical and emotional distance, the experience of love, the lover, and love-making which have, in varying measure, been left behind—lost, except as now held, in language.

The remarkable infusion of Eros into the present description of landscape typifies Marlatt's genius for carrying into the world the human condition and finding in that world resonances of her own psychological experience. And I think "carrying" and "finding" are apt terms, for at her best these are not forced correspondences, but fortuitous discoveries which make it possible if not felicitous to be in the world. That is not to say painless, for there is considerable suffering to counter the ecstasy of this and related passages. What there is, in unstinting degree, is joy—joy in the memory but also in the re/creation of love in the present moment which is never isolated, but always connected through the body, through the landscape (or nature) which allows us place, and through the language we communally inhabit. *Touch to My Tongue* is a forceful sexualizing of all these—a poetics of Eros, in which we are included, whether we are ready or not. Thus the last fragment of the section promises her lover, but I'll aver also the reader: "i am going, beyond the mountains, past the Great Divide where rivers run in opposite direction i am carrying you with me" (25).

climbing the canyon even as

the Fraser rushes out to sea and you, where you are i am, muddy with heartland silt beside the river's outward push my car climbs steadily away from and toward—where we were—each step we took, what you said, what i saw (sun in your hair on the rim of your look), smell of love on our skin as we rushed with the river's push out, out to the mouth taking everything with us / and away, as i leave you there (where i am still) to make this climb i don't want to, feel how it hurts, our pull, womb to womb, spun thin reaching Sailor's Bar, Boston Bar, reaching Lytton where the Thompson River joins, alone nosing my way into the unnamed female folds of hill, soft sage since we came down twelve days ago begun to bloom, gold and the grass gold, and your hair not gold but like as light shivers through these hills. i am waiting for the dark, waiting with us at Ashcroft, behind glass, by the river's edge: then going down to it, that bank of uncertain footing as the freight roars by, across, that black river in its rush, noisy, enveloping us as we envelop each other—and the wind took your hair and flung it around your look, exultant, wild, i felt the river pushing through, all that weight of heartlocked years let loose and pouring with us out where known ground drops away and i am going, beyond the mountains, past the Great Divide where rivers run in opposite direction i am carrying you with me. (*Touch to My Tongue* 25)

If the reader were to hear in Marlatt's lines echoes of the rapture of Whitman in his great poem "Song of Myself," which though transcendent, remains rooted in the body, in geography and place,

Is this then a touch? quivering me to a new identity,
Flames and ether making a rush for my veins,
Treacherous tip of me reaching and crowding to help them
My flesh and blood playing out lightning to strike what is hardly
       different than myself ... ;[4]

or recollections of Roberts in his "Tantramar Revisited,"

Many a dream of joy fall'n in the shadow of pain,
Hands of chance and change have marred, or moulded, or broken,
Busy with spirit or flesh, all I most have adored ... ;[5]

or the elusively simple language of Mouré's enigmatically titled poem
"Post-Modern Literature,"

But the end of a city is still
a field, ordinary persons live there, a frame house, & occasionally—
a woman comes out to hang the washing.
From a certain angle you see her
push a line of wet clothes across a suburb.
It sings in the wind there, ...
where nobody moves ... ,[6]

then the reader is prepared for the extraordinary interplay of ideas which
will be heard in the volumes of this collection. For the ideas here
expressed echo a deep care for country, language, and relations that both
transcend boundaries, and yet by their actions, re-define them. Poetics,
often constructed in the same crucible as the poems to which they are
akin, are more than statements on the craft of writing, and are at their
best also a song in the wind that quivers to a new identity whether on
Wreck Beach or the Tantramar marshes. May they be for you what
Roberts's memories were to him, and what these essays have become
for me, "all that I most adored .... "

ROBERT HOGG

Notes

1. "Flowers by the Sea" was first collected in Williams's *An Early Martyr and Other Poems*, New York: Alcestis Press, 1935. Smith likely read it in *The Selected Poems of William Carlos Williams*, New York: New Directions, 1949.

2. "The Swimmer" is one of Layton's earliest published poems (1945) reprinted here from *A Wild Peculiar Joy: Selected Poems 1945–82*, Toronto: McClelland and Stewart, 1982, 16.

3. See the Preface to Mandel's *Life Sentence: Poems and Journals: 1976–1980*, Toronto: Porcepic, 1981, where he writes: "*Life Sentence*. A way of putting it. To be a Writer. To serve the sentence. A life *of* words or a life *in* words. 'He's been given life,' the journalist exclaims" (7).

4. Walt Whitman, "Song of Myself," section 28. Included in *Leaves of Grass*, first edition in 1855, quoted here from Harold W. Blodgett and Sculley Bradley, eds., *Walt Whitman: Leaves of Grass Comprehensive Reader's Edition*, New York: W.W. Norton & Co., 1960, 3–5.

5. Charles G.D. Roberts, "The Tantramar Revisited," originally published in *In Divers Tones*, 1886. Reprinted here from Malcolm Ross, ed., *Poets of the Confederation*, Toronto: McClelland and Stewart, 1960, 3–5.

6. Erin Mouré, "Post-Modern Literature" in *Wanted Alive*, Toronto: Anansi, 1983, 16–17.

Works Cited

Allen, Donald and Warren Tallman. *A Poetics of New American Poetry*. New York: Grove Press, 1973.

Bate, W.J. *Criticism: The Major Texts*. New York: Brace Jovanovich, 1952. Reprinted in 1970.

Baym, Nina et al, ed. *The Norton Anthology of American Literature*, 2nd ed. Vol. I–II. New York: W.W. Norton & Co., 1985.

Birney, Earle. *The Creative Writer*. Toronto: CBC, 1966.

Carman, Bliss. *Letters*. Ed. H. Pearson Grundy. Kingston and Montreal: McGill-Queen's UP, 1981.

Dudek, Louis, Irving Layton and Raymond Souster. *Cerebus*. Toronto: Contact, 1952.

Layton, Irving. *The Laughing Rooster*. Preface. Toronto: McClelland and Stewart, 1964, 17–25. Reprinted in *Engagements: The Prose of Irving Layton*. Ed. Seymour Mayne. Toronto: McClelland and Stewart, 1972. 109–19.

———. *A Wild Peculiar Joy: Selected Poems 1945–82*. Toronto: McClelland and Stewart, 1982.

Livesay, Dorothy. *The Documentaries*. Toronto: Ryerson, 1968.

———. "Open Letter to Sir Charles G.D. Roberts." *The New Frontier—A Monthly Magazine of Literature and Social Criticism* 1936–37: 209–10.

Mandel, Eli. *Life Sentence, Poems and Journals: 1976–1980*. Toronto: Porcepic, 1981.

Marlatt, Daphne. *Touch to My Tongue*. Edmonton: Longspoon, 1984.

Mouré, Erin. *Wanted Alive*. Toronto: Anansi, 1983.

Ross, Malcom, ed. *Poets of the Confederation*. Toronto: McClelland and Stewart, 1960.

Smith, A.J.M. "Refining Fire: The Meaning and Use of Poetry." *On Poetry and Poets*. Ed. A.J.M. Smith. Toronto: McClelland and Stewart, 1977. 59–69.

Whitman, Walt. *Walt Whitman: Leaves of Grass Comprehensive Reader's Edition*. Ed. Harold W. Blodgett and Sculley Bradley. New York: W.W. Norton & Co., 1960.

Williams, William Carlos. *The Selected Poems of William Carlos Williams*. New York: New Directions, 1949.

Introduction

I

It is the most famous Eureka moment in Canadian literature. The season was spring, the year 1881, and the setting Trinity College, Toronto. At the time, its Archimedean figure, Archibald Lampman (1861–99), was a second-year student studying Classics, but in due course he would become Canada's finest nineteenth-century poet. In "Two Canadian Poets" (1891), a lecture delivered to the Literary and Scientific Society of Ottawa ten years later, he recalls the event with the vividness of a flashbulb memory:

> One May evening ... somebody lent me *Orion and Other Poems* [1880] [by Charles G.D. Roberts (1860–1943)] .... Like most of the young fellows about me I had been under the depressing conviction that we were situated hopelessly on the outskirts of civilization, where no art and no literature could be, and that it was useless to expect that anything great could be done .... I sat up all night reading and re-reading "Orion" in a state of the wildest excitement and when I went to bed I could not sleep. It seemed to me a wonderful thing that such work could be done by a Canadian, by a young man, one of ourselves .... A little after sunrise I got up and went out into the College grounds .... [E]verything was transfigured for me beyond description, bathed in an old world radiance of beauty, the magic of the lines that were sounding in my ears, those divine verses, as they seemed to me, with their Tennyson-like richness and strange earth-loving Greekish flavour. I

have never forgotten that morning, and its influence has always remained with me. (*Essays and Reviews* 94–95)

How soon after that momentous morning the two poets were in contact is not known, but within eighteen months Roberts was writing to Lampman at length about various literary "schemes" and about his desire to move from his native New Brunswick to Ontario in order "to get together literary and independent Young Canada, and to spread ... [the] doctrine ... [of Canadian Republicanism] with untiring hands" (*Collected Letters* 29). Under Roberts's energetic leadership, and with the help and advice of the Svengalian Newfoundlander, Edward Edmund Collins,[1] the Confederation group of Canadian poets was gradually assembled in the course of the 1880s and early 1890s. After Lampman came Bliss Carman (1861–1929), Roberts's cousin and fellow New Brunswicker, then William Wilfred Campbell (1860–1918), an Ontarian whose first two collections of poetry were published in New Brunswick while he was living there from 1888 to 1890, then Lampman's fellow Ottawan and civil servant Duncan Campbell Scott (1862–1947), and finally the most peripheral and least gifted of the seven and its only Quebecer, Frederick George Scott (1861–1944). With the exception of D.C. Scott, whose father was a Methodist, all had personal or family connections with the Church of England (in fact, F.G. Scott was an Anglican priest, as was Campbell until 1891). Without exception, they were all born in Canada in the early sixties and thus came to maturity after Confederation (and were sometimes known as "the sixties group"). And all were, of course, men—members of the sex most qualified according to the gender assumptions of the time, to celebrate in poetry the coming to maturity of the immense and young Dominion of Canada. Not all of them shared Roberts's desire to see Canada become a republic (indeed, Roberts himself soon abandoned that particular "scheme"), but all of them believed in the importance of poetry to the creation and expression of a distinctive nationality, an assumption rooted in the Romantic nationalism of which Young Ireland was an offshoot (as were Young England and Young Italy).

Integral to the belief in the interdependence of poetry and nationality that the Confederation group and their contemporaries inherited from Romanticism was the proposition that a nation's physical environment (landscape, climate) has a formative effect on the mentality of its inhabitants and, hence, its artistic productions. Neither Roberts nor Lampman was entirely convinced that the characteristics of Canadian literature were or would be environmentally determined but both gave voice to the doctrine. With his eye on the prevalent and, to him, provincial idea Canadian poets should restrict themselves to recognizably "Canadian themes" such as maple trees and sleigh rides, Roberts argued in "The Beginnings of a Canadian Literature" (1883) that, whatever the subject, the works of a genuinely creative writer will inevitably contain "the special flavour of race and clime" (*Selected Poetry and Critical Prose* 258). "Our climate with its swift extremes is eager and waking," he added in "The Outlook for Literature: Acadia's Field for Poetry, History and Romance" (1886), "and we should expect a sort of dry sparkle in our page, with a transparent and tonic quality in our thought" (*Selected Poetry and Critical Prose* 261). In "Two Canadian Poets" Lampman identified different environmental influences and literary outcomes: "In the climate of the country, we have the pitiless severity of the climate of Sweden with the sunshine and sky of the north of Italy .... A Canadian race ... might combine the energy, the seriousness, the perseverence of the Scandanavians with something of the gayety, the elasticity, the quickness of spirit of the south. If these qualities could be united in a literature, the result would indeed be something novel and wonderful " (*Essays and Reviews* 93). Never before or since in Canada have poetry, poetics, environment, identity, and national distinctiveness been more closely intertwined with one another and with a sense of achievement and potential than in the poetry of the Confederation group and, as this collection repeatedly reveals, their writings about poetry and poetics.

II

Of paramount importance to Roberts and all the other members of the Confederation group with the increasingly truculent exception of Campbell was what Roberts in different places called "craftsmanship" or "workmanship." With distant origins in the Greek idea of the poet as a maker or (Roberts's word) "workman" (*Selected Poetry and Critical Prose* 258), the concept of workmanship had Romantic and Victorian exemplars for the Confederation group in such poets as John Keats and Matthew Arnold, both of whom stood extremely high in the estimation of Lampman as well as Roberts. It had also found an influential champion in the 1870s in the English man-of-letters Edmund Gosse, whose "A Plea for Certain Exotic Forms of French Verse" (1877) includes in its celebration of the six most important of the poetic creatures of old France" a moral-aesthetic paean to the poet as artificer:

> To make immortal art out of transient feeling, to give the impression of a finite mind infinite expression, to chisel material beauty out of passing thoughts and emotions,—this is the labour of the poet; and it is on account of this conscious artifice and exercise of constructive power that he properly takes his place beside the sculptor and the painter .... If, therefore, as we must, we regard poetry as one of the fine arts, it need not surprise us to have to dismiss the purely spontaneous and untutored expression of it as of little else than historical interest. In the present age the warblings of poetic improvisation cannot expect more attention than the equally artless impromptus of an untaught musical talent. (53)

Citing A.C. Swinburne, William Morris and Dante Gabriel and Christina Rossetti as examples of a healthy flight from blank verse to fixed forms, Gosse proceeds to discuss the sonnet as an instance of the "increasing variety and richness of rhyme, elasticity of verse, ... strength of form" and "workmanship" of contemporary English poetry. "In the present generation we write sonnets on the pure Petrarchan model ... in spite of or because of its very difficulties":

> That the rhymes of the octett [sic] must be two instead of four ... encourages us to brilliant effort. We acknowledge that the severity of the plan and the rich and copious recurrence of the rhyme serve the double end of repelling the incompetent workman and stimulating the competent. This being so, why should we not proceed to the cultivation of other fixed forms of verse, which flourished in the earliest days of modern poetic literature, and of which the sonnet, if the finest, is at least but one? (56)

Of the impact on the Confederation group of Gosse's programme and the literary developments that it at once celebrated and extended there can be no doubt. By far the most common form in the oeuvres of Roberts and Lampman in the 1880s and early 1890s is the Petrarchan sonnet, and, despite a growing aversion to fixed forms, Campbell wrote dozens of sonnets, all but a few Petrarchan. The "model sonnet" that

Duncan Campbell Scott describes in his earliest extant letter, dated 19 September 1889, is Petrarchan (indeed, Scott's letter is veritably Gossean in its insistence that "one can[not] be too strict about ... form ... [W]e would have better sonnets—that is, finer thoughts better expressed—if the rules were adhered to"). Almost all of Frederick George Scott's numerous sonnets, even his "Shakespeare" (1888), are Petrarchan, as in structure and grammar are the many irregular and unrhymed sonnets that Carman wrote after the turn of the century.[2] It was during the years of the group's formation, however, that Roberts, Lampman and Carman were most infatuated with the "six ... poetic creations of old France" championed by Gosse—"the *rondel*, the *rondeau*, the *triolet*, the *villanelle*, the *ballade*, and the *chant royal*" (56–57).

The obvious bridge between the aesthetic crystallized by Gosse and the aesthetic practices of the members of the Confederation group was *Orion, and Other Poems*. From a formal perspective, Lampman's enthusiastic account of the volume's content and impact in "Two Canadian Poets" needs to be supplemented by Roberts's own considered assessment of its literary qualities and its seminal role in the aetiology of the Confederation group in "Canadian Poetry in Its Relation to the Poetry of England and America" (1933):

> All the verses it contains were written between the ages of sixteen and nineteen,—most of them before I was eighteen. They are the work of practically a schoolboy, drunk with the music of Keats, Shelley, Tennyson and Swinburne. They are distinctly 'prentice work, distinctly derivative, and without significance except for their careful craftsmanship and for the fact that they dared deliberately to steer their frail craft out upon world waters,—certain of these youthful efforts appearing in the pages of the chief English and American magazines. But the only importance attaching to the little book lay in the fact that it started Lampman writing poetry and was the decisive factor in determining Carman to make poetry his career. (80–81)

To Roberts, then, the "importance" of *Orion, and Other Poems* lay in its impact on Lampman and Carman and its "significance" in its "craftsmanship" and cosmopolitanism.[3] What is not evident even from Roberts's very astute remarks is that much of the craftsmanship, cosmopolitanism, and hence, impact of *Orion, and Other Poems* must be attributed to its formal elements: following the Tennysonian blank verse and Swinburnian hexameters of "Orion" are poems in a striking variety of forms, including a series of four ballads, a series of three rondeaux, two Keatsian odes, two Petrarchan sonnets and individual poems in several classical and English meters and stanza forms (for example, tail-rhyme, *Troilus* and Spenserian stanzas, and sapphics, choriambics and alcaics). Both in its formalistic virtuosity and in its thematic variety, *Orion, and Other Poems* set the standard for volumes published by the Confederation group in the ensuing decade and more.

Roberts was not content to lead merely by example, however. In "The Beginnings of a Canadian Literature," he not only gave a clear statement of his belief in workmanship as the *sine qua non* of worthwhile Canadian poetry, but also brought his aesthetic standards to bear on the poetry of French and English Canada, judging the former "polished and artistic, imbued with unmistakeable Canadian flavour, yet not servilely provincial in its themes," and the latter by turns "rough-hewn" (Charles Heavysege), "uneven" (John Hunter-Duvar) and lacking in "range of subject" (Kate MacLean) (*Selected Poetry and Critical Prose* 249, 252, 253). The commitment to careful and consistent workmanship that lies behind all these judgments is also evident in Roberts's comments on the work of Lampman and Carman before and during his months as editor of *The Week*, the Toronto "Independent Journal of Literature, Politics, and Criticism," in late 1883 and early 1884. On 23 September, two of Lampman's poems ("The Last Sortie" and probably "Derelict") are praised for exhibiting "the pulse of humanity" but criticized for "an evidency of haste, and too little of determined perplexing and polishing" (*Collected Letters* 30). On 31 December 1883, two of Carman's rondeaux are mentioned as having been received at the editorial offices of *The Week*, "but not yet … read closely," and on 11 January 1884 they are rejected for publication because "not quite even in merit throughout" (*Collected Letters* 38). Roberts's letters of the late fall and early winter of 1884 reveal that, although he followed Carman's lead in writing triolets and rondels at that time, this did not prevent him from critiquing his cousin's efforts in both forms. "The triolet is matchless," he told Carman on 27 November; just as

> that on the Ball Programme is one of the most perfect light triolets in the language, so this I believe to be the only really and wholly effective serious triolet. As a severe-eyed critic I have no fault to find with it. I long to get at the work of talking about such work publicly. The rondel is unquestionably beautiful, but not perfect. It has such a lyric lift and ring that one is carried over the obscurity … But the obscurity exists,

and herein lies one of your chief dangers .... Try and say what must
be said, rather than be content with what ... may be said. Try and give
the impression that nothing else could be said just there; this will give
your work the quality of inevitableness, which ... when predominant
in a poet's work, writes after his name more unmistakably than any-
thing else can, the word Master. (*Collected Letters* 46)

In addition to revealing an astute and penetrating critical intelligence
(Carman's tendency to content himself with less than "what must be
said" could indeed be identified as the chief weakness of his work),
Roberts's letters to Lampman and Carman confirm his leadership of
the emerging Confederation group in matters of form and technique
as well as ideas and politics.

Of special note in Roberts's letter to Carman is his recourse to what
he terms "the quality of inevitableness," a criterion that he would
explain in a letter to Frederick George Scott over two years later: "*every-
thing* [in a poem] must be made to look as if the difficulty of the form
had *nothing* to do with it! Every word must be *inevitable*" (*Collected Letters*
198). Even when thus explained, "inevitableness" is hard to define
precisely, though it is clearly related to the dictum that art should
conceal artifice. In practice, it seems to have meant that poets should
avoid being seen to have chosen a particular word or rhyme to fulfil the
requirements of their chosen form and metre. A result of both facility
and craftsmanship, talent and revision, its absence would be manifested
in excrescent words, awkward rhythms and clumsy rhymes, any one of
which could detract from the effect of a lyric. Writing to the American
poet Charles Leonard Moore on 16 June 1885, Roberts judges Oscar
Wilde's "general output of lyrics [to be] not of a very high quality"
because "only here and there does one come across a lyric which
contains the inevitableness which will make it live" (*Collected Letters* 49),
and it may be inferred that when he praised the "lyrics" of *Among the
Millet, and Other Poems* as "admirable" and the "sonnets" as "exquisite"
in a letter to Lampman of 18 December 1888 (*Collected Letters* 97), he did
so because he recognized in them the "inevitableness" that he had ear-
lier demanded of Carman and would later demand of Frederick George
Scott (and, very likely, other members of the Confederation group).

To some extent, the longing to express his views publicly that Roberts
confided to Carman on 28 November 1884 had already been fulfilled in
two articles that were published shortly after his departure from *The
Week*, "Notes on Some Younger American Poets" (24 April 1884) and

"Edgar Fawcett" (26 June 1884). Neither of these articles so much as mentions a Canadian poet or poem, but they are of considerable interest on two counts: as reflections of Robert's aesthetic values and as indications of his thinking on the nature of schools of poetry. Evidently intended as the first of a series of articles on "the younger school" of American poets—that is, Fawcett, Joachim Miller, Sidney Lanier, Richard Watson Gilder and others—"Notes on Some of the Younger American Poets" begins with two observations and a question: (1) "the acknowledged chiefs of American song for the most part have fallen, or have laid down their pens"; and (2) "they have formed no 'schools'" and gathered no "following[s] of pronounced disciples" (328). What accounts for this? Roberts's full answer does not come until the article on Fawcett, but it is implicit in his argument in "Notes on Some of the Younger American Poets" that of all "the acknowledged Chiefs of American Song"—Poe, Emerson, Longfellow, Whitman and Oliver Wendell Holmes—only one, Holmes, is likely to generate "a following of disciples," the reason being that no future practitioner of the type of poetry upon which Holmes left the indelible "impress of his genius" can possibly "afford to neglect his instruction" (328). That Holmes's forte was "society verse" or "*vers de société*," a type of poetry whose "characteristics ... are elegance, decorum, moderation, neatness of expression, perfection of form, and coolness of sentiment and tone,"[4] only serves to increase the likelihood that Roberts saw in him a partial parallel with himself as a technical exemplar and mentor for a new school of poets. Since Roberts had begun to develop "a warm friendship" with Holmes after the American poet responded enthusiastically to *Orion, and Other Poems* (Pomeroy 38–39), there is also a likelihood that he regarded himself as something of a disciple. Certainly, a number of Roberts's poems of the early and mid-1880s, including "La Belle Tromboniste" (1885) and "The Marvellous Work" (1886), suggest that he may have taken instruction from Holmes's work both in the light vein of such pieces as "Dorothy Q." and "the purely serious vain" of "The Chambered Nautilus" and "The Living Temple" (see Roberts, "Notes" 328).

After a brief recapitulation of the argument of "Notes on Some of the Younger American Poets," Roberts delivers himself in the preamble to "Edgar Fawcett" of an aesthetic statement that, with the substitution of Lampman and Carman for Edmund Clarence Stedman and Thomas Bailey Aldrich, could easily be an expression of his view of the state of contemporary Canadian poetry:

It is undeniable that in certain of the most distinguished of American poets exists a marked deficiency in the sense of form, in symmetry of construction, and in finish .... Stedman and Aldrich have hardly a living superior in matters of pure technique, in the essentially artistic qualifications of a poet. But these stand out as exceptions. Sometimes it looks as if the idea were of supreme importance, and to be developed at all hazard, while the medium of expression is handled with a trace of impatience or contempt. In the minor poets much more than this is apparent. One feels too often that their reverence for their art is scanty, that they have a disdain for careful and devoted labour, perhaps no perception whatever of the need of recasting, of polishing, of perfecting. An idea, an emotion, an incident, or a romance is forced into ill-fitting garments of crudely-constructed verse. (471)

Against this dismaying backdrop stands Fawcett, "a young poet ... who is essentially an artist, reverencing deeply his art, and master of all its technicalities"—a poet possessed of "the artist's intolerance of slovenly workmanship, ... an unerring sense of proportion" and "symmetry of design," and a capacity to combine "exquisite compactness" with freedom from "obscurity" (472). Roberts would soon come to see the limitations of Fawcett's work, but in the early 1880s he evidently regarded him as a poet worthy of emulation as well as "earnest regard." In fact, the model for "The Sower," the Petrarchan sonnet inspired by the painting of the same name by Jean-François Millet that Roberts first published in the July 1884 number of the *Manhattan* (New York), is clearly Fawcett's Petrarchan sonnet titled "Sleep / (For a Picture)," which Roberts discusses admiringly in "Edgar Fawcett" and proclaims superior even to Dante Gabriel Rossetti's "For a Venetian Pastoral" (472), which "is surely the most perfect sonnet-music in the language" (437). The fact that the letter of 12 December 1882, in which Roberts assumes the role of "*sacer vates*" (inspired bard) to conjur for Carman "the near approaching awakening of Canada, in politics, art, song, [and] intellectual effort generally," refers to a letter in which Fawcett has "hail[ed] [him] as a leader of the choir" (*Collected Letters* 33) suggests that the American also played a part in solidifying Roberts's sense of himself as the leader of an emerging school of Canadian poets.

Largely as a result of Roberts's personal example and critical efforts, the association of the Confederation group with careful workmanship was firmly established in Canadian literary circles by the late 1880s.

Thus Agnes Maule Machar ("Fidelis") praised Lampman's "high degree of general artistic excellence and careful technique" (251) in a review of *Among the Millet, and Other Poems* in the 22 March 1889 issue of *The Week*, and Lilly E.F. Barry, writing of the same poet in the same periodical on 10 April 1891, emphasized "the high state of finish which characterizes all ... [his] compositions" (300). For his part, Lampman had no doubt about the Archimedean moment of the aesthetic of workmanship. "[B]efore the appearance of *Orion* [, *and Other Poems*]," he wrote in "Two Canadian Poets" "all the verse writing published in Canada ... was of a more or less barbarous character. The drama of *Saul* by Charles Heavysege and some of Heavysege's sonnets are about the only exceptions which can be made to this statement .... [George Frederick] Cameron, although a poet of greater spontaneity,[5] a more passionate force, and a much higher range of feeling, than ... Roberts does not equal him in perfection of style. He neither aimed at, nor attained the same artistic excellence of workmanship" (*Essays and Reviews* 95). Nearly a quarter of a century later, Roberts's long-time friend and admirer John Daniel Logan would cement and summarize the association of the Confederation group with workmanship in *Highways of Canadian Literature*: *Orion, and Other Poems* was a source of "the First Renaissance in Canadian Literature" because it evinced "a certain ... *artistic finish* in [its] craftsmanship" that had not been present "in previous books of verse by native-born Canadians .... With the publication of his *Orion*, Roberts sounded the death knell of slovenly or indifferent technique in Canadian poetry. Working with him, and largely under the influence of his ideal of technical finish in verse, were Lampman, Carman, Campbell, Pauline Johnson, Duncan Campbell Scott, Frederick George Scott, and others. They all cared supremely for fine technique in poetry" (107).

III

Of course, the commitment of the Confederation group to "*artistic finish*" was neither as unanimous, straightforward, nor enduring as Logan suggests and, indeed, knew, for at the very inception of their correspondence in June 1888 he and Roberts had agreed that in its most rarefied form, the "passion" for French forms, the contemporary devotion to "fine technique" had exhausted itself in "satiety and weariness" (*Collected Letters* 83). As Roberts's curiously post-coital comments indicate, he was neither alone in his feeling of formal exhaustion nor bereft of reasons for experiencing it personally. In their responses to his *In Divers Tones* volume of 1886, friends and reviewers alike had taken him to task for emphasizing form at the expense of other qualities. "It is not in the dilletante rondeau of compliment, but in the treatment of themes which call forth the creative and reflective forces of his genius, that Prof. Roberts will win his way to wider recognition as a poet," wrote the reviewer for the Chatham *World* (2 April 1887). "He has ... fallen into the sin of the nineteenth-century, a fondness for formal verse such as the Ballade and Rondeau," observed T.G. Marquis in the 26 July 1888 issue of *The Week*; "the paucity of rhyme in the English Language is a sufficiently onerous chain to the muse without making artificial ones. In such styles of verse the sense must often give way to the rhyme" (559). Nevertheless, added Marquis, "in the sonnet Professor Roberts is a master, and several of his will compare with the very best in the English language."

That Roberts took such criticisms to heart is evident both from his subsequent formal choices (after 1886 he wrote and published many sonnets but no rondeaux) and from several comments in his letters and reviews of the late 1880s. "[Y]our criticism ... is just," he told his friend William Douw Lighthall on 30 September 1888; "I have long felt ... the need of my work to free itself from a certain scholasticism of subject .... Of old, I worshipped nothing but beauty .... That phase I have outgrown" (*Collected Letters* 87). "The note among our rising writers is one of more passion, more purpose, more seriousness and import than that sounded by the younger Americans," he wrote in a review of *Among the Millet, and Other Poems* in the 26 January 1889 issue of *Progress* (Saint John, NB): "[w]ith us in Canada, though we may appear to trifle a little with ballades and villanelles and triolets, there is a strenuous undercurrent almost always to be detected. The apparent trifling is but the striving after an unimpeachable technique; the underlying motive is one of deep seriousness and impassioned expectancy." In line with the "Canadianism" (see Bentley, *Confederation Group* 70–110) that he saw exemplified in the work of Lighthall and Lampman, Roberts was in the process in 1889 of abandoning the cul-de-sac of formalism into which his quest for workmanship had drawn him and began rededicating that workmanship to the Canadian subjects and themes that he had once regarded as inessential. The sense of freedom and renewal in "The Waking Earth" (1893), a sonnet first published in the *Independent* on 23 May 1889, could well be aesthetic as well as seasonal and sexual.

The evidence of Roberts having outgrown the doctrinaire formalism "phase" that had enamoured him of classical and French forms did not fully appear until the publication in 1893 of *Songs of the Common Day*, and *Ave: An Ode for the Shelley Centenary*. In the meantime, reactions against formalism proliferated and intensified both outside and within the Confederation group. "From faithful critics on all sides the cry had been going up of late years that poetry was too much given over to the worship of form," wrote Roberts in his "The World of Books" column in *Progress* on 12 October 1889:

> The cry is one of needed warning and cannot be too pertinaciously reiterated. In a vast deal of contemporary work one feels that the initial impulse has come less from a need of giving utterance to some vivid emotion or high idea than from an idle itch for experimenting in bizarre verse-forms. I am keenly alive to the fact that this experimenting in verse-forms has its value. It gives faculty, it opens one's eyes to the defects of his technique, it helps one to realize how flexible language may become; but, like all experimenting, it is perilous by reason of its fascinations. And often it happens that the writer who at first thought only of how he might best achieve a fine poem, gradually lowers his aim to the accomplishment of a delicate piece of verbal filigree that can be ticketed Rondeau, or Ballade, and judged as such mainly.

Roberts exempts the sonnet from opprobrium, but a little over two weeks later in *The Week* Edward Burrough Brownlow ("Sarepta") made no such concession: "artificial forms of verse have been resuscitated from Provençal graves to serve as winding-sheets for much wasted genius," he lamented, "and the history and analysis of all physical and psychical nature is temporarily preserved in an interminable multitude of sonnets, for which kind of composition a veritable epidemic has long set in and shows no sign of abatement" ("The Sonnet.—VIII" 760). As Collins put it in a letter of 27 August 1891 to Lampman, "there is a reaction against mere form."

Several months before Collins's letter, Lampman had in fact partici-
pated vigorously in the "reaction against mere form" in "Two Canadian
Poets," which needs to be appreciated not only for its celebration of
Lampman's momentous first encounter with *Orion, and Other Poems*,
but also for its concern to establish a moral-aesthetic contrast between
Roberts's "perfection of style" and Cameron's "greater spontaneity" that
makes Cameron the more admirable of the two poets: "[i]n Mr. Roberts'
work, notwithstanding the great ability that has gone to the making of
it, there is often a certain weightiness and deliberateness of phrase,
which suggests too strongly the hand of the careful workman, and robs
it of the fullest effect of spontaneity .... In Mr. Cameron's work ... we
come into contact with ... a man who dwells among genuine thoughts
and genuine feelings, and speaks a language full of spontaneity, force
and dignity" (*Essays and Reviews* 107–8). As admirable as they are in
many ways, including their "workmanship" (96), Lampman suggests,
too many of Roberts's poems have "a scholarly character"; he has "not
sufficient ease and flow to work well in complicated stanzas";
"occasionally [his] work is spoiled by an effect of strain and elaborate
effort"; his sonnets are "unevenly successful," and his patriotic poems
are "clever, but heavy, pompous and more of the tongue [than] the heart"
(96, 101, 102, 105, 107). In contrast, Cameron's work is "penetrating,
elastic,[6] and full of high sound," "simple, manly and bracing," "sincere"
and "genuinely poetic" (108, 113, 114). A year or two earlier, Lampman
had ended a lecture on "Style" by quoting some "unsurpassably fine"
lines from "Tantramar Revisited" (90). In "Two Canadian Poets: A
Lecture," a passage from the same poem is quoted to illustrate Roberts's
"keen sympathy with nature and his strenuous and scholarly gift of
expression," and the lecture concludes with a reading of two of
Cameron's poems, one of which, "The Week vs. Wendell Phillips," was
occasioned by "a virulent attack" on the American orator and reformer
that "appeared in ... *The Week* directly after the announcement of his
death" on 2 February 1884 (Cameron, *Lyrics* 184n)—that is, during
Roberts's editorship.

An examination of the full consequences of the rift between and
among Lampman, Roberts and other members of the Confederation
group that was becoming evident in 1891 cannot and need not be
undertaken here (see Bentley, *Confederation Group* 273–90) but the
point can be made that the animosity evident in "Two Canadian Poets"
extends even to the American poet whose workmanship Roberts had

effusively praised in *The Week* some six years earlier. In the "artifice of phrase" that they employ "to convey ... the rank warm luxurian[ce]" of the Greek landscape, observes Lampman of a passage in "The Pipes of Pan," "some of the ... lines are in a slight degree over done, [and] remind ... one in that respect of the American poet Edgar Fawcett, who is very fond of reaching natural effects by artifices of this kind" (*Essays and Reviews* 100–1). As the "reaction against mere form" grew in the early 1890s, Lampman would again use Fawcett as the target of his attacks on bloodless formalism, this time in his contributions to the weekly "At the Mermaid Inn" column that he, Campbell and Duncan Campbell Scott contributed to the Toronto *Globe* from 6 February 1892 to 1 July 1893: "the cleverest sonnets we have are those of Mr. Edgar Fawcett. They are the cleverest, the strongest, the most ingenious, and the least-touching" (17 September 1892); "his talent [is] brilliant, ingenious, productive, but artificial, overstrained, and devoid of tenderness" (20 May 1893) (152, 316). Lampman's few comments on Roberts in "At the Mermaid Inn" either damn his work with faint praise or couch praise in stringent reservations: "Chas. G.D. Roberts has written at least one sonnet of a high order, 'Reckoning,' and several others of marked and individual excellence"; "Canadian Streams" in the 1892 number of the *Dominion Illustrated* (Montreal) is "one of Professor Roberts's patriotic outbursts" that contains "many lines ... [that] are very grand ... in a way ... yet ... seem to come shouldering up with a conscious and premeditated effort," and "Ave" reveals "our master workman in verse" to be a member of the idolatrous "cult" of "Shelley worshippers" who has nevertheless produced a poem of impressive "beauty" and "fervour" that contains numerous examples of "his vivid and luxurious delight in splendid landscape and the richness of his gift as a word painter" (a term which, as will be seen in a moment, cannot be construed as an unalloyed compliment) (153, 193, 239).

While Lampman's critiques of formalism and its practitioners remained fairly constant in tenor and tone from 1891 to 1893 (and beyond), Campbell's hostility to "artificial poetry" (as he termed it and to his fellow Canadian poets) escalated to fever pitch in his contributions to "At the Mermaid Inn" in the course of 1892 and 1893. On 28 May and 1 October 1892, two American poets, James Whitcomb Riley and Thomas Bailey Aldrich, are by turns heartily complimented and gently rebuked, the former for managing to remain "sincere and natural" "in these days, when there is so much artificial verse-making," and the latter for allowing himself to become "too much the artist ... to be a great popular poet to the people, who require a stronger heart-touch than his artistic repression will allow" (80–82, 160). On 12 November of the same year, the "fad" for "finish" and "polish" in poetry has become, for Campbell, inimical to creativity and contrary to nature: "[t]he greatest genius, and the one that bids most for immortality, is the genius that is the most uneven in flight and finish. Nature requires contrast, and the greatest and strongest poetry is that which at times is rugged and bold. To spend years polishing down a man's thoughts and visions into a certain glittering monotony is just as though nature would level her hills and fill up her valleys into an immense plain .... [V]erse ... should be as near nature as possible" (*Mermaid Inn* 189). A premonition of what the following years would bring from Campbell's pen came on 10 December 1892 with his contention that what Canada needs most "at the present stage of [its] literary development ... [is] frankness of opinion and proper, unbiased judgement .... [L]iterary critics and journals [must] take the trouble to thoroughly study our literature and examine into its real merits ... [for] [t]o judge our poets as patriotic poets or human poets or nature poets or poet artists, or as disciples of this or that school, is both unnatural and absurd" (209).

Having thus established at least to his own satisfaction that his prejudices accorded with the laws of nature and reason, Campbell proceeded in his "At the Mermaid Inn" columns of 1893 to identify violations and to prosecute their perpetrators: in the plethora of recent sonnets only "half a dozen ... [are] true poems," and these are "not found among the delicate word artists who have wrought so hard in that direction" (18 March); in its review of contemporary American poetry in its tenth anniversary issue, the *New York World* is right in recognizing an absence of "great truth" and an "abundance" of "over-perfect style" in the fad for old French forms (20 May); the inheritors of Tennyson's tendency to "polish and over-refine" his poetry are a host of "college graduates ... [who] can turn out any amount of the kind of gentle, sensitive verses with a sort of delicate finish that the magazines of today seem to require" (17 June); the term "quality" has become "a sort of apology for the kind of pseudo-poetry that is marking these times, and which, in the absence of real poetic imagination and creative ability, has taken to pensive musings and landscape painting in words" (1 July) (278, 315–16, 331, 333, 341). Since Campbell's accusatory finger points more and more in these passages towards Roberts and Lampman (both of whom were, of course, "college graduates" and adept at "landscape painting in words"), they must have suspected that their poems in particular were the target of the two parodies that appeared over the name "John Pensive Bangs" in the column of 1 July (the anniversary of Confederation). Both of these, the first, titled "At Even" and contemptuously introduced as "of course ... a sonnet," and the second, titled "Pitching Hay" and similarly dismissed as the product of "no lofty thoughts or wide knowledge of nature and man," echo the poems of Roberts and Lampman in setting and phraseology as well as in form and theme, and several other aspects of the satire suggest that Campbell's "verse-maker" is at least in part an amalgam of the two: "Bangs" has been to college, he has "read Matthew Arnold," and he has garnered the extravagant praise of a critic who commends "At Even" for being "Millet-like in its terse realism"—a reference very likely to both "The Sower" and *Among the Millet, and Other Poems* (341–42).[7] It is difficult to doubt that the termination of "At the Mermaid Inn" with the 1 July 1893 column was not a consequence at least in part of Campbell's increasingly rebarbative and finally satirical attitude to his fellow poets.

Although Roberts's insistence on workmanship as the overriding criterion for Canadian poetry resulted in tensions and disagreements that contributed to the disintegration of the Confederation group in the mid-1890s, it also helped to sharpen the technical skills of the group's members and, at least as important, to direct their attention to form and its implications. Among Lampman's contributions to the "At the Mermaid Inn" column in 1892 is a piece that turns on an imaginary conversation with a "sonneteer" who "takes a sort of inhuman delight in torturing [the poet] with sonnets of his own composition on all sorts of flippant and improper subjects" (87). On being treated to readings of two sonnets that confirm his "abhorrence ... [of] persons ... who profane and misapply the sonnet"—the first a trivial account of falling asleep and the second a starkly realistic description of the ugly side of urban life—the poet censures the sonneteer in the first instance for failing to find a "form ... less ridiculously inapplicable to the smallness and homeliness of [his] subject" and in the second for "violat[ing] every law of moral dignity and literary decency" (88, 89). Clearly evident in these humorous remarks is a serious moral-aesthetic whose roots lie in the classical theory of decorum: the sonnet is more "suitable" (Lampman's word) to some themes and subjects than to others—a rule of propriety that the fictitious "sonneteer" chooses to flout in order to offend the poet's sense of seemliness and decency. That the "sonneteer" ends the encounter by breaking into "a roar of course and offensive laughter," "filliping" the "pellets" into which he has "crushed ... his papers ... into [the poet's] face," and "str[iding] rudely out of the room" (89) is a dramatic reflection of Lampman's belief as expressed in his essay on "Style" (circa 1890) and elsewhere that literary style and personal conduct are directly related. As Lampman puts it in the opening paragraph of "Style," "style ... might be defined as the habit or manner given to expression by the prevalence of a certain mental attitude peculiar to any individual or class of individuals or any age .... Style ... is not a quality peculiar to literature, but may be found in every sort of expression when carried to a certain point of culture, in action, in speech, in literature, and in all the arts. We know how noticeable the quality of style is in the conduct and bearing of many people who have a decided mental character and have mingled freely in the activities of the world .... In its finest development this style or manner ... is a revelation of character .... [P]erfection of style ... [is] the expression of a certain poetic grace of nature" (*Essays and Reviews* 72).

Although the themes and subjects "suitable" for treatment in the sonnet are not specified by Lampman in "At the Mermaid Inn," it is plausible to infer from his own formal practices that he regarded the form as appropriate only for serious and elevating materials, be these meditations on external nature, examinations of profound emotions, or statements of moral and philosophical principles (categories of which "In November," "An Old Lesson from the Fields" and "The Truth" in the sonnet section of *Among the Millet, and Other Poems* are representative examples). Only the poem titled "The Dog," with which *Among the Millet* closes, might appear to be a violation of Lampman's "law of moral dignity and literary decency" in its use of the Petrarchan sonnet form to describe the "small ... and homel[y] ... subject" of throwing "balls" for an insouciantly ugly dog (*Poems* 121); however, the exclamation with which "The Dog" opens ("'Grotesque!'") and the reflexivity of some of its phrasing ("queer feet / Planted irregularly," "we ... defied him / With ... loose criticism") indicate that it is an exercise in incongruity that aims to extract humour by treating a comically ugly subject in a serious form, which is itself rendered comical (and thus appropriate) by ridiculous rhymes ("him" for all the a rhymes in the octave, "pigs" and "legs" for one of the rhymes in the sestet).

Perhaps because he was also classically trained, Roberts evidently shared Lampman's acute sense of formal decorum. None of the sonnets in the "Songs of the Common Day" series or elsewhere violates the rules implied by Lampman's statements; and his practice vis-à-vis the ballade, rondeau, triolet and other forms confirm his awareness of their appropriateness for some but not other subjects and tones. Moreover, Roberts appears to have recognized from the outset that the Petrarchan sonnet was a suitable form for what Campbell derisively calls "landscape paintings in words"—"terse[ly] realistic" depictions of picturesque rural and architectural scenes for which the rectangular outlines of the sonnet provide the equivalent of a picture frame. Evidence for this perceived homology begins to accumulate with the two Petrarchan sonnets in *Orion, and Other Poems*, "Iterumne?" and "At Pozzuoli," both of which depict classical landscapes and themes, the latter, as Ross S. Kilpatrick has shown, partly inspired by an illustration of "the temple of Jupiter Serapis at Pozzuoli" (104–5) near Naples in James Dana's *Manual of Geology*. A clutch of sonnets of the early 1880s such as "To Fredericton in May-time" (1881) and "In September" (1881) signal a growing recognition of the suitability of the Petrarchan sonnet to picturesque Canadian scenes, but it is with "The Sower," which was probably written early in 1884, that Roberts begins fully to exploit the potential of the form's octave / sestet configuration as a vehicle for descriptions that move from background to foreground, general to particular, objective to subjective, shifts that are also evident in other much-anthologised sonnets such as "The Potato Harvest" (1893) and "The Pea-Fields." As has been argued elsewhere, (see Bentley, *Gay, Grey Moose* 40) a similar consonance between form and content is discernible in Roberts's masterpiece, "Tantramar Revisited," where the alternating lines of dactylic hexameter and pentameter accord with the scenery being described not only in their "out rolled" horizontality (*CP* 78), but also, as an early critic pointed out, in the ebb and flow movement captured by Coleridge's well-known distich on and in the form: "In the hexameter rises the fountain's silvery column; / In the pentameter aye falling steadily back" (quoted in Gummere 232).

Campbell's hostility to fixed forms and technical polish was in part a reflection of the widespread "reaction against mere form" that Collins mentioned to Lampman in August 1891 and in part a manifestation of a profound distrust of convention and artifice that arose from his Wordsworthian belief that "simplicity and directness of manner"—"direct, simple naturalness"—"are essential to the highest art" (*Poems* v). Not fortuitously, the "At the Mermaid Inn" column of 17 June 1893, in which Campbell roundly condemns what he sees as the Tennysonian tradition of "polish and over-refine[ment]," concludes with a paean to Wordsworth, as a poet of "simple, grand emotion" who "is not and never could be a minute scenic artist, such as the descriptive sonnet writers we have today" (334) (a statement that, of course, ignores the existence of Wordsworth's many descriptive sonnets). In the late 1880s, however, Campbell was probably flattered by Roberts's comment that in *Snowflakes and Sunbeams* (1888) he "shows the instincts of the crafts-man imbued with right reverence for his craft," and, as suggested in the previous chapter, he may even have been encouraged to make his second volume a collection of *Lake Lyrics, and Other Poems* (1889) by Roberts's suggestion that the "promise" of his early work was already being fulfilled in the "lyric splendor of 'The Winter Lakes' and 'A Lake Memory,'" which had recently appeared in "American periodicals" ("The World of Books," *Progress*, 9 March 1889, 6). "No other Canadian poet ... has so rendered the spirit and form of our winter scenes,—unless, perhaps, Mr. Lampman in one or two instances," wrote Roberts; "the sublime landscapes of the Great Lakes, Mr. Campbell has pre-empted as his own peculiar field; and he is likely to hold sway there without a rival, by reason of the Swinburnian resonance and the breadth of his rhythmic phrases, combined with his deep and subtle insight into eternal nature in her most impressive aspects."

As much as anything else, it may have been Campbell's preference for the sublime over the picturesque that lay behind his hostility to fixed forms, for surely the corollary of a temperamental preference for the grand and expansive in external nature and human emotion must be a rejection of the small and the circumscribed, whether it be in the realm of landscape, feeling or poetic form. Even in defending the sonnet, had not Wordsworth likened it to a "convent's narrow room," a "scanty plot of ground," a "prison" and a "cell" (3:1)? Again not fortuitously, Campbell's political movement in the 1890s from the fervent nationalism of such poems as "National Thanksgiving Chant" (1891) and "Ode to Canada" (1896) to the outspoken imperialism of "England" (1897), "Sebastian Cabot" (1897), "Victoria" (1901), "Crowning of Empire" (1901), "The Discoverers" (1904) and numerous other poems of the post-Confeder-ation group period is reflected in his choice of increasingly open, infinitely expansive and traditionally English forms such as blank verse that correspond both to the "vast spaces" of the British Empire and to the "vaster dream" of "Subduing all with iron titan will" ("Rhodes," *Selected Poetry and Essays* 390–91). Campbell would in due course give fullest poetic expression to his Imperialism in *Sagas of Vaster Britain: Poems of the Race, the Empire and the Divinity of Man* (1914), the very title of which echoes the concept of "Greater Britain" articulated by Sir J.R. Seeley in *The Expansion of England* (1883, 1895), a work that probably lies centrally in the background of the development in his political thinking in the 1890s.

Neither as temperamentally and ideologically disposed as Campbell and Carman to open spaces and forms nor as morally and politically committed to non-coercive form or order as Lampman and Frederick George Scott, Duncan Campbell Scott would prove to be the most formalistically experimental member of the Confederation group. "You could find plenty to say about metre [in my work] and I have invented not a few new stanzas," he told Pelham Edgar in 1905. "Give me some credit for logic as applied to aesthetics for I declare that I value brainpower at the bottom of everything" (*Some Letters* np). Wisely standing to one side of the aesthetic and personal controversies into which Campbell drew the other members of the group, Scott never wavered from a dedication to form that might have resulted in aestheticism if it had not been grounded in a perception of technique as functional and supportive rather than arbitrary and decorative. Objectionable though they may now be as depictions of Native peoples, "Watkwenies" (1898) and "The Onondaga Madonna" (1898) employ the Petrarchan sonnet with a keenly ironical sense of its association with idealized women, and "The Forsaken" (1905), "On the Way to the Mission" (1905), "At Gull Lake: August, 1810" (1935) and "A Scene at Lake Manitou" (1935) juxtapose various loosened and stanzaic verse patterns with a superb sense of their relative effectiveness as vehicles for kinetic, static and pictorial subject matter. As much if not more than Roberts, Duncan Campbell Scott understood the value of poetic form as a means by which a poet can exercise writerly discipline and enhance readerly pleasure to achieve what E.K. Brown called "a mixture of restraint and intensity ... [that] grasps at one and will not let go" (122)—a poetry that, at its best, involves and satisfies the reader both emotionally and intellectually.

As for Roberts himself, it is not a little ironical that he had to wait until after his departure for the United States in 1897 had sounded the death knell for the Confederation group to receive his highest compliment for achieving the workmanship that he had laboured so hard, and so often thanklessly, to emphasize and to exemplify. "There is in him a sense of artistic finish," wrote the reviewer of *The Book of the Native* (1896) in the 18 March 1897 issue of the *Nation* (New York)—"'the perfection and precision of the instantaneous line,'" in Ruskin's phrase—without which genius leaves its work still undone" (207). Whether entirely justified or not, this judgment must have greatly heartened Roberts after the previous years' assaults on his aesthetic principles and practices. Perhaps it even encouraged him in the pursuit of "artistic finish" and formal subtlety that, as demonstrated elsewhere, is very much in evidence in the volume that he published a year after moving to the United States, *New York Nocturnes and Other Poems* (1898).

IV

"I never consciously set to work to make a book of a certain type of poems .... And I have tried to avoid collecting one kind of poem in one book. I prefer variety. I have opposed Carman in this" ("Interviews" 74). Embedded in these statements by Roberts to Lorne Pierce in June 1927 are references to the second aesthetic principle shared by members of the Confederation group and to the one member of the group who rejected that principle. Almost needless to say, neither "variety" as a principle for the construction of a collection of poems nor the rejection of it in favour of a uniformity of form and/or theme originated with Roberts or Carman: Virgil, Horace, Tibullus, Propertius and Ovid are merely the best known of the Augustan poets who "took cognizance of variety" (*varietas*) in organizing their collections either to "parade ... [their] virtuosity" or to satisfy their readers' demands for "diversity" (William S. Anderson 44–49), and both the aesthetic of variety and the motives for its exercise were still very much alive in the late nineteenth century, particularly among classically trained poets and readers such a Roberts and Lampman—indeed, Kilpatrick has compellingly argued "that Roberts's chief model for his arrangement of the poems in *Orion* was the *Odes* of Horace" (xix). By the same token, the use of numerous techniques such as "structural symmetries," "thematic and imagistic metaphors among the poems" and "some pattern of serial arrangement" (for example, a seasonal or narrative progression) can be traced at least as far back as the Alexandrian poet Callimachus (Fraistat 5–6) and was also very much alive in the late nineteenth century, particularly among poets like Carman who looked to the Pre-Raphaelites for their poetic models. It is not without intriguing geopolitical implications that the issue of variety versus uniformity was a cause of both agreement and discussion in the Confederation group; in the organization of books, as in the choice of forms and the depiction of landscapes, aesthetics may be closer to politics than they initially appear.

Except for an honorific comment on "the variety of Mr. Fawcett's power" in his June 1884 essay in *The Week* (472), Roberts's published criticism and extant letters of the 1880s and early 1890s make no explicit mention of the principle that nevertheless lies centrally in the background of many of his literary judgments during this period and, more important, came increasingly to dictate the content and arrangement of his collections at this time. A preference for variety over uniformity is clearly evident, for example, in Roberts's comments on *Among the Millet, and Other Poems* and *Snowflakes and Sunbeams* in the 26 January and 9 March 1889 issues of *Progress*: Lampman's "verse ... possess[es] the essential, but Protean, quality which we indicate by the term genius," but "Campbell's note is not yet one of any great range." To the extent that this last remark was intended to be constructive as well as critical, it was probably shaped at least in part by the critical response to Roberts's own début volume, for, while *Orion, and Other Poems* was repeatedly heralded as a breakthrough and warmly endorsed in the November 1880 number of *Canadian Monthly* as a manifestation of his "varied and vivid powers" (553), it was also faulted for its bookish artistry and narrowness of theme. "Now let him read men, nature, his country and his own heart, and he can accomplish very much indeed," counselled one reviewer, and another: "now that our author is no longer at college, but a man among men, it is to be presumed that he will ... marry his muse to more modern and interesting themes" (*Capital* [Fredericton, NB], 5 October 1880; *Miramichi Advance* [Chatham, NB], 4 November 1880).

That Roberts also took these criticisms to heart is evident in the very title of his second volume. Taken from Tennyson's *In Memoriam* (1: 2), where it alludes to Goethe's mastery of "many different styles" (*Poems* 864n), *In Divers Tones* calls attention to the variety of mood and manner encompassed by the collection, which includes patriotic poems (such as "Collect for Dominion Day" and "Canada"), landscape sonnets (such as "The Potato Harvest" and "The Sower"), classical pieces (such as "Actaeon" and "The Pipes of Pan"), as well as a greater Romantic lyric ("Tantramar Revisited"), two poems on Native themes ("The Quelling of the Moose" and "The Departing of Clote Scarp"), several pieces of *vers de société* (for example, "The Poet is Bidden to Manhattan Island"), a couple of ballades, a translation of a poem by Louis-Honoré Fréchette and (note the appropriateness of the French form) a rondeau in his honour. "[A]s compared with *Orion, and Other Poems*, *In Divers Tones* reveals a broadening of the author's interest in the living world," wrote John Reade of the volume when it eventually appeared after much delay in April 1887 (see *Collected Letters* 61–65); "as the title implies, the book is the offspring of many moods, and it is addressed to many minds" (15 April 1887). Thanks primarily to *In Divers Tones*, the perception of Roberts's poetry as narrow in theme and finical in technique was replaced in the late 1880s and early 1890s with the view that he was a poet of multifaceted talent whose gifts are especially evident in his "patriotic poems," his "classical pieces" and his "sonnets of farm life" (Douglas Sladen, quoted in "The World of Books," *Progress*, 23 November 1889). In the November 1891 number of *Dominion Illustrated*, W.G. MacFarlane would write of "patriotic verse and ... Canadian nature poems" as the "two sides of [Roberts's] genius ... that make him a Canadian poet" and a third "variety of his poems" that had to be reckoned with—"those after Greek models" (494). By the early 1890s, then, Roberts had apparently overcome his reputation as a narrow and scholarly poet and come to be seen instead as a man of quite broad interests who had produced excellent poems in no less than three modes.

This was not sufficient for Lampman, however, for in "Two Canadian Poets" Roberts is faulted not only for his sacrifice of "spontaneity" on the altar of "workman[ship]," but also for his lack of breadth and diversity. True, "his poems are written upon many various subjects, and either of his books might appear on a cursory glance to be somewhat remarkable for variety," says Lampman, but in fact "only three or four really different notes are struck, and all the poems are found to be attuned to these" (*Essays and Reviews* 107). (In contrast, Cameron of course has "all the fervour, the breadth and energy of thought, the sensitive humanity that Professor Roberts lacks" [108].) In thus faulting Roberts, Lampman was merely bringing to bear on a fellow member of the Confederation group the aesthetic principle that he had articulated five years earlier in the preamble of a lecture titled "The Modern School of Poetry in England" (1886): "it seems to me that in endeavouring to reach approximately the worth of a living poet, there are two qualities to be especially looked for .... These are variety or versatility, and geniality. The work of all the greatest poets has been very varied, and it has been very genial. Looking with a wide and hearty and sympathetic eye upon all life, they have touched innumerable notes, and have absorbed themselves readily into every phase of its humour or pathos" (*Essays and Reviews* 59). When judged in the light of the interlocking (and Coleridgean) criteria of "versatility" and "geniality," no member of the "Modern School of Poetry in England"—that is, the Pre-Raphaelites—passes muster: Dante Gabriel Rossetti "had not the large mobile heart, that can throw itself into every variety of life .... He is confined in art and has no variety of flavour"; Swinburne's "vocabulary is not large, his range of imagery is astonishingly narrow," and "he has certain set images ... which perpetually recur ... with the effect of monotony in every thing he has written"; and Morris's long poems are all characterized by "universal monotony and want of hearty life" (*Essays and Reviews* 63, 64, 67).

Of all the Romantic and Victorian poets whom Lampman canvasses in his literary essays and lectures, only Tennyson and Keats (especially the latter) come close to meeting the criteria of "variety" and "geniality," which in "Poetic Interpretation" (circa 1892) become salient attributes of "the perfect poet," a figure who "would have no set style" but, rather, "a different one for everything he should write, a manner exactly suited to the subject" (*Essays and Reviews* 127). To Lampman, Keats is "the most perfect" of nineteenth-century poets because, unlike Wordsworth (his closest contender among the Romantics), "he was governed by no theory and by no usurping line of thought and feeling. He was beyond all other men disposed to surrender himself completely to the impression of everything with which his brain or his senses came into contact" (*Essays and Reviews* 128). While Lampman's preference for "variety" doubtless stemmed in part from his classical training, it also reflects other components of his intellectual make-up, including Coleridge's attribution of the multifariousness of Shakespeare's characters to his universal mind (see *Essays and Reviews* 264, 322), Arnold's association of unrelieved "mental stress" with "morbid[ity]" of mind and "monotonous[ness]" of expression (*Complete Prose* 1: 2–3), and, of course, Keats's conceptions of "negative capability" and the "chameleon poet" (see *Essays and Reviews* 322–23, 331).

Since *Among the Millet, and Other Poems* was published nearly three years before Lampman delivered his "Two Canadian Poets" lecture in 1891, the presence in the book of a great variety of styles and subjects is less likely to be a programmatic reflection of the ideas that he later adapted from Irving than merely a reflection of the preference for diversity over monotony that he had expressed in "The Modern School of Poetry in England." In retrospect, however, the variousness of the volume may well have seemed to Lampman to be an anticipation of the literature that might one day emerge from the effect of the "diversity" and "variety" of Canadian "scenery" on the Canadian character. In this light, the programmatic variety of the *Alcyone* volume, which consists of poems in an almost irreducible diversity of modes and moods interspersed at varying intervals by sonnets inspired by Canadian nature, can be construed as a reflection not just of an aesthetic principle but of the diversity that Lampman regarded as distinctive of Canada.

The fact that both *Among the Millet, and Other Poems* and the posthumously published *Alcyone* (1899) were privately funded and printed meant that Lampman did not have to contend in either case with the demands of a publisher for commercially viable material. Such was not the case with the two or more collections in which he attempted to interest American publishers in the decade between the publication of *Among the Millet, and Other Poems* and his decision in the winter of 1897–98 to "get [*Alcyone*] printed and bound in Edinburgh," with the "name [of an Ottawa firm] on the title page as publishers (*Annotated Correspondence* 195, and see 199). Precisely why only *Lyrics of Earth* (1895 [1896]) found its way into print in the 1890s is difficult to determine, but a plausible speculation is that the other collections assembled by Lampman were either too heterogeneous or too monomorphic to win acceptance in a poetry market that was already glutted with books of both types. Certainly, the collection that he assembled in the fall of 1892 under the title "Pictures and Meditations" failed to find a publisher (see *Annotated Correspondence* 49, 52), as did the "Century of Sonnets" that he assembled a year later (see *Annotated Correspondence* 125, 129, 138, 143). Thanks to Edward William Thomson's "better idea of constructing a book" for the American market, *Lyrics of Earth* took shape in the summer of 1895 as a sequence of lyrics of varying lengths organized around the seasonal cycle and conveying the sense of a spiritual journey (*Annotated Correspondence* 144, and see 141, 143, 149, 153), in which form (and, no doubt, with Thomson's friendly assistance) it was accepted by the Boston publishing house of Copeland and Day. However, Thomson's skill at "composing and naming a book" was of no avail in the case of "A Century of Sonnets": in October 1895, Lampman responded to his friend's suggestion that the sonnets be subdivided into sections with a proposal to put "the love sonnets ... almost at the front" of the sequence, to remove "ten of the descriptive sonnets and mix the rest in with the general ones ... to make a variegated collection of 90" under the Petrarchan and Rossettian title of "Sonnets of Life and Death," but in March of the next year he abandoned this scheme, telling Thomson that "in deference to commercial opinion" he had decided to "split up the volume" and include twelve of the "nature sonnets" in *Alcyone* "to make a variety" (*Annotated Correspondence* 158, 166). When Copeland and Day, prompted by poor sales of *Lyrics of Earth*, informed Lampman in the fall of 1897 that they would not honour their agreement to publish a second collection of his poems, the last remnant of his willingness "to shape [his] books with a ... view to the taste of publishers" disappeared (*Annotated Correspondence* 176, and see 192–95). If *Alcyone* "contains 'a good deal of admirable, and some very noble work' ... [as] you say ... and the publisher won't have it," he had told Thomson on 30 August 1896, "then it is the worse for the publishers. Moreover if it is as you say it will be read someday and by those who know" (*Annotated Correspondence* 176).

Because he had lived in the United States since September 1886 and worked since February 1890 as literary editor of the *Independent* (New York), Carman was even more qualified than Thomson to gauge the disposition of American publishers and readers. He was also deeply aware through his reading of Edgar Allan Poe and Walt Whitman as well as Dante Gabriel Rossetti and Swinburne of the theory and practice of the long poem as lyric sequence, a genre in which variety and uniformity co-exist in a relationship analogous to that between the parts and the whole of an extended musical composition. Indeed, it was in precisely such terms that Carman presented his début volume, *Low Tide on Grand Pré: A Book of Lyrics* (1893): "[t]he poems in this volume have been collected with reference to their similarity of tone. They are variations on a single theme, more or less aptly suggested by the title, *Low Tide on Grand Pré*. It seemed better to bring together between the same covers only those pieces of work which happened to be in the same key rather than to publish a larger book of more uncertain aim" (*Low Tide on Grand Pré* np). Together, this prefatory note and the explanatory title of *Low Tide on Grand Pré: A Book of Lyrics* indicate not only that Carman was aware of the full meaning of the term "lyric," but also that he conceived of the "book" as an ensemble based on the principle of harmonic "variation ... on a ... theme" rather than as a miscellany devoted to the display of diversity and virtuosity. It is consistent with Carman's understanding of the lyric and the book as such that he oversaw every aspect of the creation of *Low Tide on Grand Pré* from the selection of the typeface to the choice of colour for the covers and that only rarely in his creative career did he resort to the "and Other Poems" formula of *Orion, and Other Poems* and *Among the Millet, and Other Poems* for the title of a book. "The thin volumes of verse occasionally put forth by Mr. Bliss Carman have a unity not often found in such collections," William Morton Payne would observe in the "Recent American Poetry" column in the *Dial* (Chicago) on 1 September 1898; "each volume is a careful selection from a considerable mass of material, and brings together pieces of the same class" (133).

Low Tide on Grand Pré: A Book of Lyrics comprises only twenty-five poems, but, as Odell Shepard observes in a vocabulary that nicely captures the literary sensibility to which Carman appealed, "it contains half a dozen pieces of pure verbal witchery which were made for no conceivable reason in the world except for the love of beautiful sound .... [I]n this carefully winnowed and delicately harmonized collection, it was made evident that America had a new poet who could both sing and say, who combined a finished craftsmanship with unmistakable power" (34, 36). Reviews in the United States, England and Canada were "ruinous in [their] praise" (*Letters* 108), and the book sold so well that, after the New York publisher of the first edition (Charles L. Webster) went bankrupt in 1894, it was quickly published in a second and slightly enlarged edition by the new aggressive Chicago publishing house of Stone and Kimball (see *Letters* 63). By the end of 1894, Stone and Kimball had twice reprinted the book, first in a "limited (50-copy) edition" and then in a full run (*Letters* 67, 91). "[I]t sells right away," Carman told his friend and collaborator Richard Hovey on 1 March 1895 (*Letters* 91).[8] Just how successful *Low Tide on Grand Pré* was can be gleaned from the fact that, while only 270 of the 500 copies of *Lyrics of Earth* printed by Copeland and Day ever left their premises, Carman's book went to a third edition in 1895 and was subsequently reprinted five times by two other American publishers (Lamson, Wolffe and Company and Small, Maynard and Company). Little wonder that Lampman complained to Thomson on 4 December 1897 that "the books [Copeland and Day] publish are not really published, only printed and bound" (*Annotated Correspondence* 193).

Despite its critical and commercial success, *Low Tide on Grande Pré* did not entirely satisfy Roberts. "This collection, being made up of poems exclusively in the minor key, leaves unrepresented one side of Mr. Carman's genius,—a side which is of particular importance in these dilettante days," he complained in the 15 June 1894 number of the *Chap-Book* (Boston) (which Carman was by then editing); nowhere in it is heard the "joyous major note, masculine and full-throated," of "certain [of Carman's] poems in the periodicals" ("Mr. Bliss Carman's Poems" 54). Echoing the advice that he had given to his cousin a decade earlier, Roberts credits him with a distinctiveness that derives from his "mastery of the inevitable phrase, the unforgettable cadence," and his "combination of verbal simplicity and an extreme complexity of suggestion and intention," the latter a quality that points towards the diagnosis of Carman's "weaknesses" with which the review draws to a conclusion:

> His structure is often defective,—he is not always careful in regard to the architectonics of verse. Many of his poems are built as waywardly as a dream, and one sometimes feels that parts of one poem might as easily fit into the framework of another. He has a tendency to repeat his effects; and while his poems are sharply differentiated from those of other poets, they are not always well differentiated from each other. There is also, at times, a curious and bewildering intricacy of thought which may justly be called obscurity; but this is a fault which Mr. Carman is rapidly eliminating from his work. (57)

"[S]tructure ... architectonics ... framework": the disparity between these schematic terms and Carman's musical analogy is an index of the aesthetic gulf that had perhaps always separated the two poets. The fact that in 1894 Roberts was repeating the advice of a decade earlier against diffuseness and obscurity should have alerted him to the error of believing that Carman was "rapidly" mending his ways. No more could the poet whose "single" and recurring "theme" had its origins in the ebb and flow of the tides across the space between land and sea construct poems that are "sharply differentiated ... from each other" than could he rest content in the confines of poetic forms. Carman's major work of the 1880s was "Corydon," a pastoral elegy on Matthew Arnold, but it was never finished. The lyrical sequence on which he was working when he died, *Sanctuary* (1929), consists of sonnets, but they are unrhymed. The *Vagabondia* volumes that consolidated and advanced his reputation in the 1890s celebrate the pleasures of the open road in loosened verse. To the extent that there are homologies between Imperialism and sublimity and between variety and Canadian nationalism, Carman's "free-trade Tory[ism]" (*Letters* 349) and, indeed, his residence in the United States were the corollaries of the sequence of individual yet interdependent lyrics that poured from him in the wake of *Low Tide on Grand Pré*.

* * * * *

When Roberts joined Carman in New York in 1897, the Confederation group was effectively disbanded and Canadian literature left without a centre. Even during its glory days of international and then national recognition between 1893 and 1895, the group had been fragile and fissile because of geographical dispersal and internal alignments. Campbell's increasingly rebarbative remarks about fellow poets in "At the Mermaid Inn" escalated in 1894–95 into a series of anonymous and then signed articles in Toronto newspapers and magazines in which he first denigrated well-made verse, then attacked mutual boosterism among literary friends, and finally accused Carman of plagiarism. The resulting "War among the Poets," as it quickly became known, bathed the Confederation group in the revealing glare of controversy and resulted in a precipitous fall from grace that was hastened by the reading public's growing preference for fiction rather than the sort of poems against which Campbell was inveighing. Poetry did not pass entirely out of favour, of course, but the forefront of the Canadian literary stage was turned over to works such as Thomson's *Old Man Savarin and Other Stories* (1895) and Duncan Campbell Scott's *In the Village of Viger* (1896). It was a shift to which Roberts had already begun to respond with historical romances and the realistic-symbolic animal stories that, like the *Vagabondia* volumes of Carman and Hovey, promised readers temporary and therapeutic respite from the stress and tedium of work-a-day urban life and its supposed psychosomatic illnesses.

Before the turn of the new century, Lampman was dead at the Keatsian age of thirty-seven. As the First World War was drawing to a close, Campbell followed. Roberts, Carman and the two Scotts lived on, but an era had ended. "Perhaps when the war is over, and we begin to arrange our ideals of life on a new basis, we shall have some fine poetry again," Carman wrote on 5 April 1917; "[b]ut I feel that when that time arrives, only new men, young men, or those who have taken part in the struggle will be entitled to take part in the parliament of art. The Victorian days belong to history. I believe the new days will be better, but I doubt if any of the men who came to maturity before the great war will be able to find the new key, the new mode, the new tune" (*Letters* 244). He was largely right.

D.M.R. BENTLEY

Notes

1. For Collins's role in the formation and promotion of the Confederation group, see my *The Confederation Group of Canadian Poets, 1880–1897*, 24–55 and later. For the genesis, rise and disintegration of the group and for detailed discussions of their poetry and ideas, see the same study, *passim*.

2. See, for example, the fourteen-line poems in "The Green Oasis" and "New England Scenes and Seasons" sections of Carman's *Poems* (1931) and in *Sanctuary: Sunshine House Sonnets* (1929). That Carman also associated the sonnet with build structures and, concomitantly, unrhymed "sonnets" with freedom from such structures is suggested by "Escape" (1929), the sestet of which reads:

    > No cabined luxury contents the soul,,
    > Homesick for solace of its native air,
    > For healing of the wind among the pines,
    > The stilling beauty of the clear new moon,
    > The strength of hills, the joy of singing streams,
    > Take any road at hand, to Out-of-doors.
    > (*Poems* 274)

    A sense of Carman's attitude to the sonnet in the late 1880s and early 1890s can be gleaned from his correspondence with Lampman following the publication of *Among the Millet, and Other Poems*. Singling out "The Truth," he told Lampman in a letter of 28 December 1888 that he "like[d] all the sonnets very much" but "never could write a sonnet [him]self" (Simon Fraser University). A little over two years later, two sonnets that Lampman had sent to Carman for publication in the *Independent*, "In March" (1899) and "Winter-Break" (1899), occasioned the following response from him in a letter of 9 February 1891: "I like them very much; and I want to say that I think that the Shakespearian form is much better than the Italian for these transcripts from Nature that you and Roberts do so well. Roberts will not agree with me, b[ut] I dislike a landscape put in [other than (?)] Shakespearian form. 'The Potato Harvest' e.g. has no possible wave beat of Emotion, no informing Surge of Spirit to justify the ... form that has been given it. The three quatrains and a couplet [of the Shakespearian sonnet] give so much more freedom. And in picturing Nature surely one must be free to select the right word, since accuracy is necessary. But in emotional work one may be as vagrant as he pleases at the bid of the Artistic Medium and the exigencies of rhyme and movement" (Simon Fraser University). To this Lampman replied on 23 February 1891: "I had never given much thought to the question of whether the Italian or the Shakespearean form was preferable for that kind of work, but I daresay you are right in your opinion, though as in everything else, one form or the other will immediately occur to the writer as applicable to the picture he has in his mind, he can hardly define why" (quoted in

Greig, "A Checklist," Part 1, 12). Carman's notion of a "wave beat of Emotion" derives, of course, from Theodore Watts's "wave theory" of the sonnet as expressed in his much-reprinted sonnet titled "The Sonnet's Voice: A Metrical Lesson by the Sea-Shore." A discussion and refinement of the theory is provided by William Sharp in his Introduction to *Sonnets of This Century* (1886, lxi–lxiv), a volume that would almost certainly have been known to most if not all of the Confederation group (see also Maia Bhojwani, "The Tides").

3. Although the distinction between "native" (or provincial) and "cosmopolitan" (or international) traditions in Canadian writing and the privileging of the latter over the former is generally associated with A.J.M. Smith and other Canadian Modernists, it was a central tenet of the thinking of Roberts, Collins, and, behind them, Arnold (see *The Confederation Group* 17, 59–64, and elsewhere).

4. This is A.J.M. Smith's definition of "Light Verse" in the *Princeton Encyclopedia of Poetry and Poetics*, 447. Roberts's definition of *vers de société* as "earnest song with a smile upon its lips" that excludes "broad buffoonery," "the strong passions and the tragedies of life" ("Notes" 328) derives from that of F. Locker-Lampson in *Lyra Elegantiarum* (1867) as "smoothly written verse, where a boudoir decorum is ... preserved; where sentiment never surges into passion, and where humour never overflows into boisterous merriment" (ix). In "Oliver Wendell Holmes," a commemorative poem published in the *Dial* (Chicago) and the *King's College Record* a year after Holmes's death on 7 October 1894, Roberts describes "Humor's mild aristocrat" as the epitome of the "gentlest breeding of the age" and characterizes the laughter engendered by his "fun" as "never long or loud" and frequently tinged with "regret" and pathos (*Collected Poems* 200).

5. A sense of what is meant by this term can be gained from the following passage in *Canadian Literature* by the Canadian journalist, historian and poet Theodore Arnold Haultain in the first number of the *Lake Magazine* (Toronto [August 1892]): "spontaneity is the first of all the tests to be applied to anything calling itself by the name of art. If a poem or a painting, a sonata or a statue, if anything in the realm of art is not spontaneous, it is as sounding brass or a tinkling bell. If it is not the outcome of real and intense internal feeling, craving expression and careless of everything but its own instinctive adherence to truth of matter and beauty of form —in a word inspired—it is not art" (19). From this and other occurrences of the term, it is very clear that "spontaneity" as popularly conceived is a quality likely to be stifled by the careful formalism advocated by Roberts.

6. A sense of the meaning of this term can be gained from a passage in another article in the *Lake Magazine*, "The Canadian Oliver Goldsmith," by the Maritime teacher and literary journalist W.G. MacFarlane: "the ... rhyming couplet ... is ... a fine medium of expression; it has such an easy pleasant swing and its elasticity permits the swelling heart to give utterance to its feelings freely" (December 1892, 287). As was the case with "spontaneity," "elasticity" was popularly conceived as a quality likely to be stifled by adherence to a too-rigid poetic form.

7. In the Introduction to his edition of *At the Mermaid Inn*, Barrie Davies argues that the phrase "millet-like [*sic*] in its terse realism" is directed at Lampman (viii), but in a review of Davies Edition W.J. Keith points out that "Campbell actually wrote 'Millet-like' in reference to the French painter" (449). "It ought to be borne in mind," adds Laurel Boone in her edition of Campbell's *Selected Poetry and Essays*, "that Campbell may have borrowed the idea of "Millet-like" realism from W. Blackburn Harte, who (in 'Some Canadian Writers of To-day' in the September 1890 number of the *New England Magazine* 21) compared poetry with the painting of Jean François Millet, reproductions of whose peasant scenes were ubiquitous; that ditties by the American versifier John Kendrick Bangs appeared regularly in important magazines such as *The Century*; that Charles G.D. Roberts's *Songs of the Common Day* ... had recently been published to wide acclaim; and that, according to Duncan Campbell Scott, despite 'the constant watch that had to be kept upon [Campbell's] opinions,' the column 'was pretty well played out, simply because, situated as we were, there was not enough material available to keep the thing fresh'" (161, quoting Scott in McDougall, *The Poet and the Critic*, 56). It is also worth observing that, though Harte may well lie behind Campbell's "Millet-like," he was not alone in linking the landscape poems of Lampman and Roberts with the work of Millet and other painters of the so-called Barbizon school: see, for example, the review of *Among the Millet, and Other Poems* in the 9 February 1890 issue of the *Boston Sunday Herald*, in which Louise Chandler Moulton describes Lampman as "above all, a landscape poet, as [Jean-Baptiste Camille] Corot was, above all, a landscape painter" and suggests that "if Millet or Jules Breton had written their poems, instead of painting them, they would have read like these" (19).

8. Carman and Hovey collaborated on the four *Vagabondia* volumes of 1894–1901 and, though Hovey was the principal author, in the series of linked essays on poetics that preceded and accompanied them: "Delsarte and Poetry" (1891), "The Technic of Poetry" (1892), "The Technic of Rhyme" (1893) and "The Elements of Poetic Technic" (1894). See my "Carman and Mind Cure" for a discussion of Carman's and Hovey's theory of poetry in the context of the mind-cure movement that developed in the late nineteenth century as a response to the psychosomatic diseases of modernity.

Works Cited

To avoid unnecessary bibliographical repetition, the sources of quotations from newspapers and periodicals contemporary with the Confederation group are given only in the text at the point of citation.

Anderson, William S. "The Theory and Practice of Poetic Arrangement from Vergil to Ovid." *Poems in Their Place*. Ed. Neil Fraistat. Chapel Hill: U of North Carolina P, 1986. 44–65.

Arnold, Matthew. *Complete Prose Works*. Ed. R.H. Super. 11 vols. Ann Arbor: U of Michigan P, 1960–77.

Barry, Lilly E.F. "Prominent Canadians—XXV: Archibald Lampman." *The Week* [Toronto] 8 (10 April 1891): 298–300.

Bentley, D.M.R. "Carman and Mind Cure: Theory and Technique." *Bliss Carman: A Reappraisal*. Ed. Gerald Lynch. *Reappraisals: Canadian Writers* 16. Ottawa: U of Ottawa P, 1990. 85–110.

———. "Charles G.D. Roberts's use of 'Indian Legend' in Four Poems of the Eighteen Eighties and 'Nineties," *Canadian Poetry: Studies, Documents, Reviews* 51 (Fall/Winter 2002): 18–38.

———. *The Confederation Group of Canadian Poets, 1880–1897*. Toronto: U of Toronto P, 2004.

———. *The Gay, Grey Moose: Essays on the Ecologies and Mythologies of Canadian Poetry, 1690–1990*. Ottawa: U of Ottawa P, 1992.

———. "Nervous ReincarNations: Keats, Scenery, and Mind Cure in Canada during the Post-Confederation Period, with Particular Reference to Archibald Lampman and Related Cases." Forthcoming in *Nervous Reactions: Victorian Recollections of Romanticism*. Ed. Joel Faflak and Julia M. Wright. New York: State U of New York P, 2003.

———. "Roberts' Series of Sonnets in Songs of the Common Day." *Dalhousie Review* 69 (1989): 393–412.

Brownlow, Edward Burrough ("Sarepta"). "The Sonnet.—VIII." *The Week* [Toronto] (1 Nov. 1889): 760–1.

Cameron, George Frederick. *Lyrics of Freedom, Love and Death*. Ed. Charles J. Cameron. Kingston: Lewis W. Shannon; Boston: Alexander Moore, 1887.

Campbell, William Wilfred. *Poems*. Toronto: William Briggs, 1905.

———. *Selected Poetry and Essays*. Ed. Laurel Boone. Waterloo: Wilfrid Laurier UP, 1987.

Campbell, William Wilfred, Archibald Lampman, and Duncan Campbell Scott. *At the Mermaid Inn: Wilfred Campbell, Archibald Lampman, Duncan Campbell Scott in The Globe, 1892–93.* Ed. Barrie Davies. Literature of Canada: Poetry and Prose in Reprint. Toronto: U of Toronto P, 1979.

Carman, Bliss. *Letters.* Ed. H. Pearson Grundy. Kingston and Montreal: McGill-Queen's UP, 1981.

———. *Low Tide on Grand Pré: A Book of Lyrics.* New York: Webster, 1893.

———. *Poems.* Arranged by R.H. Hathaway: New York: Dodd, Mead, 1931.

Carman, Bliss, and Richard Hovey. *Last Songs from Vagabondia.* Boston: Small, Maynard & Co., 1901.

———. *More Songs from Vagabondia.* Boston: Copeland and Day, 1896.

———. *Songs from Vagabondia.* Boston: Copeland and Day, 1894.

———. *Songs from Vagabondia.* 1894. Boston: Copeland and Day; London: Elkin Mathews, 1895.

Forman, W[illia]m Henry. "Jasper Francis Cropsey, N.A." *Manhattan* [New York] 3 (April 1884): 372–81.

Fraistat, Neil. "Introduction." *Poems in Their Place: The Intertextuality and Order of Poetic Collections.* Ed. Neil Fraistat. Chapel Hill: U of North Carolina P, 1986. 3–17.

Gosse, Edmund. "A Plea for Certain Exotic Forms of Verse." *Cornhill Magazine* [London] 36 (1877): 53–71.

Grieg, Peter E. "A Check List of Lampman Manuscript Material in the Douglas Library Archives," Part 1. *Douglas Library Notes* 15 (Winter 1967): 8–16. Part 2. *Douglas Library Notes* 16 (Autumn 1967): 12–27.

Haultain, Theodore Arnold. "A 'Canadian Literature.'" *Lake Magazine* [Toronto] 1 (Aug. 1892): 17–20.

Hovey, Richard. "Delsarte and Poetry." *Independent* [New York] 43 (27 Aug. 1891): 3–4.

———. "The Elements of Poetic Technic." Part 1. *Independent* [New York] 46 (27 Sept. 1894): 5–6; Part 2. 46 (4 Oct. 1894): 7–8.

———. "The Technic of Poetry." Part 1. *Independent* [New York] 44 (7 April 1892): 9–10. Part 2. 44 (21 April 1892): 4.

———. "The Technic of Rhyme." *Independent* [New York] 45 (19 Oct. 1893): 3–4.

Hurst, Alexandra J., ed. *The War among the Poets: Issues of Plagiarism and Patronage among the Confederation Poets.* London: Canadian Poetry Press, 1994.

Kilpatrick, Ross S. "Introduction." *Orion, and Other Poems*, by Charles G.D. Roberts. Ed. Ross S. Kilpatrick. *Post-Confederation Poetry: Texts and Contexts*. London: Canadian Poetry Press, 1999. ix–xxxii.

Lampman, Archibald. *An Annotated Edition of the Correspondence between Archibald Lampman and Edward William Thomson (1890–1898)*. Ed. Helen Lynn. Ottawa: Tecumseh, 1980.

———. *Essays and Reviews*. Ed. D.M.R. Bentley. London: Canadian Poetry Press, 1996.

———. *Poems*. With a Memoir by Duncan Campbell Scott. Toronto: Morang, 1900.

Lampman, Archibald, and Edward William Thomson. *An Annotated Edition of the Correspondence between Archibald Lampman and Edward William Thomson (1890–1898)*. Ed. Helen Lynn. Ottawa: Tecumseh, 1980.

Logan, J.D., and Donald G. French. *Highways of Canadian Literature: A Synoptic Introduction to the Literary History of Canada (English) from 1760 to 1924*. 1924. 2nd ed. Toronto: McClelland and Stewart, 1928.

MacFarlane, W.G. "The Canadian Goldsmith." *Lake Magazine* [Toronto] 1 (Dec. 1892): 285–9.

———. "New Brunswick Authorship." *Dominion Illustrated* [Montreal] 7 (21 Nov. 1891): 494–5.

Machar, Agnes Maule ("Fidelis"). "Some Recent Canadian Poems." Review of *Among the Millet, and Other Poems*, by Archibald Lampman. *The Week* [Toronto] 6 (22 March 1889): 251–2.

Marquis, T.G. "Roberts" *Canadian Magazine* [Toronto] 1 (Sept. 1893): 572–5.

McDougall, Robert L., ed. *The Poet and the Critic: A Literary Correspondence between D.C. Scott and E.K. Brown*. Ottawa: Carleton UP, 1983.

Payne, William Morton. "Recent American Poetry." *Dial* [Chicago] 25 (1 Sept. 1898): 132–36.

Pomeroy, E.M. *Sir Charles G.D. Roberts: A Biography*. Toronto: Ryerson, 1943.

Roberts, Charles G.D. "Canadian Poetry in Its Relation to the Poetry of England and America." Ed. D.M.R. Bentley. *Canadian Poetry: Studies, Documents, Reviews* 3 (Fall/Winter 1978): 76–86.

———. "Charles G.D. Roberts' Review of *Among the Millet*." Ed. Tracy Ware. *Canadian Poetry: Studies, Documents, Reviews* 29 (1991): 38–45.

———. *Collected Letters*. Ed. Laurel Boone. Fredericton: Goose Lane, 1989.

———. *Collected Poems*. Ed. Desmond Pacey and Graham Adams. Wolfville, NS: Wombat, 1985.

———. "Literature." In "Review of Literature, Science and Art." *The Dominion Annual Register and Review for the Seventeenth Year of the Canadian Union, 1883*. Ed. Henry J. Morgan. Toronto: Hunter, Rose, 1884. 206–19.

———. "Edgar Fawcett." *The Week* [Toronto] 1.30 (26 June 1884): 437–38.

———. "Mr. Bliss Carman's Poems." Review of *Low Tide on Grand Pré*, by Bliss Carman. *Chap-Book* [Chicago] 1.3 (15 June 1894): 53–57.

———. "Notes on Some of the Younger American Poets." *The Week* [Toronto] 1.21 (24 April 1884): 328–29.

———. *Orion, and Other Poems*. 1880. Ed. Ross S. Kilpatrick. *Post-Confederation Poetry: Texts and Contexts*. London: Canadian Poetry Press, 1999.

———. *Selected Poetry and Critical Prose*. Ed. W.J. Keith. Literature in Canada: Poetry and Prose in Reprint. Toronto: U of Toronto P, 1974.

Rossetti, Dante Gabriel. *Works*. Ed. William M. Rossetti. London: Ellis, 1911.

Scott, Duncan Campbell. *Poems*. Toronto: McClelland and Stewart, 1926.

———. *Some Letters of Duncan Campbell Scott to Archibald Lampman and Others*. Ed. Arthur S. Bourinot. Ottawa: Bourinot, 1959.

Shepard, Odell. *Bliss Carman*. Toronto: McClelland and Stewart, 1923.

Stedman, Edmund Clarence. *Poets of America*. 1885. New York: Johnson Reprint, 1970.

Tennyson, Alfred. *Poems*. Ed. Christopher Ricks. Longman's Annotated English Poets. London: Longmans, Green, 1969.

Woodworth, Harry A. "Roberts' Poetry of the Tantramar." Anniversary Number. *Chignecto Post and Borderer* [Sackville, NB] (Sept. 1895): 1–7.

Wordsworth, William. *Poetical Works*. Ed. E. de Selincourt. 1940. 5 vols. Oxford: Clarendon, 1963.

WILFRED CAMPBELL

WILFRED CAMPBELL (1858–1915)

Biographical Notes

William Wilfred Campbell was born in Berlin (now Kitchener), Ontario, 1 June 1861, a descendant through his father, the Rev. Thomas Swaniston Campbell, of the first Lord Campbell of the House of Argyll through whom he was related to the poet Thomas Campbell and the novelist Henry Fielding. Campbell grew up in Wiarton, attended high school in Owen Sound, and studied at University College from 1881 to 1882 (where he wrote for the student newspaper the *Varsity*). He studied at Wycliffe College in Toronto from 1882 to 1883, and finally at the Episcopal Theological School in Cambridge, Massachusetts. In 1884 he married Mary Louisa Dibble, the daughter of a physician in Woodstock. After his ordination in 1886, Campbell spent several years as a rector for Episcopal parishes of West Claremont, New Hampshire, and for the Anglican parish in St. Stephen, New Brunswick.

His faltering religious faith caused Campbell to abandon his ministry in 1891 and accept a position in the office of the Secretary of State in Ottawa, which led a few years later, in 1909, to a posting in the Dominion Archives. During this period he became a contributor to the *Atlantic Monthly*, the *Century* and *Harper's*, and in 1906, received an honorary LL.D. from the University of Aberdeen. Along with Archibald Lampman and Duncan Campbell Scott, he contributed articles to the "Mermaid Inn," a literary column of the Toronto *Globe* that ran from 1892–93, several examples of which are found herein. In 1892 he was elected to the Royal Society of Canada. In 1905, the best of Campbell's lyrics and sonnets were published in a substantial volume titled, *The Collected Poems of Wilfred Campbell*; the opening sentence of his Introduction to this volume reminds us how in tune he was with the work of the emerging Modernists in the U.S. and Britain in terms of his technique, despite his conservative opinions. He writes: "Simplicity and directness are essential to the highest class of verse. In the judgment of poetry this principle must never be lost sight of." Campbell eschews the valorizing of daintiness and dreamy romanticism which was often praised by literary critics of his age, and calls instead for a hard-hitting, realist approach to experience. Campbell's prose evidences an acerbic wit, and he is not beneath taunting his fellow Confederation Poets for their tendency to idealize the farmyard while ignoring the suffering of humanity.

In 1913 Campbell edited the *Oxford Book of Canadian Verse*. His own early volumes of poetry were *Sunshine and Snowflakes* (1888) and *Lake Lyrics* (1889), for the latter of which he became known as "the poet of the Great Lakes." By far the most conservative of the Confederation Poets, Campbell was an outspoken supporter of the British Empire, a staunch advocate for Canadian participation in World War I, and he was proud of his son, Basil, who became a major in the 2nd Canadian Pioneer Battalion in the Great War.

William Campbell died from pneumonia in 1918, aged fifty-seven, in Ottawa where he is buried in Beechwood Cemetery.

Publications

Snowflakes and Sunbeams. [S.l.: s.n., 1888?]. Reprinted Ottawa: Golden Dog, 1974.

The Dread Voyage and Other Poems. Toronto: W. Briggs, 1889; Montreal: C.W. Coates, 1889.

Lake Lyrics and Other Poems. St. John, NB: J. & A. McMillan, 1889.

Mordred and Hildegrand—A Book of Tragedies. Ottawa: J. Durie, 1895.

Beyond the Hills of Dream. Boston: Houghton Mifflin, 1899.

Atlantean Lyrics. [S.l.: s.n., 1905].

The Poems of Wilfred Campbell. Toronto: W. Briggs, 1905.

Canada. Toronto: McMillan, 1906.

Xlan of the Orcades, or the Armourer of Grinigoe. New York and Toronto: F.H. Revell, 1906.

Poetical Tragedies. Toronto: W. Briggs, 1908.

A Beautiful Rebel: A Romance of Upper Canada in Eighteen Hundred and Twelve. Toronto: Westminster, 1909.

The Beauty, History, Romance, and Mystery of the Canadian Lake Region. Toronto: Musson, 1910, [enlarged and revised reprint in 1914].

Sagas of Vaster Britain: Poems of the Race, the Empire and the Divinity of Man. Toronto: Musson, 1914.

Canada's Responsibility to the Empire and the Race. 1858–1918. [Canada: s.n., 1915?].

War Lyrics. Ottawa: s.n., 1915.

Lyrics of Iron and Mist. Ottawa: s.n., 1916.

Lyrics of the Dread Redoubt. Ottawa: s.n., 1917.

The Poetical Works of Wilfred Campbell. Ed. W.J. Sykes. London: Hodder and Stoughton, 1923.

Vapour and Blue: Souster Selects Campbell: The Poetry of William Wilfred Campbell. Ed. Raymond Souster. Sutton West, ON: Paget P, 1978.

William Wilfred Campbell: Selected Poetry and Essays. Ed. Laurel Boone. Waterloo, ON: Wilfrid Laurier UP, 1987.

Books Edited

The Oxford Book of Canadian Verse: Chosen by Wilfred Campbell. Toronto: Oxford UP, 1913.

Critical Materials

Book Length

Klinck, Carl F. *Wilfred Campbell: A Study in Late Provincial Victorianism.* Toronto: Ryerson, 1942.

Articles

Ower, John. "Portraits of the Landscape as Poet: Canadian Nature as Aesthetic Symbol in Three Confederation Writers." *Journal of Canadian Studies* 6 (1971): 27–32.

Whalen, Terry. "Wilfred Campbell: The Poetry of Celebration and Harmony." *Journal of Canadian Poetry* 1, no. 2 (1978): 27–41

Online Resources

Bentley, D.M.R. "Charles G.D. Roberts and William Campbell as Tour Guides." (This interesting portrait of Wilfred Campbell as an ultra-imperialist) may be found at: http://www.uwo.ca/english/canadianpoetry/confederation/wwcampbell/criticism/tour_guides.htm

Malloch, Faith. "An Intimate Picture of Wilfred Campbell." in D.M.R. Bentley's http://www.uwo.ca/english/canadianpoetry/confederation/wwcampbell/intimate_picture/index.htm

Wicken, George. "William Wilfred Campbell (1858–1918)." *Canadian Writers and Their Works* (1982). http://eir.library.utoronto.ca/rpo/display/poet49.html

From the Globe
11 June 1892

Reprinted from *At the Mermaid Inn: Wilfred Campbell, Archibald Lampman, Duncan Campbell Scott in The Globe 1892–93*, intro. by Barrie Davies, Toronto: U of Toronto P, 1979, 90–92.

There are two kinds of poetry that may develop in a country, one born of the soil, and yet dependent on universal sympathy for its audience; the other largely of local growth, and the result of the various vicissitudes of national development. They may both be great in their way, but the latter is the most certain to acquire a quick sympathy. It is patriotic, cast in a large and heroic mould, and a necessary part of the pulse-beat of the day. Such a school was the great New England one of the era prior to and following the civil war. It was human and popular, and the writers were necessarily strong men, with large human instincts and enthusiasms. But it might be said that the time made them as much as they helped to make the time, and that much of their largeness of mould and high ethical vision was due to the high pitch of the national spirit at the time they wrote. Then again, their work contained much sentiment that was merely local and passing, but of no effect now when the community is not pitched to appreciate it. They had a note that was impossible in a less heroic day, but it carried them beyond the natural which endures, and so rendered their work necessarily ephemeral. Much of the work of Whittier, Longfellow, and Lowell is of this class, and, as literature of immediate interest, perished with the passing of the time and events that gave it being. When we go back to the works of these poets to find poems of enduring beauty on subjects that might be treated about, and have been treated about, in all ages of our literature, we find that what they have left is small indeed. If we look for complete poems that will rank with the old English masterpieces we have to be chary in our choice: Longfellow has many tender and heroic tales in verse, and his [*Song of*] *Hiawatha*, while not original in construction, is almost an epic, but it has not that haunting beauty of expression to be found in the best work of many of the great poets. It is diffuse and full of mannerisms, and grows tiresome after much repeating. The opening and closing lines of "Evangeline" are fine, but the poem as a whole also is diffuse, and lacks solidity even in the nature descriptions, for which there was great scope given. It is a decided failure as a great poem, if not as a story, and much of the charm lies in the pathos of the incident embodied. Many of his shorter pieces are by far his best. A noted reader for a famous New England publishing house told me that he always considered Longfellow did his best work in *Voices of the Night*, his first small published volume, and I think he was right, though for pure beauty and simplicity, in my opinion, "The Wreck of the Hesperus" is his finest bit of work. This poem, while not by any means his most ambitious attempt, is such as a poet might accomplish in any age, even of less heroic pitch than that in which he wrote. To Whittier and Lowell this test is even more applicable than to Longfellow. Freedom was the great inspiration that gave the keynote to both, and yet poems like "Snowbound," "In School Days," and "Maud Muller" are the gems that one leaves to posterity, while the other will endure in such poems of deep insight as "Extreme Unction," and nature descriptions as found in "The Dandelion," and in "Indian Summer." The former class of verse, which I mentioned at the beginning of this article, is that produced in an unheroic age, such as ours is today in Canada, when the ethical pulse is even below the normal, certainly not above it, and when to be a true poet one must be a born singer, without the aid of any unusually strenuous environment to inspire the song. This class of singers run no great chance of being overrated in their generation. They may leave no lofty epics or funeral paens to mark the historical eras, but their note, if true, is liable to be deep and lasting. They are interpreters rather than chroniclers, and their message from humanity or nature, or from both, if they are great enough, is sincere and direct. There is a shallow idea that the length of a poem is the test of a poet's greatness. But, on the contrary, most of the greater poets have written at the most half a dozen poems, and most of them less than a hundred lines, that have given them their claims to immortality. The greatest epics in all languages are but, as someone said of Milton's *Paradise Lost*, rare oases of beauty in a desert of verbiage. Like in all other cults, there is no end of writing and of the making of books, and happy is the man who has produced one poem that can be classed with those of even a century's endurance.

From the Globe
5 *November 1892*

Reprinted from *At the Mermaid Inn: Wilfred Campbell, Archibald Lampman, Duncan Campbell Scott in The Globe 1892–93*, intro. by Barrie Davies, Toronto: U of Toronto P, 1979, 185–86.

It has been claimed by many critics that a man cannot be a truly great writer unless he pictures what is hopeful in humanity and passes over what is dark and tends to despondency and despair. We hear so often of what is called the healthy imagination, which is essential to and is found in all the greater writers. All the literary works from those of Shakespeare and Milton to Browning have been scoured for extracts carrying out this theory. But I would just here like to note that the very opposite is true, and that, strange to say, all that is strongest and most lasting in literature depicts not the bright and joyous side of life, but rather what is gloomy, despairing, and tragic. For all the theories of the critics of today, the poets who have endlessly sung life is happy because I am happy have been of the weaker and more ephemeral class. The work of a great poet, like that of any other great man, is not to hypnotize the world into a false or fancied dream of security and selfish indifference, but rather to show life as it is in all its reality—but as a god would show it. The great man is he who truly knows life but still sees the divine back of the most hideous manifestations of its existence. Were the season always springtime and the day always morning, we all would be lotus-eaters. But it is the struggles and the longings, the memories and the might-have-beens that make us great. This wonder and awe of the greatness of life in its sombre aspects is impressed on us by the greatest writers of all ages.

Beginning with Homer, called the greatest epic poet of any age, we find him depicting almost wholly endless battle, which, with all its good side, is perhaps the most awful spectacle humanity can dwell upon. Battle and deceit, rapine and despair is what he gives us. The downfall and destruction of a great people, the Trojans, is his chief theme. Virgil, the noble Roman who followed him, is certainly greater in his epic, which is largely influenced by the *Iliad*, than when he described piping shepherds and fleecy flocks. Dante, the next great poet, has dedicated his whole magnificent genius to the description of hell. Milton, the literary descendant of the Greek, the Roman, and the Florentine, and the greatest English poet after Shakespeare, made the fall of man and the attendant evils the subject of his great epic, which has rendered him immortal. Shakespeare has four or five masterpieces among his marvellous dramas, and what are the subjects of the greatest? We will name them: *Macbeth, Lear, Hamlet, Othello, Julius Caesar, Richard the Third, Romeo and Juliet*. I have named seven, which include all of his greatest works. Now what are the bare subjects of these dramas? The hideous murder of a king, and the attendant horror and punishment of the murderers. The despair and death of a despised old king ruined by his own children. Madness, death, graves, and spooks are the stock in trade of *Hamlet*, and so on through all of these remarkable productions. The dark, the hideous, the tragic side of life is shown in these plays, if they have ever been depicted in literature. Surely if any poet ever lived in the weird, the awful, and the despairing in humanity that man was Shakespeare. And yet we hear so much about the healthiness of the minds of the greatest poets. All that is great in literature will always be connected with the tragedy of human sin and human despair as long as the humanity we are walks this earth. In this lies the greatness of genius. And true genius must always be sad, because it sees the true state of things so acutely. "The man who went down into hell," it was said of the great Florentine as he walked the streets, and so it will be unto the end—greatness must suffer.

From the Globe
25 February 1893

Reprinted from *At the Mermaid Inn: Wilfred Campbell, Archibald Lampman, Duncan Campbell Scott in The Globe 1892–93*, intro. by Barrie Davies, Toronto: U of Toronto P, 1979, 263–64.

It is quite interesting to notice the different attitudes with regard to such poets as Wordsworth and Tennyson assumed by the general public and the cultured poetical critics. And it is strange to note how much the former have been imposed on by the latter. The general public regards a poet to the extent that he thrills and pleases. The poetical critics have a different standard of judgment. The general public cares little or nothing about the evolution of nature or morals, or spiritual intuition. It accepts poetry for its great human qualities, its grasp of or sympathy with the general pathos of human life. And here I must say that to a great extent I agree with the general public. With all due regard to those who would lay so much stress on the inner consciousness, it is not by straining the inner ear for the voice of the Nameless that life is made great, but by clothing the realities of existence with that grandeur and divinity that belong to it.

It was his mastery of the humanities that made Shakespeare the greatest poet of modern times. Wordsworth says:

> For I have learned
> To look on nature, not as in the hour
> Of thoughtless youth; but hearing oftentimes The still, sad
> music of humanity.

It is a pity that Wordsworth did not "look on humanity" more than he did. He had too little affinity to the common toiling souls; he lived apart and brooded too much. Wordsworth was too self-centred to be a great human poet. The great human poet must feel within the common love and the common joy, and be ever aware of the pulse of humanity as human. He must not write of men as beggars and gentlemen, but as men. Now the cultured critic is not at all an appreciator, he rarely discovers a new poet, but is, on the other hand, such a blind worshipper of the poetical god he adores that his first aim is to find in new work some affinity to his idol. He judges verse by what he calls the "quality" in it, which means nothing more than a certain vague finish. His eye and ear are all wrapped up in style, and he is keen to discover any sin of omission or commission in this regard. He is always talking about the file, and did he have his way would attenuate all modern poetry to a thin flute note of twilight melancholy. The truth is that this idea is perfectly fitted for the guidance of minor poetry, which, devoid of great imagination and creative gift, can afford to spend the time in tuning its gentle and mellow reeds to the required softness that is pleasing to the sensitive ear of the modern critic, who is himself generally a minor poet. But the larger and more sublime landscapes—the rugged skies, the woes and battles of earth—are not for it.

The general public are not yet tired of life, even if the critics are, and they still are interested in the storm and stress, the hopes and despairs, of human life. The true worth of the poet, or rather the joy of the poet, is to dwell on and depict the divinity that is everywhere existent in our common humanity. As he does this, so does he succeed in or fail in being great.

From the Globe
18 March 1893

Reprinted from *At the Mermaid Inn: Wilfred Campbell, Archibald Lampman, Duncan Campbell Scott in The Globe 1892–93*, intro. by Barrie Davies, Toronto: U of Toronto P, 1979, 277–79.

I do not pretend to be one of those who make a special study or worship of the sonnet as a form of verse. I have often thought, as many others have, that this form of verse has been done to the death, especially by our minor poets of the last two decades. We all admit that there are a number of beautiful sonnets, but the few gems are no excuse for the myriads of poems of this sort that have poured forth in England and America during the last twenty years. Anyone who picks up an anthology of sonnets will perceive the truth of my remarks. You may in such a collection note the clever conceits of the corps of mediocre verse writers, young and old. But you soon grow to realize that the greatest poets have paid the least attention to the sonnet as an art. There are some extremely clever sonnet artists in America and England, especially in America, who have wrought hard to perfect this form of verse. But what does it all amount to? After all is said and done, the reader goes to an anthology of these poems, and he finds at the most half a dozen in hundreds that appeal to him and haunt him as true poems, and it is not strange to say that these half dozen are not found among the delicate word artists who have wrought so hard in this direction, but exist among the few sonnets of the greater writers in both countries who made use of this form as a lyric interlude between more ambitious flights of creation.

In England we know that the half dozen or so highest creations in this form are from the pens of Shakespeare, Wordsworth, Keats, Milton, and Tennyson. In America the case is similar, the few good sonnets being the productions of our leading poets. In my estimation the three or four greatest American sonnets have been written by Gilder, Longfellow, and the Canadian Heavysege. Their sonnets which I will quote were not written with the premeditated idea of producing a fine sonnet, but show on their faces suggestions of power that are not found anywhere else in this form to the same extent. Gilder's sonnet, "On a Life-Mask of Abraham Lincoln," is, I believe, the greatest by an American, and one of the few great sonnets in the language. It is a little epic:

> This bronze doth keep the very form and mould
> Of our great martyr's face. Yes, this is he;
> That brow all wisdom, all benignity;
> That human, humorous mouth; those cheeks that hold
> Like some harsh landscape all the summer's gold;
> That spirit fit for sorrow, as the sea
> For storms to beat on; the lone agony
> Those silent, patient lips too well foretold.
> Yes, this is he who ruled a world of men
> As might some prophet of the elder day—
> Brooding above the tempest and the fray
> With deep-eyed thought and more than mortal ken.
> A power was his beyond the touch of art
> Or armed strength: his pure and mighty heart.

Longfellow's "Nature," though less powerful, is, next to the one quoted, a great American sonnet; like Gilder's, it shows "a power beyond the touch of art," beginning, as it does:

> As a fond mother when the day is o'er
> Leads by the hand her little child to bed.

The sonnets by Heavysege are "Annihilation," "The Dead," and "Night." In the first occur the lines:

> All round about him hanging were decays,
> And ever-dropping remnants of the past.

In "The Dead" are lines of great power and beauty, as:

> Even as gigantic shadows on the wall
>   The spirit of the daunted child amaze,
> So on us thoughts of the departed fall.

He speaks of "Night" as:

> Like a nude Ethiop 'twixt two houris fair,
> Thou stand'st between the evening and the morn.

In all of these sonnets we get glimpses of the power of great poets. They are not little frameworks, so polished and overwrought as to make the critic wish the idea framed were a little more prominent and the adornment a little less clever. But they lead us by a few lines into the presence of the holy of holies of genius itself. This, to my mind, is the office of the sonnet, which has been over-much abused in these latter days of artificial writing.

From the Globe
17 June 1893

Reprinted from *At the Mermaid Inn: Wilfred Campbell, Archibald Lampman, Duncan Campbell Scott in The Globe 1892–93*, intro. by Barrie Davies, Toronto: U of Toronto P, 1979, 331–34.

A serious deficiency in current literature, and especially in the department of verse, is an utter lack of imaginative creative ability. We have an overplus of dainty conceits and delicately spun lyrics, and far too much of verse of a purely descriptive quality. The magazines and weeklies are stocked with such verse, and it is regarded as the characteristic poetry of the age; but of original conceptions of a high order we are almost utterly destitute. Many have been educated into the idea that Tennyson at his best was a poet of rugged power and original conception, but the fact is that his extremely brilliant and successful poetic career was one of marked decadence in this respect, and few realize that the day of great creative genius went out with Byron. What Tennyson did for English verse was to polish and over-refine it. He made verse-reading possible, and even pleasing, to the strict morality of the average middle-class English household. His "May Queen" took the place of "The Bride of Abydos," as the romantic gradually passed into the prosaic that succeeded it. It is true that he gave us some stirring ballads, but his influence on English verse-making did not fall on this side. The successors of Tennyson are a lot of small men, who owe much of their positions as poets to culture and leisure. These men have many masters; some, the nature school, claim Wordsworth as their supreme idol; but, did the simple old man live today, they would flee in horror from his lack of style. Some follow Keats, and claim for him qualities he never assumed or deserved. Keats was a man who had a sort of archaic madness; but a knowledge of, and an interest in, the real life about him is entirely lacking in his work. Keats will always remain an interesting story in English poetry. But woe to the man of today who tries to build a literary fame with such as Keats as a master. Keats is as evanescent and elusive as his own goddesses, and his imagination is purely of the fantastical order, as would be natural in a man who dares to approach any mythology with an utter lack of the religious genius that gets at the real greatness and human interest that alone can make any mythology important. The man who absorbs Keats gets a sort of honied literature without any comb, and his poems become a series of literary confections. But the brawn and muscle are not there. Such poetry may do well to adorn the current magazines, for gentlewomen to gush over, or to be admired by a certain order of critics, but it never will move or inspire the world. There is another class of poets who make an idol of Matthew Arnold. They swallow all of his literary creeds, and assume his austere melancholy towards life. They strain to think and write as he did, forgetting that Arnold's real power lay not in all this, but rather in the fact that the man was there himself in all he said and felt. Arnold had many weaknesses of style and limitations of voice as a poet. His marked greatness is as a thinker, who had deeply imbued himself with his own ideals and conceptions. His very egotism is his strength. When he attempted to follow Keats or Wordsworth he made an utter failure. It is impossible for this reason for any man to be a successful follower of such a poet as Arnold, and yet be original. Others of the current schools follow Rossetti and Swinburne, while some essay Browning, with little more success than the attainment of the merely grotesque. That they are all followers of Tennyson in reality goes without saying, which is evidenced by the utter lack of any real new thought or creative imagination in current work, coupled with the evident straining after what is called style or finish. One man gets the trick of Keats's phrasing, his peculiar way of building a line, the adjectives he used and their unique effect. Another assumes Wordsworth's simplicity of attitude toward nature, another aims at Shelley's elusive and airy buildings out of nothingness, with brilliant success. Another strains to express some subtle thought, or personal contempt of the great horde, after the Matthew Arnold plan. But they all forget that to be great a man must first and last be himself, and that borrowed clothing, no matter how it may suggest the original, sits as badly on the borrower's back as the skin of the lion did on the body of the ass. To be called the American Byron or Wordsworth or Tennyson is not certainly a compliment to a man's originality, however it may redound to his powers of imitation. Such a phrase concerning a man's work should cause the reader to look up the work so compared and note wherein the comparison lies. But such a state of things is the result of making mere words and their picturesque groupings for artistic effect the first and most important end of the would-be poet. Subject matter seems somehow at a discount, and what is called quality has taken its place. Strip most of the so-called poetry of its borrowed plumage and very little would remain; yea, not even the dignity of a backbone of thought or incident. The day of the great writer is when we have the great creative power and lofty imaginative genius. A very good test of our current writers would be to search their volumes for evidence of original mental qualities and large sympathetic grasp of our common humanity. A writer may drench himself with the form of expression used by Shelley or Rossetti, and then apply the peculiar mannerism to the analysis of his personal feelings concerning certain aspects of a spring day or of a sea picture, and yet not have a great mind. That is one reason why there are so many successful writers of verse today. The fact is that a large mass of college graduates with literary susceptibilities have discovered the trick, and can turn out any amount of the kind of gentle, sensitive verses with a sort of delicate, finish that the magazines of today seem to require. A remarkable instance is that the greater amount of this kind of work is done by women. Of course I would not rob all of these poets of a certain amount of even poetic genius, but it is another thing to compare the writers of this sort of verse with the minds that conceived such poems as Byron's "Address to the Ocean," or "The Dying Gladiator," Coleridge's "Ancient Mariner," Shelley's "Cloud," Keats's odes to a "Grecian Urn," and "To a Nightingale," Burns's "Lines to a Mountain Daisy," and "Tam O'Shanter," Hood's "Bridge of Sighs," and the many beautiful poems by Tennyson and Browning, such as "The Lotos-Eaters," "The Moated Grange," "The Revenge," "The Funeral of Wellington," "Herve Riel," "The Ride from Aix to Ghent," all of which are poems of great original conception, and show powers that culture alone could not produce. On turning our attention to America, we have Poe's "Raven," Bryant's "Thanatopsis," Whittier's "Maud Muller," Longfellow's "Wreck of the Hesperus," all exquisitely rare as poetry, and containing in themselves in various degrees those evidences of the rare mind, with its grasp of humanity in a lesser or greater degree, coupled with the true dramatic capability of being able to crystallize the individual conception or thought in such a way that it could never be improved upon. Now, let us apply this test, and search our current literature for work of this order, and we fail to find it. Many critics who are acute enough to see this lack try to explain it away when writing up their especial idols by claiming that this is not the highest order of poetry, or that the times are changing, and that "pensive meditation" and "acute observation" amount to genius of a high order. That may "go down" with the people who have not taken the trouble to weigh current literature in the balance in which I have just weighed it. But the fact remains the same, that the truest poets the language has as yet produced have ever been deeply interested in the issues of life and death, and these are the paramount ideas with which they will ever dwell. Wordsworth, who has been called the greatest nature poet, has never divorced nature from humanity in any of his work, and it is really, after all, man with whom he deals. The true greatness of Wordsworth lies in his simple, grand emotion, his power of entering into the humanities of the scene about him. He is not and never could be a minute scenic artist, such as the descriptive sonnet writers we have today. Emerson had also some of this peculiar quality. In both men it was a great pressing in, as it were, of nature's impressiveness on their souls. Such men never could write of nature in cold blood. They were too deeply impressed with its reverence to do so. In the highest sense they were impressionists.

Many of our writers of today, on the other hand, are cold-blooded, professional writers for the magazines, who, many of them, turn out any amount of stuff, more from ambition than from a desire to produce what is in them.

They set themselves a task, as many of their brother-writers in prose do, with the result we have just described.

From the Globe
1 July 1893

Reprinted from *At the Mermaid Inn: Wilfred Campbell, Archibald Lampman, Duncan Campbell Scott in The Globe 1892–93*, intro. by Barrie Davies, Toronto: U of Toronto P, 1979, 341–43.

We notice that the term, "quality" is used to-day in connection with our current minor verse. And, while I would object to it as an unfair and misleading expression as applied to true poetry, yet it comes in very handy as a sort of apology for the kind of pseudo-poetry that is marking these times, and which, in the absence of real poetic imagination and creative ability, has taken to pensive musings and landscape painting in words. The real critic when he meets this article, which is as easy for some men to make as it is to whittle a stick, he passes it over with the slight mention it merits. But there is another class of critic, who, bearing the same relation to true criticism that this kind of verse-maker does to poetry, and stumbling up against a sort of poetical miracle of this kind, he is dumbfounded. Of course, it is a sonnet, and is possibly called

At Even

I sit me moanless in the somber fields,
The cows come with large udders down the dusk,
One cudless, the other chewing of a husk,
Her eye askance, for that athwart her heels,
Flea-haunted and rib-cavernous, there steals
The yelping farmer-dog. An old hen sits
And blinks her eyes. (Now I must rack my wits
To find a rhyme, while all this landscape reels.)

Yes! I forgot the sky. The stars are out,
There being no clouds; and then the pensive maid!

Of course she comes with tin-pail up the lane.
Mosquitoes hum and June bugs are about.
(That line hath "quality" of loftiest grade.)
And I have eased my soul of its sweet pain.

—John Pensive Bangs, in the Great Too-Too Magazine for July

The critic stumbles, I repeat, on this remarkable effusion, and this is what he remarks: "This is verse of a high poetic quality. It is Millet-like in its terse realism. Mr. Bangs is not one of your common flabgasters in rhyme. He is a monk in literature, and wears the hair-shirt of realism. Mark his delicate touches, his firm hand. No laying on with a white-wash brush for him. Oh! It is rare; it is restful. It makes me— w— . No, the disciple of realism and Arnold does not weep; he only groans. I will hang on to myself." He then consigns all of the other poets who may be standing around stopping up Bangs' literary way to early poetical graves, and black oblivion, while he notes the mellow moon of this his particular poet radiating the heavens with its beams, and rising higher and higher into universal favor. But the funniest part is that the critic should give Mr. Bangs so much praise for his realism. He surely would not have Bangs make the cows drive the landscape, the dog do the roosting, and get the hen, the maid and the June bugs mixed up promis-cuously. Hardly! John Pensive Bangs has too much horse-sense for that since he went to college, read Matthew Arnold, cut his hair and got toned down a bit. Nor should the critic expect that Mr. Bangs ever did sit thus, "moanless," in the fields, a martyr to blackflies and damp grass, in order to capture this most rare and fleeting glimpse for the uplifting of his lesser human brethren. Not by any means. John Pensive has a patent on this sort of business, and ten to one he wrote it in his back office, two flights up, with a cigar in his mouth, and the spittoon two points on the weather-bow. Nor should the critic think it anything remarkable to rig or hitch such a landscape together, so as not to forget even the June bugs. This is simple enough. We might give him some more examples. They need no lofty thoughts or wide knowledge of nature and man. This is another, called

Pitching Hay

Hitched to the waggon by the grimy hands
Of the horny-fisted farmer, stands the team,
Filling the drowsy air with languid dream

> Of gone, last-winter oats: Aloft there stands
> The lusty farm-hand, and he mops his brow,
> And says, 'We'll hustle in this last load now.'

Or these lines of "singular discernment," says our critic:

> Far up the road, where once a waggon was,
> Lies all deserted where the toilers sped,
> The foot-path leading to the dun cow's shed
> Has but a solitary hobbling toad.

Fancy such a picture of desolation and bleakness, and so on.

We have no space here to quote from many such landscapes as "Raking Chips," "The Lonely Clam," "Morn," "Beetles," "Hoeing Potatoes," "Bunch-Grass," "Tadpoles," "Sharpening the Bucksaw," and other equally interesting and peculiar subjects for word-landscape, and all found in John Pensive Bangs' new volume of poems, called "Red Top and Radishes," and all containing that remarkable attribute called "poetic quality" in a marked degree.

Views on Canadian Literature

From *The Week*, March 16th, 1894. Reprinted from Laurel Boone, ed., *William Wilfred Campbell: Selected Poetry and Essays*, Waterloo, ON: Wilfrid Laurier UP, 1987, 167–69.[*]

As a writer it is difficult for me to speak frankly without incurring the risk of being misunderstood by many who may not look at our literature from my point of view. Like all writers I have my literary ideals, which govern my development, and it is from the standpoint of these that I will look at our literary conditions.

There is no doubt that we have the beginnings of a literature, in poetry at least. But that we have produced much serious work that is liable to live is another question. We have several clever men, who have made their names as magazine writers, but just what impression their work is having on the national life it is very hard to discover. A writer may acquire considerable reputation in certain literary circles to-day and yet never be in touch with the great reading public at all, his standing as a man of letters being fixed by his fellow writers, many of whom he in turn helps to celebrate in the same manner. In fact, it has become quite fashionable among certain literary cliques to rather scorn the work of a man who has the power of impressing the public, as being work of

[*] Boone comments: "Professor L.E. Horning organized a Canadian Literature Evening at Victoria University in Toronto. In preparation for this event, he 'asked a number of Canadian authors to give ... their views on the present state and outlook for the future of our literature.' In *The Week*, he published 'substantially as received' the responses of five authors. Those of Charles Mair and J.M. LeMoine appeared on March 9, 1894 (344–46) and those of J.G. Bourinot, Wilfred Campbell and Duncan Campbell Scott came out on March 16, 1894 (368–69). In his contribution, Campbell sums up various ideas which he had developed at greater length in his 'At the Mermaid Inn' essays, especially those of May 28, 1892 (Davies 80); October 1, 1892 (Davies 160); November 12, 1892 (Davies 188); and July 1, 1893 (above 166)." (Davies references above are from *At the Mermaid Inn: Wilfred Campbell, Archibald Lampman, Duncan Campbell Scott in The Globe 1892–93*, ed. Barrie Davies, Toronto: U of Toronto P, 1979.)

a secondary order. But this power of impressing the public is to my mind the true test that marks out the real poet from the mere clever verse writer. While there are myriads of skilful versifiers in the neighboring Republic there is only one man, James Whitcomb Riley, who is in real touch with the people as a whole. It is his power of putting the humanities into his verse that makes him what he is, a true poet. On the other hand, Thomas Bailey Aldrich, perhaps the most polished verse-writer this continent has produced, with all his delicate skill and power as a word-builder in verse, is today no more the American national poet than is the "Sweet Singer of Michigan." He can turn quaint fancies into musical lyrics, can write polished sonnets as far as technique is concerned that would have shamed many of the great poets, but he has utterly failed to acquire a national fame as a poet. The simple reason for this is that he is not a real poet at all, but merely a skilled verse-maker. He is remarkably clever, but you may turn his volumes over from cover to cover and rarely if ever find anything to appeal to the heart. His soul is unresponsive to the deep mysteries of existence, to the terrible problems of life. He is a word artist, pure and simple, but he is not and never could be a great poet. I would now, with these comparisons in mind, turn your gaze to Canada, and I would say that our writers, to give us a literature worthy of the name, must have higher ideals than the carving of magazine cameos. The greatest poets in all ages have been dramatic and epic, and no poet can be called great who has not reached high grade in one of these departments of literature. Of course there have been great lyrical poets, like Burns, but they have been great in the humanities. Nature-poetry, or rather landscape-verse, as the most of it really is, has been overdone. It is a sure sign of decadence in literature, when this kind of verse is given overmuch prominence. This is a kind of literature that will always be strictly minor in its characteristics, though a writer who, with the painter's eye, devotes himself to it assiduously, may more easily, in this field, reach what some call perfection than in any other branch of literature. I cannot speak for our other writers, as I am not aware of their ideals, but speaking for myself, I must say that I would have little hope for our literature did I think it were merely to produce a few polished sonnets and delicate lyrics. I know this is an age when great ideals and efforts in all the arts are scoffed at by men who have no ideals save perfection in reproducing the commonplace, and that my hopes and ambitions for our literature may be laughed at as absurd, but in spite of all this decadent tendency, I sincerely believe that if a man has the large ideas and great conceptions within him, that he has just as much right and chance today to produce great poetry as at any other age or condition of the world's history.

One of the great stumbling blocks in the way of developing good literature is the contemporary magazine verse. It claims to represent current poetry and in this way is gradually weaning the public who read it from any great ideal of poetry. The professional magazine verse-writer monopolizes the place of the real poet. True genius too is shamed out of public notice by the glittering finish and the clever sneer of the magazine verse-makers [sic] and his friend, the newspaper critic, who worships the little tin-art god. If a real poem at rare intervals appears in the magazines it is by chance indeed. The best proof of the general contempt for magazine verse is shown in the refusal of leading publishers to publish in book form verses that were to a large extent printed in their own magazine. It is not a very difficult matter for a clever versifier to get his little lyrics and sonnets accepted by magazine editors, but he is a fool who dreams this to be the road to fame as a poet. This is not how the great line from Shakespeare to Tennyson made their fame. Magazines and polished verses were an unknown quantity in the days of Bryant, Poe, Longfellow, Whitman and Whittier. It is needless for me to compare the poetry of these strong individualities with the mediocre current verse that goes for poetry in various magazines nowadays. I speak from the strongest conviction when I say that there can be no real poetic development in this or any other country until the great reading public is ready to buy a book of verse, not as a means of light recreation, not because the critics admire its style or finish, but because they feel the author has a great inspiration to interpret the sublime and the beautiful to his fellowmen, and that the volume in question contains but a part or stage of his development in this impulse. My ideal of the great poet is he of the great heart, strong intellect, and wide and deep knowledge, who with an exquisite sympathy towards all the tragedy and beauty of existence, reaches out and down into all the recesses of the human heart with a natural instinct that knows and feels what other men often take a lifetime to learn. All this coupled with a born desire and power to translate these tragedies and beauties into the majestic forms and moods of human language, constitute, to my mind, the chief characteristics of a poetic genius. The poet must be, first and foremost, a man of ideas and ideals, a burning soul, lifted above the ordinary plane by a passionate interest in the race as a whole, and in the relationship of the individual to the great Unknown. He should be ahead of his age in knowledge and aspiration, and should know history as other men know their own times. This has been so of all the great poets of the past, in part at least. Patriotism is also an indispensable quality of poetry. But the great patriotic poetry is not found in stiff odes, but in the battle, death and folk songs of a people. Such poems can only be written under pressure of a great crisis and can only be produced by poets of strong human sympathy. Finally, I would say that our present literature has been affected far too much by the neighboring decadent American school, and that our opinions of literary values have been guided too much by their false magazine standards. Under these influences our literature is in great danger of deterioration, even before it has found its wings. When the people begin to take our poetry seriously and look more for the sublime and less for the merely beautiful or rather pretty in its leading characteristics, then will our literature begin to be a great formative influence in the national life.

Introduction to
The Collected Poems of Wilfred Campbell

From *The Collected Poems of Wilfred Campbell*. Toronto: Briggs; Toronto: Ryerson; New York and London: Revell, 1905, v–viii. Reprinted from Laurel Boone, ed., *William Wilfred Campbell: Selected Poetry and Essays*, Waterloo, ON: Wilfrid Laurier UP, 1987, 179–80.

Simplicity and directness are essential to the highest class of verse. In the judgment of poetry this principle must never be lost sight of.

Goethe, perhaps the greatest literary mind since Shakespeare, is noted for his simplicity and directness of manner. The effort to dwarf the writing of verse into an obscure cult, will fail so long as the people keep themselves familiar with the verse of the great poets of the past—whose work is true and beautiful because of its very character of direct, simple naturalness.

It may be difficult to explain to the layman the conditions which produce poetry but no person of a poetical temperament (and I believe that the greater mass of readers have such an inclination) can fail to appreciate a true poem. The failure to appreciate verse today is not owing so much to the inability of the public to recognize a poem, as to the attempt of certain critics to force upon the public as poetry, what is after all at the most only clever verse. The result is a sort of confusion in the mind of the ordinary reader who in the past was accustomed to judge by his own feelings.

There is no doubt that poetry is first and last a high emotion. It is a sort of instrument which thrills the soul not only by what it reveals but by what it suggests. For this reason, a mere esthetic word-picture, no matter how carefully wrought, is not in the true sense poetry.

It may emulate the careful photograph which seemingly loses nothing, yet fails to catch the one necessary insight which the painter who is a genius puts into his picture—that light that never was on sea or land, yet which all men see sometime or other in what the average world may call the dull and commonplace. There may be a danger, however, that a cult to see beauty in the commonplace will grow from the affectation to seem artistic and poetical. After all, the beauty we see in a special verse is in ourselves. There is the universal beauty which all see. That is the real, the lasting beauty. There is the greatness of life as life, the greatness inherent in noble actions and noble aims; the pathos of a great love, a great self-denial or a great despair. There is the greatness of a struggle for a lost cause (how mankind loves a lost cause). There is a majesty of life and death; the majesty of ocean and shore and lofty hills. All of this is universal, and of this poetry is made.

After all, the real root of all poetry from Shakespeare to the latest singer is in the human heart. The mind is cold and critical. It plans and plots. It examines and sifts. Man with the mind alone were but a mean creature. Man the planner and plotter, the schemer and builder, may move mountains and yet be little better than the ape. It is man the hoper, man the dreamer, the eternal child of delight and despair whose ideals and desires are ever a lifetime ahead of his greatest accomplishments, who is the hero of nature and the darling of the ages. Because of this, true poetry will always be to him a language, speaking to him from the highest levels of his being and a sort of translation from a more divine tongue emanating from the mystery and will of God.

Poetry may have many messages; but above all stands the eternal appeal from life and nature. All descriptions of water and land, sky and earth, summer and winter, are not necessarily poetry, any more than are all verses on life and death and love and despair. But the greatest poetry is that dealing with the human soul. The highest class of poetry, that of Shakespeare, that of the Old Testament, of Goethe, is that dealing with the eternal tragedy of life in the universe. The eternal theme of man is man. But all poetry may not stand on this high level. There are lesser degrees of the divine emotion, and much that is true, beautiful and majestic in the verse of the eighteenth and nineteenth centuries.

In the work of the great nature poets, the very strength and beauty of the verse is owing to the fact that the thought and imagination dwell upon the human, and nature as affecting the human, rather than upon the mere objective nature, as solely an esthetic aspect. The greatness of such verse consists in its lofty emotion, whereby it conveys to the soul an impressive sense of the majesty of life and death. It is not merely the work of the literary artist, who paints in words on a sort of literary canvas; but whether the idea be death or a season, the mood is a creation of a soul strongly imbued with a feeling of the sublimity of life. In such verse one is lifted out of the common into an atmosphere of spiritual exaltation, such as only true poetry has the power to create.

In dealing with a volume of verse it is perfectly right that the reader should be guided only by the highest standards in the selection or rejection of poetry as such. To find the true poetry needs no subtle insight into the intricacies of language and the laws of prosody. The soul of the man of pure sentiment and cultured mind is at once attracted to true poetry through those very impressive qualities which mark it out from the body of mere rhyme or unrhymed effusions and literary exercises with which, even in the volumes of our noblest poets, it is sometimes mingled.

Literature, Music and the Arts:
The Argument from Literature

Originally published in *The Collected Poems of Wilfred Campbell*, Toronto: Briggs; Toronto: Ryerson; New York and London: Revell, 1905. Here reprinted from Laurel Boone, ed., *William Wilfred Campbell: Selected Poetry and Essays*, Waterloo, ON: Wilfrid Laurier UP, 1987, 194–97.

It is a remarkable fact that all of the greatest human literature is a part of antiquity and quite out of touch with all that is modern. In short, it is all prehistoric either in text or in subject. Job, Homer, Shakespeare, Milton, all deal with subjects which connect man with the Gods, demigods or the primal elemental, and universal tragedy of the ancient people and the early world.

Lear and Macbeth are certainly not modern; but where in modern literature is there as great an ethical ideal as is found in these great dramas. Homer is still the chiefest of Epics, and the very epic itself as a form of literature is essentially great, and a witness to greatness in a people, and is eternal evidence of ancient greatness. Next to the Biblical account, which is the greatest literature the world has ever known, the intellect of man has worshipped and will always worship the great world epics, placing side by side with them the great world dramas of Greece, Britain and Germany.* These are, and ever remain, the lofty mountain peaks of literature, around which cluster the lesser foothills and plateaus of national letters and culture.

Great as these are, it is also quite certain that literature even greater must have existed in remote ages. The muse of Ossian the famed Celtic Bard gives a slight idea of what may have existed in ancient Britain, when that country was at its greatest long before even Arthur and the Round Table.

---

*   Campbell's note: "Refer to Prometheus."

It is not easy to explain why this titan literature is so universally revered and admired, save that it is titan, in all respects being essentially of the ancient mountains and hill slopes of Avernus and Atlantis.

There is a nobleness inherent in all great literature, just as there is in primitive nature, and the Greek art. There is also a sense of the sublime, which permeates the whole of the Hebrew Literature in those old epics and plays, an atmosphere of the great human tragedy, that is found nowhere else, outside of the prehistoric literature of the world.

No one really knows where these old literatures had their first beginnings; they are and always will remain a mystery just as Shake-speare in Britain is a mystery, and yet the chiefest glory of the race, for which the Shakespeare literature stands. But they all point to a remote past of the golden age of earth when men were god-like and great in their destiny and undertakings.

They all point to a vast culture a primitive age of a high perfection of life and ideal, and a period of colossal effort, and accomplishment, when, as we are told, men would be as the gods and ascend once more to heaven.

They deal with and are part of a Promethean age, of lofty struggle, when the godlike in self-sacrifice for some divine purpose, came down from the heaven to earth and took upon it the earthy and the imperfect, and the infinite suffered and was caged in the prison of the finite so that, the earthy might be likened to the heavenly, and, the Caliban climb up to the level of Prospero. This is all a great mystery, but none the less a living fact, as felt in all earth's true literature as the expression of beauty and character and the Christ doctrine of self-denial, and the divine discontent, that has set the higher soul of man off on a long journey, whence there is no returning.

Be not dismayed. God never intended his broad and shining roadway to end in a mere cul de sac. All His paths lie upward and outward and the destiny of the man and the race of today, still possess all of the primal divine possibilities of emancipation and achievement. This is found in all of earth's great literature. Its god-like attributes are those of conscience or the sublimity of character, as the result of the imperfect, struggling both toward the perfect, or, the intense sense of the infinite sin in the self that will not absolve itself, as in the case of Lady Macbeth—"Not all the seas .... "

Here we have one of literature's greatest examples of the presence of the divinity, in man, judging with god-like greatness the unpardonableness of its own sin or deeds of evil. Here we find the terrible clash between the two natures in the one personality—the Caliban and the Prospero—in the one being. The Caliban would be the eternal child and smash everything to please its animal nature, ... to seize all things, as it did in its low slime. But the other nature, stands apart from itself and is outraged, is ashamed, is afraid to meet God, in the garden, as at the fall. Here we see this great and terrible inevitable law working out in the human entity of the fallen and risen man, as shown in earth's greatest literature. The realization of this great truth raises religion once more to the highest plane and puts it in its true place as pervading all of our world environment.

All this is seen in the revelation of Prospero and Caliban, the struggle between the divine and the earth heredity, in the one human personality. And it is this struggle that is the great drama of man on this earth, and it depends on us all as to which shall conquer. This is a wonderful picture, a remarkable contrast, as seen in the pagan races and the loftier races, or those where conscience rules in the individuals.

This dual personality runs through all of our great and true poets. It is that divine, that immortal sadness, over wrecked civilizations, or great opportunities lost. It is the shadow of God himself—called evil—haunting man. How else explain the titan unhappiness of our great poets such as Shakespeare, Byron, Shelley, and Poe, or Milton's conception of Satan, the fallen demi-god, or the Prometheus of Eschylus or the Manfred or Childe Harold of Byron. The powers of the early godman were infinitely vaster than anything, suggested by our limited imaginations. So much was this so, that all known instances of genius are but breedings back, as it were, to that greatness gone, that divine condition of earth's primeval unfallen man. The language of poetry, called inspired, is no doubt but a harking back to the common speech of the Gods.

All that man ascribes to the so-called supernatural is explained in this way.

We are now, through our earth heredity, as far below that one-time godlike plane of existence as are the lower creatures now below our level. Christ himself was but a reincarnation of what man was in the beginning, in Earth's divine morn, when he walked with God, and was not yet taking upon himself, the condition of the earthy. This sublime mystery is all explained in St. Paul's wonderful passage used in the Burial service.

Much has been written concerning the reverting back of the human
to the lower levels. But there never has been realized the possibility of
the reverse upward to the higher, as in all our genius and its influences:
Every great man, from Homer to Shakespeare is but an example of this.
The so-called discovery of music was but a remembering in part of the
race heredity reverting back through the medium of what has been
called genius, to its one true inheritance of God-like harmony, when the
morning stars sang together, and the tritons sang in old ocean's caves,
and the God Pan on Earth. It may not be realized that in the perfect state
all the universe was music and melody, and that is why ever since, in the
winds of Autumn and in Old Ocean's voice there is that haunting
sadness, which beats its surfs on the iron shore of this human tragedy.
One can imagine mighty organ notes in the wind vents of Ocean's Caves
round Saturn's wondrous Isle.

Then, when fallen humanity and all nature became [sic] to come back
to itself after the first dark ages following the dread catastrophe of the
first or spiritual fall.* There would be titan attempts, of the God-presence
in man marred by the brutal to once more emulate those divine
harmonies, and exquisite memories, this would be all mingled with a
sadness of the pure soul, in vain striving once more to be as the gods,
and so has it lingered in music and poetry and art down to our day.

In art we see a strong example of this influence in the marvellous
creations of Turner. In the works of this great artist are found the
greatest proof of the Ancient Atlantean, Trojan, Egyptian, Greek, and
pre-Roman personality of the Modern Briton at his highest. The race
that produced a Turner—and a Shakespeare—invented a marvellous
culture, long ere Rome and the Modern world of the last two thousand
years existed. Shakespeare was of the demi-gods, and Turner has his
spirit, coeval with Ulysses and the search for the golden fleece. His work
is full of unconscious dreams of the golden age of the Atlantean world.
Shakespeare is of that age and condition all compact. Prospero and the
Magic Isle and Caliban is no mere dream. There is an idea here of the
loftier god like man with powers over the nature around him, in keeping
with his great, more god like conscience, a divine ruler as it were over
the lesser creatures of the creation.

---

* I am inclined to read this sentence: "Then, when fallen [,] humanity and all
nature began [not became] to come back to itself after the first dark ages follow-
ing the dread catastrophe of the first or spiritual fall."

SIR CHARLES G.D. ROBERTS

SIR CHARLES G.D. ROBERTS (1860–1943)

Biographical Notes

Sir Charles G.D. (George Douglas) Roberts was born in Douglas, New Brunswick, on 10 January 1860 and grew up near the Tantramar marshes by Sackville. Along with his cousin, Bliss Carman, he attended the Fredericton Collegiate Grammar School from 1874 to 1876, and studied under the tutelage of headmaster and classical scholar George R. Parkin. Roberts went on to attend the University of New Brunswick from 1876 to 1879 where he graduated with honours in Mental and Moral Science, and Political Economy. During his studies there he won a scholarship in Latin and Greek, and a medal for Latin composition. While at UNB, Roberts wrote several poems including "Memnon," which was published in the *Century* in the summer of 1879, and by the following year published his first, quite influential collection of verse: *Orion, and Other Poems*. He stayed on at UNB to complete an M.A. in 1881, and from there he moved to Toronto, where he edited Goldwyn Smith's periodical *The Week* for two years until a disagreement over Smith's pro-American politics caused him to leave.

Roberts passed up an opportunity to go to Oxford in 1880, to wed Mary Isabel Fenet with whom he had five children by 1892. After working as schoolmaster in Chatham and Fredericton, Roberts became a Professor of English and French Literature at King's College in Windsor, Nova Scotia, from 1885 to 1888, and then Professor of English and Economics in the same college from 1888 to 1895. Three volumes of his poetry were published during this period and Roberts was elected a Fellow of the Royal Society of Canada in 1890. Disillusioned with teaching, and increasingly unhappy in his marriage, Roberts determined to live by his wits as a freelance writer. He resigned from King's College in 1895, then two years later, separated from his wife and children, and moved to New York City, where he worked from 1897 to 1898 as associate editor of *The Illustrated American*. He subsequently left for Europe, living first in Paris, and later for two years in Munich, before moving to London, England, in 1912 where he remained until 1925. During this period he earned his living writing fiction, especially populist animal stories and romances, and non-fiction prose. Though primarily known today as a poet, he is also credited with being one of the founders of the "animal story."

Although fifty-six years old at the outset of WWI, Roberts joined up as a private in the British army with the 16th Battalion of the King's Regiment; at the close of the war he was made captain and served at the Canadian War Records Office in London, England until 1925. While living outside Canada, Roberts produced four volumes of poetry. When he returned to Canada in 1925 he lived in Toronto, where he continued his involvement in the Canadian literary scene. He lectured, published and promoted emerging Canadian writers, and served as national president of the Canadian Authors' Association and as editor of the *Canadian Who's Who*. He gave poetry recital tours in 1925 to 1926. Late in his life, when Roberts was recognized as the "father of Canadian literature," he brought out four more substantial volumes of poetry.

Roberts received many honours: he was awarded the Royal Society of Canada's first Lorne Pierce Medal, was elected president of the Canadian Authors' Association in 1926, and knighted on 3 June 1935. He had received an honorary LL.D. from UNB in 1906. When his estranged wife Mary died, Roberts married Joan Montgomery on 28 October 1943. He died on 26 November 1943, and is laid to rest in Fredericton.

Publications

Orion, and Other Poems. Philadelphia: Lippincott, 1880.

In Divers Tones. Montreal: Dawson; Boston: Lothrop, 1887.

Poems of Wild Life. London: W. Scott, 1888.

Songs of the Common Day and Ave! An Ode for the Shelley Centenary. Toronto: Briggs; London: Longmans, 1893.

Enigmas. Boston: Lamson, Wolffe & Co., 1896.

New York Nocturnes and Other Poems. Boston: Lamson, Wolffe & Co., 1898.

The Kindred of the Wild. Toronto: Copp, Clark; Boston: L.C. Page & Co., 1902.

The Book of the Rose. Toronto: Copp, Clark, 1903.

Poems. New York: Silver Burdett, 1901; rev. 1907.

New Poems. London: Constable, 1919.

The Vagrant of Time. Toronto: Ryerson, 1927.

Eyes of the Wilderness. Toronto & New York: Macmillan; London: Dent, 1933.

The Iceberg, and Other Poems. Toronto: Ryerson, 1934.

Selected Poems. Toronto: Ryerson, 1936.

Canada Speaks of Britain and Other Poems of the War. Toronto: Ryerson, 1941.

Selected Poetry and Critical Prose. Ed. W.J. Keith. Toronto & Buffalo: U of Toronto P, 1974.

The Collected Poems of Sir Charles G.D. Roberts. Ed. Desmond Pacey and Graham Adams. Wolfville, NS: Wombat, 1985.

Critical Materials

Book Length

Adams, John Coldwell. *Sir Charles God Damn: The Life of Sir Charles G.D. Roberts.* Toronto: U of Toronto P, 1986.

Cappon, James. *Charles G.D. Roberts*. Toronto: Ryerson, 1923.

———. *Charles G.D. Roberts and the Influence of his Times*. Ottawa: Tecumseh, 1975.

Keith, W.J. *Charles G.D. Roberts*. Toronto: Copp, Clark, 1969.

Martell, Carol E. *Sir Charles G.D. Roberts: The King's College Years*. Sackville, NB: Mount Allison UP, 1978.

Pomeroy, Elsie May. *Sir Charles G.D. Roberts: A Biography*. Toronto: Ryerson, 1943.

Sir Charles G.D. Roberts Symposium. Ed. Glenn Clever. Ottawa: U of Ottawa P, 1984.

Whalen, Terrence. *Charles G.D. Roberts and his Works*. Toronto: ECW, 1989.

Articles

Bentley, D.M.R. "Roberts's 'Series of Sonnets' in Songs of the Common Day (1893)." *Dalhousie Review* 69.3 (1989): 393–412.

Precosky, Don. "'Need that irks': Roberts' sonnets in Songs of the Common Day." *Canadian Poetry* 22 (1988): 22–31.

Rogers, A. Robert. "American Recognition of Bliss Carman and Sir Charles G.D. Roberts." *The Humanities Association Review* 22.2: 19–25.

Roper, Henry. "High Anglican Pagan" and His Pupil: Charles G.D. Roberts, Robert Norwood and The Development of A Nova Scotian Literary Tradition, 1885–1932." *Dalhousie Review* 75.17 (1997): 51–73.

Strong, William. "Charles G.D. Robert's The Tantramar Revisited." *Canadian Poetry* 3 (1978): 26–37.

Online Resources

http://www.ucalgary.ca/UofC/faculties/HUM/ENGL/canada/poet/c_roberts.htm)

http://eir.library.utoronto.ca/rpo/display/poet278.html

http://digital.library.upenn.edu/women/garvin/poets/robertscgd.html

http://www.lib.unb.ca/archives/roberts/MGL10.html#bio

The Outlook for Literature:
Acadia's Field for Poetry, History and Romance

First published in the *Halifax Herald* on 1 January 1886; reprinted from *Selected Poetry and Critical Prose,* ed. W.J. Keith, Toronto: U of Toronto P, 1974, 260–64. *

Having been asked for a brief forecast as to the future of literature in Nova Scotia, let me in the first place declare my faith that that future must be the future of literature in Canada. We must forget to ask of a work whether it is Nova Scotian or British Columbian, of Ontario or of New Brunswick, until we have inquired if it be broadly and truly Canadian. It is the future of Canadian nationality with which every son of Canada is most concerned; and our literature will be false to its trust, will fail of that very service for which young nations have ever relied upon their literature, if it does not show itself the nurse of all patriotic enthusiasms, and the bane of provincial jealousies. This being premised, my subject becomes a consideration of the part likely to be played by Nova Scotian talent in the making of our national literature. But the subject is one on which it would be hard to speak with much definiteness or confidence. The utmost to be looked for here is perhaps a little suggestiveness.

It is fair to expect that our contribution will be to the higher and more imaginative claims of literature, seeing that, to a greater degree than any other province save Quebec, we have wealth of tradition, variety of surrounding, and a soil well tempered by human influences,—a soil that has been cradle and grave to a now fair number of generations. This last means much, for a raw soil seems rarely to flower into fine imaginative work. As we have inspiring material in our past, and in our

---

*   Keith notes: "The paragraph divisions are editorial, since the newspaper employed standardized and idiosyncratic layout procedures that are not followed here. The text is reprinted in full."

hopes for the future, so we have also picturesque and striking material in some aspects of the present, in the lives of our fishing populations, for instance; and in our lumber camps and drives. In our landscape, earth and sea and sky conspire to make an imaginative people. These stern coasts, now thundered against by Atlantic storms, now wrapped in noiseless fogs, these overwhelming tides, these vast channels emptied of their streams, these weird reaches of flat and marsh and dike, should create a habit of openness to nature, and by contrast put a reproach upon the commonplace and the gross. Our climate with its swift extremes is eager and waking, and we should expect a sort of dry sparkle in our page, with a transparent and tonic quality in our thought. If environment is anything, our work can hardly prove tame.

Referring to our material in history and tradition, perhaps the source from which most is commonly expected is our store of Indian legend. There is continual demand for the working of this field, and continual surprise that it should be so long unharvested. Both the demand and the surprise are as old as literature in North America, and are likely to grow much older before being satisfied. The legends are, some of them, wildly poetic, and vigorous in conception; and they are easily attainable, both from the lips of their hereditary possessors and from such books as Leland's admirable "Legends of the Algonquin Indians." But the stuff seems almost unavailable for purposes of pure literature. The Indian has left a curse in his bequest, and the prize turns worthless in our grasp[*] The host of American poems and romances with the Indian as inspiration form, "Hiawatha" being excepted, a museum of lamentable failures. They are the crowning insult to a decaying race. Even "Hiawatha," in spite of easy story-telling and bright description, can hardly be called quite worthy of its author's genius. It is bizarre and fanciful rather than imaginative; and it lacks the grave beauty and the air of reality essential to great verse. Only indirectly, by association and suggestion, is Indian legend likely, I think, to exert marked influence upon our creative literature. But there is room to do invaluable work in the collection and comparative study of Indian folk-lore and kindred matter, for the results of which there is now a ready appreciation. Leland has left behind him some very good gleaning, owing to the wideness of the field which he has occupied.

---

[*] Keith notes: "The reference is to *The Algonquin Legends of New England*, by Charles Godfrey Leland (1824–1903), published in 1884."

With the story of the French in Nova Scotia, which reads less like history than romance, the case is far otherwise: The eager searchings, the bold exploits, the strange adventures, the hardships and the triumphs interwoven in the old Acadian annals, together with the deep pathos of the end, these are matters so near us that we can feel their warmth, and at the same time remote enough to admit of full poetic treatment. They are in that distance which catches

> The light that never was on sea or land,
> The consecration and the poet's dream.*

This material, too, has already proved itself adapted to exquisite treatment. The fact of Longfellow having come to it for one of his chief inspirations, though this might seem to make it presumptuous for another to dip into the same source, in reality only makes that source so much the more available. Most of the greater power of our literature, and of all literatures, has been wrought upon subjects familiarized by previous handling. Nearly all great themes show a certain inexhaustibility, and admit of being more than once or twice splendidly treated. It is he has the hardest task who breaks a new field; but his successors as a rule reap the richest harvests. Longfellow's handling of Acadian story has simply glorified the theme for later singers. Every dike and ancient rampart, and surviving Acadian name, and little rock-rimmed haven, from the wind-rippled shifting sepulchre of Sable Island to the sunny levels of Chignecto, should be breeding ground for poem, and history, and romance. It is hard to imagine a region more fascinating to the thought, more suffused with the glamour of a splendid imperishable past half veiled in mystery, than is the Island of Cape Breton. The ear is greedy for the faintest echo of the trumpets and the stir that once were Louisburg; and an insistent spell is in the silence, broken only by tinkle of sheep-bells, that has come down upon the place of the vanished city.

But not only in the past of another people should our pens find motion; for our own ancestors have left us noble themes. In the coming of the Loyalists there is a treasury of subjects hardly inferior to that which New England has found so rich in the deeds of her Puritan fathers. Perhaps these are matters scarcely yet remote enough to take

---

[*   Keith notes: "Wordsworth, 'Elegiac Stanzas, Suggested by a Picture of Peele Castle.'"

the highest treatment; but surely now is the time for doing, in this connection, the work which will make purely creative work a possibility in the future. Those minute and loving records of the past of particular localities, those accurate studies of this or that county, town, or village, such as count no detail too petty, and grudge no labour of research, are needed now to preserve traditions, which year by year are dying out, and of which the ultimate value is as yet hardly to be realized. For work of this sort well done, not prostituted to the requirements of the subscription book advertisement scheme, there is always a steadfast welcome, and a position honorable if not among the highest. Great literary skill is not essential to the production of such works, but it is a secure investment in the future to have written a book, upon which after-workers in the field shall find themselves of necessity dependent. If it is nothing very definite which I have dared to prophesy, I trust that this brief note may at least serve to indicate a probable and suitable direction for our literary effort. It may serve also to ground a reasonable confidence that the Nova Scotian element in that Canadian literature which our hearts are set upon building will not fail of being important and of rare quality.

Notes on Some of the Younger American Poets

Originally published in *The Week* 1:21, 24 April 1888: 328–29. Reprinted from D.M.R. Bentley, http://www.canadianpoetry.ca/confederation/roberts/non-fictional_prose/younger.htm.

Just at this day, when the acknowledged chiefs of American song for the most part have fallen, or have laid down the pen, it may be of interest to examine the qualifications of some of those younger poets on whom the leadership will next devolve. It is evident, at first glance, that the new generation is not following the traditions of the old. On this account, before dealing directly with my subject, I may be permitted to review very briefly those names which have become representative in American poetry. Between these poets and their contemporaries in England a striking difference exists, in the absence on the American side of that quality which goes to the formation of "schools," or gathers a following of pronounced disciples. This really proves less than might at first be imagined, but it suggests and emphasizes several points of difference, besides accounting for what was noticed above—that the methods of the new men are new.

Of all the earlier singers, the pioneers of American verse, Edgar Poe is perhaps the one who has stamped himself most on the work of other men; but it is certain that he has founded no school, such as those that carry on the traditions of Keats or Wordsworth, Tennyson, Browning, or Rossetti. He has left his impress to a certain extent on the music of other masters, even upon that of Tennyson himself, and has exerted an influence on some of the later French singers; but in America even less than elsewhere will he be found to have gathered disciples. Upon Bryant is the mark of Wordsworth more ineffaceably than upon any writer is stamped the mark of Bryant. Emerson himself, who has indeed a devoted and illustrious following, can hardly be said to have a single imitator, or any who could directly assert that from him they had learned their art.

Again, what poet owes as much to Longfellow as does Longfellow to the German Romanticists? So far as I have been able to observe, Longfellow has scarcely left a trace on those of the younger verse writers who are worth taking into account. Where his influence is perceptible it shows mainly in the fashion of quaint similes—a fashion of which he knew how to wear to advantage and with new and exquisite effect, but which most readily grows offensive upon a lesser wearer. Let me not be misunderstood as joining in what is just now quite prevalent, a whole-sale depreciation of Longfellow's genius. Some slight depreciation at the hands of the literary class was inevitable, from his fervent accepta-tion by the masses. But his best work—unfortunately very restricted in quantity—possesses qualities which have perhaps quite failed to hit the sight of the admiring people, excellences other than those which have won him his wide-spread popularity. These are, a consummate grace of thought and diction, an undistorted vision, and sweetness and purity of tone, which, with his wholesome naturalness and his universal tender-ness, must set his fame secure, if not high, as time goes on, even among those who now somewhat decry him. His individuality, though much less obtrusive and insistent than, for instance, that of Emerson, is none the less a fact. And that his genius is, to some extent, begotten of German romanticism on one of the finer developments of New England culture, no more detracts from his originality than does the general theory, that Tennyson is the outcome of Wordsworth and Keats make Tennyson's title less secure. But neither has there arisen, nor from the nature of his genius is there likely to arise, from among Longfellow's throng of admirers a group of disciples to perpetuate his style and traditions.

As for Whitman, who, in the judgement of many of the finest intellects of the day stands out the most prominent figure in American poetry, with all his admirers he has no imitators, for which we are devoutly thankful. Yet Whitman's genius is so great that, in spite of his immodesties, his irritating egotism, his extravagant affections, his reckless constructions, his inapt and awkward coinage of unnecessary words—in spite of the deadly dullness of his catalogues, his pages on pages of utter failure, at length the most hostile critic, unless blind of the mind's eye, is constrained to yield him homage. When most truly himself, the inspired interpreter of Nature in her largest and freest moods, his genius refuses to be hidden by the rags wherewith he decks it. The elemental strength and the truth of it will out. Whitman's song has the power to set one face to face with nature. It is perhaps the fullness of satisfaction to be obtained, in certain moods, from Whitman, which has made his advocates so unqualified, almost furious, in their advocacy. Yet how rarely is he at his best, or even at his second best! And who could tolerate his manner in a smaller poet? Himself we accept gratefully, with all the bitterness he will sometimes force down our throats. But the prospect of feebler Whitmans who could endure? Therefore it is a matter for congratulation that his admirers, some of whom themselves are poets, display no tendency to become his imitators.

It is Dr. Holmes, I think, of whom it may most safely be predicted that a follower will not be lacking to him while cultured society in America continues to exist. He is the unquestioned master in this country of what is called "society verse"; and no future writer in this form can afford to neglect his instruction. His following indeed will probably ever be small, as the qualifications for a successful society poet are most rare; but it will be select, discriminating, and also very devoted. Dr. Holmes has written a few poems in the purely serious vein—poems like "The Chambered Nautilus" and the "Iron Gate"—which take their place with the best of American song; but his title will be derived from his most characteristic and individual work, his vers de societé, a form of verse which has been moulded and altered in his hands, and on which he has set the impress of his genius indelibly.

Why is this species of verse so hard to fit with a name? No one appears quite satisfied to call it "society verse." But this title, under protest as it were, has been universally adopted, and must, I think, stand as the best attainable. It has been suggested, and not without a grain of wisdom, to call it "evening verse"—this earnest with a smile upon its lips, this laughing song that is never quite unmindful of life's pathos. Such a definition is particularly applicable to Dr. Holmes's verse, of which the tone and manner and language are those of such refined and informal social intercourse as an evening gathering alone can best afford. Of such society, whence broad buffoonery is excluded, where the strong passions and the tragedies of life, though recognized, are not dwelt upon, where hearts are sound and flippancy is not acceptable, the verse of Dr. Holmes is the expression.

Further particularizing is not necessary to show that among our elder poets, as compared with their brethren in England, there has been some lack of those characteristics which are apt to exert deep influence on future song. Whether they have adequately stamped themselves on the mass of their fellow-countrymen is quite another question. For instance, we see no trace of Whittier upon the new verse, yet undoubtedly his influence has been wide and deep in American life and sentiment.

We may omit discussion, therefore, of Stoddard and of Bayard Taylor; as well as of the essayist-poets Lowell and Stedman, the former of whom is less a master in his verse than in his prose, while the latter, speaking to us as our wisest critic of song, proves his title to this office, now and again, by the production of [a] perfect lyric. Passing over, also, a later poet, Mr. Aldrich, whose standing has been fully secured to him, whose gem-like richness and elaborate art have long been widely recognized, we come at last to what may be considered as distinctively the younger school. The most prominent members of this are:—Joaquin Miller, Edgar Fawcett, Sidney Lanier, Richard Watson Gilder, Charles de Kay, Miss Ellen Mackay Hutchinson, H.H. Boyesen, Maurice Thompson, F.S. Saltus, Starr H. Nichols, Miss Edith M. Thomas, with others who may be referred to later.

I have mentioned here the name of Miss Thomas, although as far as I am aware her poems are not yet gathered in book form, and are therefore only to be obtained, few in number, by gleaning from the magazines and periodicals. Yet so red-blooded are these verses, of thought and of imagination all compact, so richly individual and so liberal in promise, that the name of their author is already become conspicuous. Miss Thomas's work, in some of its best characteristics, recalls to me Shakespeare's sonnets. We are justified in expecting much from her genius.

Pastoral Elegies,
or Shelley's "Adonais"

"Pastoral Elegies" appeared first in the *New Princeton Review* 5:3, May 1888, 360–70; King's College Record 15: 137, March 1893, 64–68; and was also published with minor variants as the Introduction to Shelley's *Alastor and Adonais*, ed. Charles G.D. Roberts, New York: Silver Burdett, 1902, 22–37. The text below is reprinted from *Selected Poetry and Critical Prose*, ed. W.J. Keith, Toronto: U of Toronto P, 1974, 282–95.[*]

In the spring of 1821, at the Baths of Pisa, where "the mountains sweep to the plain like waves that meet in a chasm," was composed the "Adonais." The circumstances and motives that inspired its composition are best conveyed in Shelley's own preface to the Pisa edition. Reared upon a stable foundation and with careful heed to artistic requirements of structure, the product of a mature and fertile period, the adequate expression of a sublime idea, this poem was regarded by Shelley as one of his most indefeasible titles to fame. He writes of it thus to his publisher, "I confess I should be surprised if that poem were born to an immortality of oblivion." In its attitude of impassioned reverence, its highly spiritualized philosophy, in many regards akin to that which forms the basis of Christianity, it furnishes an effective refutation of the charges of those who still hold Shelley for an atheist. Besides the paramount consideration of its absolute beauty as a poem, it is of importance to the student as marking the highest reach of a form of verse in which our poetry has attained peculiar distinction.

[*]   Keith notes: "Roberts wrote a short preface, an introduction in two parts, 'Biographical' and 'Adonais and Alastor'; and detailed notes for both poems. According to Elsie M. Pomeroy (*Sir Charles G.D. Roberts: A Biography*, introduction by Lorne Pierce, Toronto: Ryerson, 1943, 105), this incorporated an essay on the pastoral elegy published elsewhere. I have been unable to trace this earlier version, but have here extracted the relevant section on 'Adonais' and related poems. The biographical section and a brief discussion of 'Alastor' are omitted; otherwise the text is reprinted in full."

The chord of pastoral elegy, first struck by Bion in his "Lament for Adonis," is one which, through varying expansion and modification, has kept its resonance down to the present day: The "Lament for Bion" by Moschus, the "Lycidas" of Milton, the "Adonais," the "Thyrsis" of Arnold, the "Ave atque Vale" of Swinburne, these all have their origin, more or less distinctly, in that brief and simple idyl. In order to gain a right understanding of the "Adonais," my purpose here is to seek out the relations existing between these several poems, and to endeavour to indicate the development of this species of verse. Neither the purely subjective "In Memoriam" nor the impersonal reverie of the "Elegy in a Country Churchyard" falls within my scope, as neither adopts any part of the conventional framework upon which the pastoral elegy relies.

The form taught by Bion has shown itself adaptable and expansive. For the expression of a grief which is personal but not too passionately so, and which is permitted to utter itself in panegyric, it has proved exactly fitted. A rapid inter-transition between subjective and objective treatment, a breadth of appeal, a reliance upon general sympathy, these are characteristics which endow this species of verse with its wonderful flexibility and freshness. The lines of its structure, moreover, are such as to admit of an almost indefinite degree of decoration, without an appearance of overabundant and extrinsic detail, or departure from the unity of the design.

Of the "Lament for Adonis" the design is marked by extreme simplicity. The singer vibrates between musical reiterations of his own sorrow and reiterations of the sorrow of Aphrodite. Her grief, together with the beauty and the fate of Adonis, is dwelt upon with a wealth of emotional description, and reverted to again and again; while, in the intervals, are heard lamentations from the rivers and the springs,—from the hounds of the slain hunter, and the nymphs of his forest glades,— from the mountains, the oak trees, the flowers that redden for anguish,— from the Loves who clip their locks, the Muses, the Graces, and Hymenaeus with benignant torch extinguished. The most passionate passage in the poem comes from the lips of Aphrodite herself; and even this, dramatic as it is in expression, is held strictly within the bounds of self-conscious and melodious utterance. Throbbing irregularly through the verse, as a peal of bells borne in between the pauses of the wind, now complete, now fragmentary and vanishing, come the notes of the refrain:

Woe, woe for Adonis, the Loves unite in the Lament.

When we turn to the work of Moschus, we see what an expansion has been wrought in the slender pastoral, and that wholly with gain in unity and artistic effect. The advance is toward more definite purpose in the use of reiteration, a more orderly evolution, a wider vision, a more vivid and human interest, and a substitution of the particular for the general. Here, in place of undistinguished springs and rivers, we find the "Dorian water," the fountain Arethusa, and Meles, "most melodious of streams." It is now not the flowers in general that redden in their anguish, but each manifests its pain in its own fashion—the roses and the wind-flowers flush to a deeper crimson, the hyacinth breathes more poignantly the *ai ai* upon its petals, and the trees throw down their young fruit. It is no longer to the unnamed array of nymphs that appeal is made, but with far more potent spell to Galatea herself, to the nymphs Bistonian, to the damsels of Œagria. The heifers reject their pasture, the ewes withhold their milk, and the honey has dried up for sorrow in the wax. Apollo himself is added to the mourners, with the Satyrs and the Fauns. The illustrious among cities bring their tribute, Ascra lamenting more than for her Hesiod, Mytilene than for her Sappho; and Syracuse grieves through the lips of her Theocritus. The nightingales of Sicily join their song, and the Strymonian swans, and the bird of Memnon—the halcyon, the swallow on the long ranges of the hills, and in the sea the music-loving dolphins. Finally the poet, recalling the descent of Orpheus into Hades and how his song there sped him, laments that he himself cannot travel the same path on like errand, and dreams that Persephone were already half won to grant his suit, seeing that she too is Sicilian and skilled in the Doric song. All this is development upon the same lines as those laid down in the "Lament for Adonis." The method is still almost wholly emotional and pictorial, but two or three new elements begin to hint their advent. The strain of philosophical meditation, later to assume a preponderating influence in this species of verse, here begins in a passage of exquisite loveliness which is expanded from a single phrase in the "Lament for Adonis." In the latter poem Cypris cries out to Persephone, "all lovely things drift down to thee"—

τό τε πᾶν καλὸν ες σέ καταρρεί

Observe what this becomes in the treatment of Moschus:* "Ah me, when the mallows wither in the garden, and the grey parsley, and the curled tendrils of the anise, on a later day they live again, and spring in another year, but we men, we the great and mighty and wise, when once we have died, in the hollow earth we sleep, gone down into silence; a right long, arid endless, and unawakening sleep." A new note, too, is touched in the references to Homer, wherein a swift comparison is instituted between the epic and the idyl, and their respective sources of inspiration; and here is the first appearance of the autobiographic tendency which in later poems of the class becomes a prominent feature. In the matter of direct verbal borrowing Moschus owes but little to his master, his indebtedness in this respect being as nothing in comparison with that of Milton and Shelley. The refrain as used by Moschus has not quite the same functions as in the song of Bion. It is used with greater frequency and regularity, as a sort of solemnly sweet response marking off stanzaic divisions, and is in its substance not so interwoven with the body of the poem.

In "Lycidas," generally speaking, the like lines are pursued. The personal note is intensified, which follows from the fact that the lament is for a well-loved friend rather more than for a fellow singer. The conventional masquerade of the art of song under "the homely shepherd's trade" is more insisted on; it becomes now the basis of every detail, and in the manner of the Virgilian Eclogues the parallel is carried out to its limits. A higher degree of complexity is attained, but not without a loss in congruity and clearness. The verse is not less responsive to the touch of external nature, but it has acquired a new susceptibility to the influences of learning, of morals, and of the tumultuous questions of the day. It cannot refrain from polemics; it allegorizes upon the slightest excuse; and it indulges in an almost pedantic amount of abstruse and remote allusion. It is scholastic poetry; but informed, nevertheless, with such imaginative vigour, filled with such sympathy for nature, attuned to such sonorous harmonies and modulated to cadences so subtle, as to surpass in all but simplicity the distinctive excellences of its models. The treatment is still frankly objective, transparently free from introspection; the atmosphere and colouring of a noonday vividness; the descriptions drawn at first hand from that affluent landscape which

---

*   Roberts's footnote: "The Extracts from Bion and Moschus are ... in the words of Mr. Lang's admirable translation."

the poet's early manhood knew at Horton. As in its predecessors, the objects of familiar nature are appealed to, the "Dorian water" and other classic streams, the dolphins, the nymphs, the muses, and Apollo himself; but, by a strange anomaly, comes St. Peter too, amid the pagan train, and pronounces a scathing diatribe against the opponents of Milton's theological school. This is a lesson learned of Dante, perhaps; and it is quite in keeping with medieval methods that the passage of most exalted spirituality which the poem affords should be placed in the lips of Apollo. An element which now makes its first appearance in the pastoral elegy is discovered in the lofty rejoicings of the conclusion. The note of hope was wanting in the pagan laments, and their sorrow deepens to the end. But "Lycidas" is the expression of a confident immortality, and hence the temporal grief which it bewails passes at length into a solemn gladness of consolation.

In regard of style Milton has little conformed to his originals. The departure is from a direct to an indirect utterance, the singer being, ostensibly, not the poet himself, but the "uncouth swain," depicted in that matchless bit of purest Greek objectivity which, in terminating the poem, appears to throw it out into clear relief. The refrain has dwindled into nothing more than the unobtrusive repetition of a few phrases; and for the fluent, direct, pellucid Sicilian hexameters we have the measured and delaying pace of the iambic pentameter. The measure is one of high and stately loveliness, but bearing little resemblance to the line of Bion and Moschus.

Arriving at the "Adonais" we find ourselves in another atmosphere. Hitherto our course has lain along the valleys and low hill slopes, where nature is all fertility and peace, where the winds are soft, the waters slow-winding, the meadows thick with flowers, and the sunshine heavy with fragrance. We have kept within the region of the pipe, the safe flocks, "the azure pillars of the hearth." However much the strain may have been, laden with allegory and with symbol, yet the joys recalled, the griefs lamented, the hopes and desires rehearsed, have all been definite, not only measurable but measured and stated. It is with material conceptions that the singer has been occupied. But Shelley hurries us out upon the heights, where the air is keen and stimulating, where the horizon is so vast that our gaze grows wide-eyed and eager, and where the more minute details of life are lost as the shifting pageantry of night and day is unrolled in dazzling nearness. The colouring is transparent, of a celestial purity, and ordered in strangely vivid contrasts; and instead of a pastoral stillness we have the unrest of winds, the aspiration of flame.

The many points of resemblance between the "Adonais" and its models, though obvious enough to force themselves upon the most casual attention, are yet far more superficial than those existing between those models themselves. So extraneous, indeed, is the likeness that I am tempted to illustrate it by the comparison of a seed of pulse, which is immediately recognizable after its germination because it carries with it, upon its expanding seed leaf, the remnants of its husk. To identify it is a simple matter, but its transformation is none the less complete. In the "Adonais" we find verbal borrowings so ingenuous and so abundant that the censor of literary morals has not breath enough left to cry "stop, thief!" In truth Shelley has not scrupled to appropriate the gold of his predecessors as a setting for his jewels. In the place of the Paphian Goddess we now find Urania, the Heavenly Muse; instead of the Loves and Nymphs, the Desires, Adorations, and Dreams of the dead poet; and for the shepherds, under thin disguise, come the contemporary singers, Byron, Moore, Hunt, and Shelley himself. After the fashion of the Loves in Bion, a dream seeks to break her bow and shafts, while another clips her locks; as in Moschus, Echo feeds on the dead singer's music, and the trees cast down their expanding buds; and one of Shelley's "Ministers of Thought" is heard to cry, with a voice not all unlike that of the shepherd in "Lycidas," "Our love, our hope, our sorrow, is not dead." These parallels, and many others like them, are sufficiently emphatic; but their scant importance is to be estimated from the fact that they may all be obliterated without destroying the unity of the poem, without even making serious inroad upon its highest and most distinctive beauties. The material conceptions of his predecessors Shelley has adopted, but he has made them subservient to an intensely spiritualized emotion and aspiration. The very imagery of the poem is to a great extent psychological in its origin, yet as vivid as if derived from the most familiar of physical phenomena.

The summit of attainment in the "Adonais" is not reached until the poet's passion of thought has carried him clear of his models. So long as his song was of loss and sorrow, he was, perhaps, neither greater nor less than they, only more metaphysical, more fierce in invective, less serenely and temperately beautiful. But when he comes to speak of consolation, the theme even in "Lycidas" of only one brief passage, he straightway attains his full measure of inspiration. The white heat to which this thought has kindled his imagination transfuses nearly every line of the concluding seventeen stanzas. This consolation is based upon a sort of spiritualized and emotional Pantheism, vivified by a breath of the essence of Christianity, and finds its fullest expression in Stanzas XLII and XLIII. The unsatisfying element in this faith is compensated by the creed of personal immortality, expressed in Stanzas XLIV, XLV, and XLVI. Then follows an inspired digression, describing the loveliness of that last resting-place of the mortal vesture of Keats,—a loveliness suggesting the dead poet's own utterance: —

I have been half in love with easeful Death.

The poem concludes with a majesty which has been thus finely analyzed by Mr. Symonds* "Yet again the thought of Death as the deliverer, the revealer, and the mystagogue, through whom the soul of man is reunited to the spirit of the universe, returns; and on this solemn note the poem closes. The symphony of exaltation which had greeted the passage of 'Adonais' into the eternal world is here subdued to a grave key, as befits the mood of one whom mystery and mourning still oppress on earth. Yet even in the somewhat less than jubilant conclusion we feel that highest of all Shelley's qualities, the liberation of incalculable energies; the emancipation and expansion of a force within the soul, victorious over circumstances, exhilarated and elevated by contact with such hopes as make a feebler spirit tremble."

The "Thyrsis"** of Matthew Arnold, in temper one of the most modern of poems, maintains nevertheless a closer relationship than does the "Adonais" to the work of the Sicilian elegists. With a far less degree of external resemblance, it makes at the same time a far less marked spiritual departure from the field and scope of its models. The conventional metonymy of shepherd and pipe is still adhered to; still figure the names of Corydon and Daphnis. But the heterogeneous train of mourners is gone; and the solitary singer makes no call upon Nymphs or Loves, Dreams or Desires, Deities or the phenomena of Nature, to assist his sorrow. The use of iteration still remains, much modified, but the refrain has vanished utterly. Save for Stanzas IX and

---

*   Keith's footnote: "The quotation is from the volume on Shelley in the English Men of Letters series by John Addington Symonds (1840–93), *English poet and critic.*"

**   Roberts's footnote: "In memory of Arthur Hugh Clough."

X, which read almost like an adorned and expanded paraphrase of the conclusion of the epitaph on Bion, there is scarcely an instance of adaptation or verbal borrowing. So much for the comparison of externals. But, in a sense of something like finality in the mourner's loss, a profound internal resemblance makes itself felt. There is, indeed, in the "Thyrsis," a search made for consolation, but the result is inadequate. This consolation excites no such singing fervour as does that found by Milton or by Shelley. The proof is scarcely such as to carry conviction, and the faith it upholds is somewhat thin and pale after the creeds of "Adonais" and "Lycidas." Nevertheless, though cold, it is a high and severe philosophy which informs the "Thyrsis":

> A fugitive and gracious light he seeks,
>   Shy to illumine; and I seek it too.
>   This does not come with houses or with gold,
> With place, with honour, and a flattering crew;
>   'Tis not in the world's market bought and sold—
>   But the smooth-slipping weeks
> Drop by, and leave its seeker still untired;
>   Out of the heed of mortals he is gone,
>   He wends unfollowed, he must house alone;
>   Yet on he fares by his own heart inspired.

It goes beyond any motive or aspiration expressed by the Sicilian singers. But the philosophy lightly suggested in Stanza VIII is not far from identical with that of the passage quoted from Moschus; and the elysium claimed for Thyrsis ("within a folding of the Apennine" to "hearken the immortal chants of old") is not fundamentally different from that to which Bion and Adonis were snatched, reluctant, away.

The modern temper of the "Thyrsis" has been referred to. This is manifested in its undertone of skepticism, in its profound consciousness of the weariness and the meagre rewards of effort. The heroic and stimulating element in the poem consists in the lofty courage with which this depressing consciousness is kept at bay, in order that it may not exert a demoralizing influence on human life and conduct. Another peculiarly modern quality is that which Mr Hutton describes as "a craving after a reconciliation between the intellect of man and the magic of nature." The keen and ever present perception of this magic of nature is the source of what constitutes perhaps the crowning excellence of the work—its faithful and yet not slavish realism—interpretive, selective, imaginative—which forms the basis of all the most enduring and satisfying poetry. In its most selective phase it pervades Stanza VII, which furnishes an interesting parallel to the exquisite flower passage in "Lycidas."

A minor difference between the "Thyrsis" and its predecessors, yet a difference reaching far in its effects, is to be found in the quality of its colour. This has little of the flooding sunlight and summer luxuriance to which Moschus and Milton introduced us; it has none of the iridescent and auroral splendours which steep the verse of Shelley. It is light, cool, and pure, most temperate in its use of strong tones, matchless for its tenderness and its exquisite delicacy of gradation. This colouring contributes in an appreciable degree to what I take to be the central impression conveyed by the "Thyrsis"; the impression of a serious and lofty calm, resulting, not from joy attained, but from clearsighted and unsanguine endurance.

Arriving at Mr. Swinburne's "Ave atque Vale"* we seem to have rounded a cycle. While structural resemblances have all but vanished, in substance of consolation we stand once more where Bion stood, and Moschus. In motive there is a vast descent from the "Thyrsis" to this poem. No longer is there any high endurance to spiritualize the hopelessness of the mourner and hold him above the reach of despair. There is but the very negative prospect of a sort of perpetual coma, or at most the sensuous solace of a palely luxurious peace.

> It is enough: the end and the beginning
> > Are one thing to thee, who art past the end.
> > O hand unclasped of unbeholden friend!
> For thee no fruits to pluck, no palms for winning,
> > No triumph and no labour and no lust,
> > Only dead yew leaves and a little dust.
> O quiet eyes wherein the light saith naught,
> > Whereto the day is dumb, nor any night
> > With obscure finger silences your sight,
> Nor in your speech the sudden soul speaks thought,
> > Sleep, and have sleep for light.

But while motive has been lessened and conception lowered, execution has risen to an almost unsurpassable height. With the possible

---

*   Roberts's note: "In memory of Charles Baudelaire."

exception of the "Lament for Bion," no one of the poems previously considered can equal this in perfection of structure. It has complete unity of effect, it has strong continuity of impulse. Never varying from its majestic restraint, it achieves such matchless verbal music as that of Stanza II, such serious breadth of imagination as that exemplified in Stanza VI, and such haunting cadences of regret as those which find expression in Stanza IX. Of what may be called the machinery of mourning, with which the Sicilians set out so well equipped, we find here little remnant. It has nearly all seemed superfluous to the later elegist. A fragment appears in Stanza XII, where still

> ... bending usward with memorial urns,
> The most high Muses that fulfill all ages
> Weep.

Still Apollo is present, and

> Compassionate, with sad and sacred heart,
> Mourns thee of many his children the last dead.

And Aphrodite keeps place among the mourners; but she is no longer either the spiritual Venus Urania, or the gladly fair and sanely passionate Cytherea of the Greeks. She has become that bastard conception of the Middle Ages, the Venus of the Hollow Hill, "a ghost, a bitter and luxurious god."

To recapitulate, it would appear that the pastoral elegy as originated by Bion reached its complete structural development at the hands of Moschus; and that in its inner meaning the work of these two poets was adequate to the spiritual stature of their day. The "Lycidas" was an inspired adaptation of like materials to the needs of a more complex period. In the "Adonais" we find the structure undergoing a violent expansion, and a new and vast departure made in the spheres of conception and motive. In hopefulness, in consolation, in exalted thought, in uplifting emotion, Shelley's poem occupies the pinnacle of achievement for this species of verse. In the "Thyrsis" we see structural conformity diminishing, but at the same time a reapproach to the religious attitude of its Greek originals. The elements of spirituality and hope have declined, but to support us till the coming of "the morningless and unawakening sleep" some inward consolation yet remains, in a spirit akin to the best wisdom of the Greek philosophies. In this poem we discern, too, if not the complete contemporary adequacy of the work of Bion and Moschus, yet a most sympathetic expression of the intellectual tendencies of the period. Finally, in the "Ave atque Vale," with a structural resemblance reduced to its lowest terms, we find a remarkable return to the spirit of Bion and Moschus. To the sorrow of this elegy there is no mitigation suggested. The goal it seems to point to is but a form of annihilation, or such grey pretence of immortality as that of the ghosts in the abode of Hades. Nevertheless, though without the impregnating force of impassioned spiritual purpose, the poem is endowed, I believe, with a perpetuity of interest by the sincerity of its lyric impulse, its adoration of beauty, its imagination, and its flawless art.

The Poetry of Nature

First published in *Forum* (New York) in December 1897. Reprinted from *Selected Poetry and Critical Prose*, ed. W.J. Keith, Toronto: U of Toronto P, 1974, 276–81.

"The poetry of earth is never dead," wrote Keats; and, though the statement sounds, at first thought, a dangerously sweeping one, there is no doubt that if he had been called upon to argue the point he would have successfully maintained his thesis. Regarded subjectively, the poetry of earth, or, in other words, the quality which makes for poetry in external nature, is that power in nature which moves us by suggestion, which excites in us emotion, imagination, or poignant association, which plays upon the tense-strings of our sympathies with the fingers of memory or desire. This power may reside not less in a bleak pasture-lot than in a paradisal close of bloom and verdure, not less in a roadside thistle-patch than in a peak that soars into the sunset. It works through sheer beauty or sheer sublimity; but it may work with equal effect through austerity or reticence or limitation or change. It may use the most common scenes, the most familiar facts and forms, as the vehicle of its most penetrating and most illuminating message. It is apt to make the drop of dew on a grass-blade as significant as the starred sphere of the sky.

The poetry of nature, by which I mean this "poetry of earth" expressed in words, may be roughly divided into two main classes: that which deals with pure description, and that which treats of nature in some one of its many relations with humanity. The latter class is that which alone was contemplated in Keats's line. It has many subdivisions; it includes much of the greatest poetry that the world has known; and there is little verse of acknowledged mastery that does not depend upon it for some portion of its appeal.

The former class has but a slender claim to recognition as poetry, under any definition of poetry that does not make metrical form the prime essential. The failures of the wisest to enunciate a satisfactory definition of poetry make it almost presumptuous for a critic now to attempt the task; but from an analysis of these failures one may educe something roughly to serve the purpose. To say that *poetry is the metrical expression in words of thought fused in emotion,* is of course incomplete; but it has the advantage of defining. No one can think that anything other than poetry is intended by such a definition; and nothing is excluded that can show a clear claim to admittance. But the poetry of pure description might perhaps not pass without challenge, so faint is the flame of its emotion, so imperfect the fusion of its thought.

It is verse of this sort that is meant by undiscriminating critics when they inveigh against "nature poetry," and declare that the only poetry worth man's attention is that which has to do with the heart of man.

Merely descriptive poetry is not very far removed from the work of the reporter and the photographer. Lacking the selective duality of creative art, it is in reality little more than a presentation of some of the raw materials of poetry. It leaves the reader unmoved, because little emotion has gone to its making. Poetry of this sort, at its best, is to be found abundantly in Thomson's "Seasons." At less than its best it concerns no one.

Nature becomes significant to man when she is passed through the alembic of his heart. Irrelevant and confusing details having been purged away, what remains is single and vital. It acts either by interpreting, recalling, suggesting, or symbolizing some phase of human feeling. Out of the fusing heat born of this contact comes the perfect line, luminous, unforgettable, with something of mystery in its beauty that eludes analysis. Whatever it be that is brought to the alembic—naked hill, or barren sand-reach, sea or meadow, weed or star,—it comes out charged with a new force, imperishable and active wherever it finds sympathies to vibrate under its currents.

In the imperishable verse of ancient Greece and Rome, nature poetry of the higher class is generally supposed to play but a small part. In reality, it is nearly always present, nearly always active in that verse; but it appears in such a disguise that its origin is apt to be overlooked. The Greeks—and the Romans, of course, following their pattern—personified the phenomena of nature till these, for all purposes of art, became human. The Greeks made their anthropomorphic gods of the forces of nature which compelled their adoration. Of these personifications they sang, as of men of like passions with themselves; but in truth it was of external nature that they made their songs. Bion's wailing "Lament for

Adonis," human as it is throughout, is in its final analysis a poem of nature. By an intense, but perhaps unconscious, subjective process, the ancients supplied external nature with their own moods, impulses, and passions.

The transitions from the ancient to the modern fashion of looking at nature are to be found principally in the work of the Celtic bards, who, rather than the cloistered students of that time, kept alive the true fire of poetry through the long darkness of the Middle Ages.

The modern attitude toward nature, as distinguished from that of the Greeks, begins to show itself clearly in English song very soon after the great revivifying movement which we call the Renaissance. At first, it is a very simple matter indeed. Men sing of nature because nature is impressing them directly. A joyous season calls forth a joyous song:

> Sumer is icumen in,
>> Lhude sing, cuccu.
> Groweth sed and bloweth med
>> And springth the wude nu.

This is the poet's answering hail, when the spring-time calls to his blood. With the fall of the leaf, his singing has a sombre and foreboding note; and winter in the world makes winter in his song.

This is nature-poetry in its simplest form,—the form which it chiefly took with the spontaneous Elizabethans. But it soon became more complex, as life and society became entangled in more complex conditions. The artificialities of the Queen Anne period delayed this evolution; but with Gray and Collins we see it fairly in process. Man, looking upon external nature, projects himself into her workings. His own wrath he apprehends in the violence of the storm; his own joy in the light waves running in the sun; his own gloom in the heaviness of the rain and wind. In all nature he finds but phenomena of himself. She becomes but an expression of his hopes, his fears, his cravings, his despair. This intense subjectivity is peculiarly characteristic of the nature poetry produced by Byron and his school. When this Titan of modern song apostrophizes the storm thundering over Jura, he speaks to the tumult in the deeps of his own soul. When he addresses the stainless tranquillities of "clear, placid Leman," what moves him to utterance is the contemplation of such a calm as his vexed spirit often craved.

When man's heart and the heart of nature had become thus closely involved, the relationship between them and, consequently, the manner of its expression in song became complex almost beyond the possibilities of analysis. Wordsworth's best poetry is to be found in the utterances of the high-priest in nature's temple, interpreting the mysteries. The "Lines Composed a Few Miles Above Tintern Abbey" are, at first glance, chiefly descriptive; but their actual function is to convey to a restless age, troubled with small cares seen in too close perspective, the large, contemplative wisdom which seemed to Wordsworth the message of the scene which moved him.

Keats, his soul aflame with the worship of beauty, was impassioned toward the manifestations of beauty in the world about him; and, at the same time, he used these freely as symbols to express other aspects of the same compelling spirit. Shelley, the most complex of the group, sometimes combined all these methods, as in the "Ode to the West Wind." But he added a new note,—which was yet an echo of the oldest, —the note of nature-worship. He saw continually in nature the godhead which he sought and adored, youthful protestations and affectations of atheism to the contrary notwithstanding. Most of Shelley's nature-poetry carries a rich vein of pantheism, allied to that which colours the oldest verse of time and particularly characterizes ancient Celtic song. With this significant and stimulating revival, goes a revival of that strong sense of kinship, of the oneness of earth and man, which the Greeks and Latins felt so keenly at times, which Omar knew and uttered, and which underlies so much of the verse of these later days.

That other unity—the unity of man and God, which forms so inevitable a corollary to the pantheistic proposition—comes to be dwelt upon more and more insistently throughout the nature poetry of the last fifty years.

The main purpose of these brief suggestions is to call attention to the fact that nature poetry is not mere description of landscape in metrical form, but the expression of one or another of many vital relationships between external nature and "the deep heart of man." It may touch the subtlest chords of human emotion and human imagination not less masterfully than the verse which sets out to be a direct transcript from life. The most inaccessible truths are apt to be reached by indirection. The divinest mysteries of beauty are not possessed exclusively by the eye that loves, or by the lips of a child, but are also manifested in some bird-song's unforgotten cadence, some flower whose perfection pierces the heart, some ineffable hue of sunset or sunrise that makes the spirit cry out for it knows not what. And whosoever follows the inexplicable

A Note on Modernism

Originally published in *Open House*. Ottawa: Graphic Publishers Limited, 1931, ed. by W.A. Deacon and Wilfred Reeves. Included as part of the Prefatory Note to *Selected Poems*, 1936. Reprinted from *Selected Poetry and Critical Prose*, ed. W.J. Keith, Toronto: U of Toronto P, 1974, 302–3.

Modernism is reaction. That sounds like a paradox. But in reality, as applied to the arts—poetry, painting, sculpture, music, dancing—it is a mere statement of fact. To architecture, of course, it does not exactly apply, because what architecture creates is based primarily on material needs; and though these may slowly evolve, they cannot fundamentally change any faster than the nature of man changes. Architecture is a matter of long vision. New materials of construction may come into use, to meet new conditions and make possible new forms; but the most fantastical skyscraper of modern Germany (the home of fantastical skyscrapers), built of chrome-steel instead of stone, does not make the cathedrals of Cologne, Chartres, or Canterbury seem out-of-date.

Modernism, a strictly relative term, has gone by different names in different periods, but always it has been, and is, a reaction of the younger creators against the too long dominance of their older predecessors. One or more great poets, two or three great painters, win their way to general acceptance and authority in their period. Their genius raises up a swarm of disciples and imitators, who can reproduce their form, though not their fire. Their form comes to be regarded as the only proper medium of expression. By that time the virtue, the impulse, has gone out of it. It has hardened into a fetter. Then comes the reaction— which, for a generation, is modernism, by whatever name it may be called and whether the phenomenon occurs in the 18th, 19th, or 20th century. The more complete and prolonged the dominance, the more violent and extreme the reaction. Wordsworth, Shelley, Coleridge, Keats were "modernists" in the beginning, rebelling against the sway of Pope and his school. Slowly they became accepted and supreme. The great Victorians, continuing and developing their tradition, made that supremacy so absolute that it seemed as if no poetry could be written save in the manner, more or less, of Tennyson or Swinburne, of Arnold, Browning, Morris or Rossetti. In painting, too, the mode of Reynolds, Romney, Raeburn, of Constable and even of Turner, carried on with a difference by Millais, Leighton, Burne-Jones, ruled with an unquestioned authority. Then began, tentatively at first, the reaction. The seeds of it, in poetry, were scattered unawares by Browning, and even by Arnold; and in painting by Turner, always a law unto himself. Here and there revolt lifted its head. Rodin appeared, a portent tremendous and magnificent. Debussy began to weave his seemingly lawless arabesques of sound. And then, of a sudden, "modernism" was upon us—a chaos of startling, elusive beauty and defiant ugliness, of strange, wild harmonies and ear-splitting dissonances, of stark simplicities and grotesquely unintelligible obscurities; and those who could not immediately be famous could, it appeared, with much more profit be notorious.

In all this present day welter of productivity, wherein genius, and near genius, and loud mediocrity, and thinly veiled insanity, jostle for recognition and are sometimes hardly to be distinguished from each other, the critic is at least delivered from monotony. His wanderings become a ceaseless adventure. He may be confronted by absolute beauty, radiant as if new risen from the sea. He may lose himself in a vast maze of words, or forms, or sounds which none can understand— though many profess to! Or he may run into some miracle of obscene hideousness before which he can no more than cringe and gape. Cubism, imagism, futurism, have had their fantastic way with the people, who, ashamed to acknowledge their bewilderment, have hastened to acclaim them lest they be thought conventional. Some younger persons have, figuratively speaking, danced in the streets without their trousers, and thereby achieved a reputation for originality. I know an artist, a man of indisputable talent, who now acknowledges that he painted his cubist nightmares with his tongue in his cheek, but with such profit to his purse that he can now afford to do the work by which he hopes his name will live. In sculpture we see, though happily but seldom, such monstrous abortions as the great Epstein, his fingers to his nose, frequently permits himself to perpetrate. But on the other hand, to give us heart and faith again, we have poets and painters who achieve a serene and captivating loveliness to which certain oddities of expression are only an enhancement.

To Canada modernism has come more slowly and less violently than elsewhere. This applies more particularly to poetry, and indeed to literature in general. The older generation of Canadian poets, Carman and Scott—and Lampman in a lesser degree because his career was so untimely cut short—had already initiated a departure, a partial departure, from the Victorian tradition of poetry, years before the movement began in England. They had been profoundly influenced by the transcendentalism of Emerson and the New England school of thought. They were more immediately in contact with nature, and they looked upon her with less sophisticated eyes. And in the deep but more or less unconscious optimism of a new country whose vision is fixed upon the future, they had no time for the pessimism and disillusionment of the old world. Therefore there was no violence of reaction. They kept one hand, as it were, on the Victorian tradition while they quietly stepped aside and in advance of it. Carman had long ago developed the seeds of change which he found in his master, Browning, and had harked far back to Blake for his further inspiration. Lampman, in his great sonnets, had not changed the sonnet but had carried it on beyond the point where Wordsworth had left it. Scott had developed those "seeds of change" which he, for his part, had found in Meredith; and had kept in the forefront of his time. He remains always, by a process of imperceptible gradations, a contemporary of the youngest generation.

And so it has come about that since there was no repression, there has been no revolt. Eager young spirits who thirsted to imitate Miss Sitwell or E.E. Cummings have disgustedly felt themselves patted on the back instead of pasted in the breeches. Modernism has come softly into the poetry of Canada, by peaceful penetration rather than by rude assault. We all lie down together very amicably, the lions and the lambs; and no one is quite sure which is which, except that here and there a lamb may growl and a lion essay a propitiatory bleat.

What I have said of Canadian poetry applies also to Canadian prose fiction. The Canadian temperament is set against extremes. It will go far along new lines, but it balks at making itself ridiculous. I am prudently resolved to avoid personalities in this paper. But I must make an exception in one instance because it so well illustrates my point. Mr. Morley Callaghan is reported as having declared himself a humble disciple of Mr. Hemingway—as having learned his art from Mr.

Hemingway. If this is so, the disciple has on many counts excelled the master. Compare the two novels, *Strange Fugitive* and *The Sun Also Rises*. The latter is marred by eccentricities in the vogue of the moment. You find yourself skipping whole pages of conversation whose only purpose is to display the reiterant vacuities of the drunken mind. Able as it is in many respects, the book will hardly, I think, survive a change of fashion. It carries too great a burden of mere words. Mr. Callaghan's story, on the other hand, carries no such burden. There is not a superfluous word in it. The style is clear, bare, efficient. It is modernism—the subject matter is very "modern." But it has sanely avoided the modern fault of striving after effect. It does not date itself; and it may well appear as readable a hundred years hence as it does today.

In the case of painting and sculpture there is a difference, but rather of degree than kind. The reaction against older manners and methods is more sharply defined and much more controversial. That is because the movement is more organized, self-conscious, and militant. There is the "Group of Seven," for instance, well armed and more than ready for battle. But its militancy finds so little to militate against that it doffs its armour and hides its hatchet under its blouse. Somewhat to its disappointment, perhaps, it finds the exponents of the older school of art for the most part more curious than hostile. Some of them, even, coming to curse, remain to bless. The reason for this happy consummation is not far to seek. It lies in the Canadian dislike for extremes. These young rebels are essentially sane. They love not ugliness for its own sake, or incomprehensibility for the sake of being thought profound. Neither do they care for those petty affectations which are designed only to emphasize aloofness from the common, kindly race of men. Now and again, to be sure, there may be a gesture, of defiant propagandism or of impatient scorn. But in the main they are altogether preoccupied with beauty. And beauty they not only see with new eyes, but show it to us with simplicity and truth.

Canadian Poetry in its Relation to the Poetry of England and America

Lecture: 18 March 1933. D.M.R. Bentley writes that: *Roberts gave this address at a testimonial dinner in his honour on 18 March 1933. He sent the first draft of this address to Cecil Charles Jones, the president of the University of New Brunswick, for the Canadiana collection which Roberts had virtually forced Jones to start in 1926.* The copytext is the signed holograph manuscript held by the D.B. Weldon Library at the University of Western Ontario, as published for the first time *Canadian Poetry* 3 (Fall/Winter 1978): 76–86, with comments by D.M.R. Bentley. Reprinted from *Non-Fictional Prose*, by Charles G.D. Roberts, edited by D.M.R. Bentley and Laurel Boone, http://www.canadianpoetry.ca/confederation/roberts/non-fictional_prose/address.htm.

I have no words to thank you—no words to half express my deep and heartfelt appreciation of the very great honour done me here tonight and of the more than generous gift with which I am overwhelmed. You have given a most eloquent and emphatic contradiction to that old whining complaint about a prophet not being without honour except in his own country. For you have made it plain that in his own country a prophet may have both honour and—profit. May I try to show my appreciation, and to justify myself in the role of profit, by prophesying a distinguished and distinctive future for Canadian Poetry.

I have taken as the subject of my address tonight, "Canadian Poetry in its relation to the Poetry of England and America." I purposely refrain from saying "of the rest of the English-speaking world," because the poets of Australia, New Zealand and South Africa seem to be linked more closely and more exclusively with the Mother Country than we are in Canada. Their poetry has less of a separate corporate existence than ours, has a more decided tendency to look to the Mother Country for recognition than has ours. This, for two main reasons, is only to be expected. They are, all three, much younger and less populous peoples than Canada. For all practical purposes they are under but one stream of influence, they inherit from but one source, the Mother Country; while we inherit from three sources, in varying degree,—from the Mother Country, America, and France. The influence of France has been, as yet, comparatively slight upon the poetry of English-speaking Canada, which alone I am considering here,—though I hope it may be greatly extended in the future, when the cultural characteristics of the two great races from which we spring may come to be more intimately interfused. But American influence, though altogether secondary to that of England and growing more so as our national consciousness matures, has been strong upon us in two ways. The mass immigration of that strong and dominant Loyalist American stock, influential out of all proportion to its numbers, provided us with a great proportion of our spiritual and intellectual endowment, that element of character which is the ultimate test of a people's stature; and our social relations with modern America have had their effect, not invariably a happy one, upon our verse structure and forms.

Our English Canadian Poetry may be divided, very loosely, and for the purposes of this address, into two periods,—the pre-war and the post-war. The pre-war period may be considered as beginning in the '80s, with the publication of Crawford's *Old Spookses' Pass*, and Lampman's *Among the Millet*, 1888. At this point, if you will forgive me, I am compelled to become personal for a moment. In the course of this survey I am going to disregard entirely my own various books of verse and their influence, if any, on the development of Canadian Poetry. But it is necessary, to avoid misunderstanding, that I should refer to my little volume of juvenilia, *Orion and Other Poems*, which appeared in 1880. This book, which obtained in Canada and abroad a recognition out of all proportion to its merits, has been accepted as a sort of landmark. All the verses it contains were written between the ages of sixteen and nineteen,—most of them before I was eighteen. They are the work of practically a schoolboy, drunk with the music of Keats, Shelly, Tennyson and Swinburne. They are distinctly 'prentice work, distinctly derivative, and without significance except for their careful craftsmanship and for the fact that they dared deliberately to steer their frail craft out upon world waters,—certain of these youthful efforts appearing in the pages of the chief English and American magazines. But the only importance attaching to the little book lay in the fact that it started Lampman writing poetry and was the decisive factor in determining Carman to make poetry his career.

The distinctively Canadian poetry, of significance beyond the borders of Canada, therefore, may be considered as beginning with Isabella Crawford's *Old Spookses' Pass*, 1884; Charles Mair's *Tecumseh*, 1886; Archibald Lampman's *Among the Millet*, 1888; F. G. Scott's *The Soul's Guest*, 1888; W.W. Campbell's *Lake Lyrics*, 1889; D.C. Scott's *The Magic House*, 1893; Bliss Carman's *Low Tide on Grand Pré*, 1893. Pauline Johnson's *White Wampum*, 1894; [and] Arthur Stringer['s] *Watcher of Twilight*, 1894; but it must be borne in mind that for seven or eight years previous to 1893 Carman's poems had circulated widely in privately printed broad-sheets, and had exerted an immense influence, before his first publication in book form.

Though Mair's *Tecumseh* appeared in 1886, it seems to stand apart from the new movement inaugurated by Crawford, Lampman, Carman and Scott. It marks the end of the old period,—Mair's first and only other volume of verse, *Dreamland and Other Poems*, having appeared in 1868. It looks backward rather than forward. Deriving, in its conception and its structure, straight from Shakespeare himself, but with its verbal music borrowed from Keats, it is a dignified and massive closet-drama, dramatic in form but narrative in spirit; and it stands up as great isolated rock against the incipient tide of Canadian lyric verse. Isabella Crawford, on the other hand, seems to me to be looking forward rather than back. Her verse, though so different, belongs with that of Lampman, Carman, and D.C. Scott. It has a distinction and strength which have not yet been sufficiently recognized. Her early death was a great misfortune to our literature.

Now, having thus cleared the way, I will try to trace the influences which affected Canadian verse during this first period, and to point out wherein Canadian verse was distinctive from the verse of England and of America. Of course it is obvious to us all, that Canadian verse, like American verse, is but a branch of the one splendid parent stem. American verse, beginning to thrust forth from the parent stem nearly two hundred years ago, has by now attained a stature which fairly rivals that of its parent. Today it would be hard to say which shows the loftier and more sturdy growth. It is my claim that Canadian Poetry, a young shoot which began to bud forth not fifty years ago, started under happier auspices, developed more rapidly, and has already attained an authentic separate existence. It is of course overshadowed by its great rivals, but it is not obliterated by them. When the long but beneficent tyranny of the Tennysonian tradition in England—buttressed rather than shaken by Swinburne, Arnold, Morris, Rossetti (rudely assaulted but not overthrown by Browning) at last began to fall into saccharine decay, English poets seemed somewhat at a loss for guidance. Masters of craftsmanship like Stevenson, Le Gallienne, John Davidson, William Watson, Henley, Wilde, seemed to be groping in all directions for themes on which to exercise their craft. Francis Thompson wrote one magnificent and immortal poem; Alice Meynell produced a tiny sheaf of exquisite and stringently reserved verse, but both sounded their poignant notes upon approximately one theme. The choir had brilliant individual singers, but there was no leader, and the result was a mere confusion of sweet sound. To be sure there were no blatant discords. These were to come later!

Meanwhile, how was it faring with poetry in Canada? For one thing, there was singularly little confusion of purpose, or casting about for themes. In the main it was Nature poetry, of one sort or another. The Canadian scene and the Canadian atmosphere, were always present, sometimes as a very conspicuous background to the subject, sometimes as the subject itself. It was frankly enthusiastic. It was patently sincere. There was never any need to whip up the inspiration. From the "Bite deep and wide, O axe, the tree," of Isabella Crawford, to the "There is something in the autumn that is native to my blood," of Carman, there is the note of looking forward, of the optimism of a young and confidently aspiring people. The pervasiveness of this note gave a certain unity to the work of all the otherwise differentiated Canadian singers. It was a note that had practically faded out from the infinitely louder American chorus.

The influence of Tennyson—with the one brief exception already noted,—is not evident in this Canadian Poetry. It is descended rather from Wordsworth, Milton of the earlier poems, Landor, Keats, Shelley, Blake, and from Arnold in form and language though manifestly not in spirit. It also drew one strong stream of influence from Emerson and the New England school of transcendentalists, to whom it is heavily in debt for its philosophy and for its employment of the plain, blunt words of common speech. It owes something also to that very great American poet, Sidney Lanier. Whitman's influence both in thought and in form upon our poetry of this period is entirely negligible. And if I may be permitted to differ flatly from a very distinguished critic, Dr. Cappon, the wonderful poems of Edgar Allen Poe, were almost as negligible in their effect upon us. Even Carman, contrary to Dr. Cappon's thesis, was not greatly interested in Poe's form, and with Poe's philosophy of life he was emphatically out of sympathy. I can detect Poe's influence upon one only of our Poets, Tom McInnes, and he belongs to our later period. Carman was influenced in one portion of his career by Browning, but that influence ultimately worked itself out. And Duncan Campbell Scott now and again shows traces of having fallen under the spell of George Meredith's more inspired verse. And it may be noted here that our poets were doing thirty or forty years ago what certain of the quieter and more serious poets of England have been doing since the war.

There is another consideration which gives unity to our Canadian poetry of this period. In doctrine, in dogma, in creed, our poets may differ very widely, from strict orthodoxy, through a sort of mystical theosophy, to a Neo-Platonic pantheism or Nature worship. But they all worship. They are all religious, in the broad sense, in their attitude toward this life and the future. They are all fundamentally antagonistic to everything that savours of materialism, and even of such high and stoical pessimism as that of Matthew Arnold. They are all incorrigible and unrepentant idealists.

I think I have traced the chief sources from which our poetry has sprung, and indicated, in the main, those characteristics which differentiate it from the work of contemporaries in England and America. I will conclude the survey of this first period by reading a sonnet of Lampman's and a lyric of Carman's, two poems which, of their kind, have not been surpassed by any of their contemporaries in England or America. They may serve to illustrate certain of the points which I hope I may be considered to have made:

"Outlook"

Not to be conquered by these headlong days,
But to stand free: to keep the mind at brood
On life's deep meaning, nature's attitude
Of loveliness, and time's mysterious ways;
At every thought and deed to clear the haze
Out of our eyes, considering only this,
What man, what life, what love, what beauty is,
This is to live, and win the final praise.
    Though strife, ill fortune and harsh human need

Beat down the soul, at moments blind and dumb
With agony; yet, patience—there shall come
Many great voices from life's outer sea,
Hours of strange triumph, and, when few men heed,
Murmurs and glimpses of eternity.

A. Lampman

"Exit Anima"

"Hospes comesque corpis
Quae nunc abitis in loca?"

Cease, Wind, to blow
And drive the peopled snow,
And move the haunted arras to and fro,
And moan of things I fear to know
Yet would rend from thee,
  Wind, before I go
On the blind pilgrimage.
Cease, Wind, to blow.

Thy brother too,
I leave no print of shoe
In all these vasty rooms I rummage through,
No word at threshold, and no clue
Of whence I come and whither I pursue
The search of treasures lost
When time was new

Thou janitor
Of the dim curtained door,
Stir thy old bones along the dusty floor
Of this unlighted corridor.
Open! I have been this dark way before;
Thy hollow face shall peer
In mine no more ....

Sky, the dear sky!
Ah, ghostly house, good-by!
I leave thee as the gauzy dragon-fly
Leaves the green pool to try
His vast ambition on the vaster sky,—

Such valor against death
Is deity.

What, thou too here,
Thou haunting whisperer?
Spirit of beauty immanent and sheer,
Art thou that crooked servitor,
Done with disguise, from whose malignant leer
Out of the ghostly house
I fled in fear?

O Beauty, how
I do repent me now,
Of all the doubt I ever could allow
To shake me like an aspen bough;
Nor once imagine that unsullied brow
Could wear the evil mask
And still be thou!

Bone of thy bone,
Breath of thy breath alone,
I dare resume the silence of a stone,
Or explore still the vast unknown,
Like a bright sea-bird through the morning blown,
With all his heart one joy,
From zone to zone.

B. Carman

Between the first and second periods of Canadian poetry there is no break, but rather a very gradual transition. Some members of the first group are in full singing vigour today, as in the cases of Duncan Campbell Scott, and have, indeed, more or less identified themselves with the mood and temper, even the external forms, of the second period. Others were already becoming well known in the decade preceding 1914. Preeminent among these is Tom McInnes, standing somewhat apart from the stream of our poetry, and tracing the inheritance of his very individual talent to François Villon and Edgar Allan Poe, with an occasional dash of Keats. And I must mention here that remarkable woman Mrs. Harrison, known as "Seranus," who began her political career with "the stretchèd metre of an antique song" in *Pine, Rose and Fleur de Lis*, 1891, using old French verse forms and seeking to interpret the spirit of French Canada to English Canada; and who now, in *Songs of Love and Labor* and in *Penelope and Other Poems*, brings herself thoroughly abreast of modern movements and methods.

During and since the War new forces began to make themselves felt in Canadian verse, influencing both its matter and its manner. But in our verse, as in our painting and sculpture, the pervading sanity and balance of the Canadian temperament, its obstinate antagonism to extremes, saved us from the grotesque excesses indulged in by some of our English and American contemporaries. Modernism, so called, came without violence to Canada. It was with us not revolution but evolution. The slender but exquisite genius of Marjorie Pickthall seemed to flourish apart, hardly affected by latter day changes. I can do no more in this paper than touch upon some half dozen of the many singers who now form our choir. Katherine Hale, with her extremely meager output, is nevertheless very significant, because thoroughly modern in theme and treatment. Nature, with her, is always strictly subordinate to human nature. Charlotte Dalton treats big themes in a big way, her intellect and her genius being of the major order. A.M. Stephen, in the breadth and variety of the subjects which he treats, combines both the younger and the older schools. He is at times a Nature poet, at times a poet of humanity. But in the matter of form he has not as yet fully escaped the influence of Amy Lowell and Carl Sandburg. There are many others of whom I would wish to speak but the familiar "exigencies of time and space" forbid. And, of course, my lips are sealed in regard to the poetry of Lloyd Roberts and Theodore Roberts, my son and my brother.

But there are three poets whom I feel called upon to discuss more in detail, because they represent three distinct trends in modern Canadian poetry, and differ from each other fundamentally. I refer to Doctor E.J. Pratt, Mr. Wilson MacDonald, and the late Dr. Robert Norwood.

Dr. Pratt is the most predominantly intellectual. Under whatever he writes the thought processes are definite and precise, whether the writing be lyrical or narrative. Yet the thought is always adequately fused in the emotion. And he has the saving gift, the vital gift, of humour. He is easily the greatest master of pure narrative that Canada has produced. In *The Witches' Brew*, with its vast Rebelaisian [sic] humour and grotesque fantasy. "The Cachalot," with its splendidly robust and red-blooded imagination; and "The Roosevelt and the Antinoe," with its sustained strength, its gripping directness, its severity of diction and its unflagging interest,—he has given us poetic narratives hardly to be matched in contemporary letters. He is almost exclusively *objective*.

Mr. Wilson MacDonald is purely a lyrist, with a very wide range of form and theme. His best work is forged in the white heat of emotion, and is always definitely stamped with his own personality. It is primarily subjective. In his shorter, personal lyrics, such as "Exit," he achieves at times an unforgettable poignancy. In his passionately humanitarian poems he is modern in spirit, but in form he is distinctly classical. He has been so bold as to experiment frankly with Whitman's peculiar form and content, and he has justified the experiment. He has succeeded at times in breathing into that harsh form a beauty of words and cadences which Whitman never achieved.

The late Robert Norwood is, first, last and always mystic. His great narrative poem, "Bill Boram," is a lyrico-mystic creation masquerading under a thin disguise of realism. Its emotional fervour is always breaking through the disguise. His religious dramas, *The Witch of Endor* and *The Man of Kerioth*, are great lyrical poems rather than pure drama. His book of dramatic monologues, Browningesque in form but at the opposite pole from Browning in thought, content and approach, are mysticism intellectualized. That peculiarly individual poem, "Issa," is a mystical autobiography in lyrical form, sustained with almost unflagging fervour throughout seven cantos. It is a remarkable *tour de force*. The three volumes of lyrics and sonnets contain poems of varying merit, from mediocre religious rhetoric to the highest quality of craftsmanship and lyric significance. But always in the web and texture of them is the pervading sheen of that mysticism which was Norwood's breath of life. The keynote to all his work is in the line "And let there be a going up to stars."

And now let me conclude with a few words about our younger poets, those who are just winning their spurs. And let me say at once that I survey their work with the profoundest satisfaction, feeling that the future of our poetry is in safe hands. It is the prerogative of youth to rebel. But our Canadian youth has sufficient sanity to save it from the extravagant and grotesque excesses of rebellion. I find here and there among the young poets a tendency to hark back to the artificiality of the post-Elizabethans,—a tendency, also, to stress the intellectual at the expense of the equally important emotional side of poetry. Some of them show the effect of a study of the works of the so-called metaphysical school, which derives from Ben Jonson rather than from Shakespeare.

But I am not sure that this is altogether to be deplored, as a reaction against over sentimentalism. To Beauty, however, if not always to simplicity, they are faithful. There is none of that deliberate sabotage of beauty, that adulation of ugliness in the name of realism, in which certain wild-eyed extremists in other lands are wont to riot. I find traces of T.E. Brown, de la Mare, and Hopkins,—the influence of Emily Dickinson, Elinor Wylie, Edna Millay. I do not, God be thanked, find the influence of E.E. Cummings or Marianne Moore. Among these our younger poets I will not take the responsibility of selecting any names for mention here, lest I should do some an injustice by omitting them,—or prove myself a false profit. I will only say that I believe some of them will go very far. Indeed, I think I will even go with them a little way, if my years—and my decrepitude—will permit!

"The old order changeth, yielding place to new."

From the Prefatory Note to Selected Poems

Originally the Preface to *Selected Poems*, Toronto: Ryerson, 1936. Reprinted from *Selected Poetry and Critical Prose*, ed. W.J. Keith. Toronto: U of Toronto P, 1974, 302–3. Keith notes that an introductory section discussing the ordering of the poems in this edition has been omitted.

From early youth to the present day I have always been alive to the moment, keenly aware of contemporary currents of thought, action and emotion. There is a vast change to be noted between the rigid Ovidian elegiac metre of the "Tantramar Revisited" and the "Pipes of Pan" (1887), with their formal alternation of hexameter and pentameter lines, and, on the other hand, the freedom of structure of "The Iceberg," the interstanzaic fluidity of "The Squatter" (1934). I am far from claiming that this change is of necessity growth. But it is divergence, and as such might, I think, be taken into account in any serious evaluation of my verse which the critic may find it worth while to make.

As there is just now a good deal of difference of opinion—a healthy difference, if at times somewhat acrimoniously expressed—in regard to what constitutes poetry both in form and in content, it may not be unfitting for me to indicate my own position in the matter. The following sentences from a Preface by Mr. Humbert Wolfe[*] seem to me relevant:

> There is no such thing (as modern verse) and never has been. Nor is there ancient verse. There are only oldish men in each generation misunderstanding what is being written now, side by side with youngish men misunderstanding what was written then. Verse itself cares noth-

[*] Keith's note: "Humbert Wolfe (1885–1949), a minor English poet of the Georgian school. The extract is taken from *The Unknown Goddess* (1925)."

ing for the oldish men nor the youngish men, nor indeed for anything but itself.

It seems to me it is all a matter of the succeeding cycles of reaction. Reaction is life. The more healthy and vigorous the reaction, the more inevitably does it froth up into excess. The excess dies away of its own violence. But the freshness of thought or of technique that supplied the urge to the reaction remains and is clarified, ultimately to be worked into the tissue of permanent art.

BLISS CARMAN

BLISS CARMAN (1861–1929)

Biographical Notes

William Bliss Carman was born in Fredericton, New Brunswick, 15 April 1861 to William Carman, a barrister, and Sophia Bliss Carman, the descendent of a Loyalist family from Long Island who was related through an American kinsman, Daniel Bliss, to the American poet and essayist, Ralph Waldo Emerson. She was also the aunt of Charles G.D. Roberts. Bliss Carman was first tutored at home and later studied along with his cousin, Charles, at the Collegiate Grammar School in Fredericton. From 1878 to 1881 he was enrolled at the University of New Brunswick from which he graduated with an Arts degree. Accepted as a student by Oxford, Carman, who became known for such restless behaviour, left for the University of Edinburgh after only three days on campus; there he studied mathematics, physics and philosophy, but again left without completing a degree. Instead, he returned to Fredericton and taught at the Collegiate Grammar School for a couple of years.

In 1886 he went to Harvard to study philosophy, but again grew disillusioned with a disciplined lifestyle, and dropped out after two years. Nonetheless, while at Harvard Carman was strongly influenced by Josiah Royce and George Santayana, and began reading the work of his distant American relation, the transcendentalist Emerson. It was during this period that Carman began publishing some of his poetry: "Ma Belle Canadienne" was published in Godwin Smith's *The Week* under Roberts's editorship in 1884, while two years later "Low Tide on Grand

Pré" received its first printing in the influential *Atlantic Monthly*. In 1888 Carman left Harvard to work as an editor for several publications in New York and Boston; these included: the *Atlantic, Cosmopolitan, Current Literature, Chap-Book, Independent, Literary World* and *Outlook*. Carman took the opportunity while editing the *Independent* to include poems by several of his Canadian contemporaries: Pauline Johnson, Archibald Lampman and Duncan Campbell Scott, among others.

In 1893 a first poetry collection, *Low Tide on Grand Pré*, was published to international acclaim, and is considered by many to be his best work. This was followed over the next several years with a three-volume set of poems completed between 1894 and 1900 and published as *Songs from Vagabondia*. In 1896 Carman became close friends with Dr. Morris Lee King and his wife, Mary Perry King, with whom Carman collaborated in the writing of several books and articles, including those found in *The Making of Personality* in 1908, some of which are published here. That year, Carman moved to New Canaan, Connecticut, in order to be near the Kings' estate. Unable to hold any position for a sustained period, Carman was reliant on their goodwill and patronage for the rest of his life, and lived either with them or, during summers, in a cabin nearby. A prolific writer of verse, he published more than fifty books throughout his lifetime; these included five collections of essays and thirty-six books of poetry. Though Carman spent most of his mature years in the U.S., he undertook several reading tours across Canada, and became something of an unofficial first poet laureate of the country. He was made a member of the Royal Society of Canada in 1925, was awarded the Lorne Pierce medal for literature three years later, and received honorary degrees from McGill University and the University of New Brunswick. Influential in publishing and promoting poetry as well as a writer of it himself, Carman edited *The World's Best Poetry*, a ten-volume project in 1904, and many years later in 1927, an edition of *The Oxford Book of American Verse*. Shortly after his first cross-Canada tour he produced, along with Lorne Pierce, *Our Canadian Literature: Representative Verse, English and French* in 1922.

Publications

A Seamark: A Threnody for Robert Louis Stevenson. Boston: Copeland and Day, 1875.

Low Tide on Grande Pré: A Book of Lyrics. New York: C.L. Webster, 1893.

Low Tide on Grande Pré: A Book of Lyrics. 2nd, expanded ed. Cambridge, MA: Stone and Kimball, 1894.

With Richard Hovey. *Songs from Vagabondia.* Illus. Tom B. Meteyard. Boston: Copeland and Day, 1894.

Behind the Arras: A Book of the Unseen. Illus. Tom B. Meteyard. Boston: Lamson, Wolffe & Co., 1895.

Ballads of Lost Haven: A Book of the Sea. Boston: Lamson, Wolffe & Co., 1897.

By the Aurelian Wall: And Other Elegies. Boston: Lamson, Wolffe & Co., 1898.

With Richard Hovey. *Last Songs from Vagabondia.* Illus. Tom B. Meteyard. Boston: Small, Maynard & Co., 1901.

Ballads and Lyrics. London: Bullen, 1902.

Ode on the Coronation of King Edward. Boston: L.C. Page & Co., 1902.

From the Green Book of the Bards. His Pipes of Pan, No. 2. Boston: L.C. Page & Co., 1903.

From the Book of Myths. His Pipes of Pan, No. 1. Boston: L.C. Page & Co., 1904.

The Kinship of Nature. Boston: L.C. Page & Co., 1904.

Sappho: One Hundred Lyrics. Intro. Charles G.D. Roberts. Boston: L.C. Page & Co., 1904.

Songs from A Northern Garden. Pipes of Pan, No. 4. Boston: L.C. Page & Co., 1904.

Songs of the Sea Children. Boston: L.C. Page & Co., 1904.

From the Book of Valentines. Boston: L.C. Page & Co., 1905.

Poems. London: Chiswick P, 1905.

The Poetry of Life. Boston: L.C. Page & Co., 1905.

The Friendship of Art. Toronto: Copp Clark Co., 1904; Boston: L.C. Page & Co., 1908.

The Making of Personality. Boston: L.C. Page & Co., 1908.

The Rough Rider: And Other Poems. New York: M. Kennerley, 1909.

With Mary Perry King. *Daughters of Dawn: A Lyrical Pageant or Series of Historic Scenes for Presentation with Music and Dancing.* New York: M. Kennerley, 1913.

Echoes from Vagabondia. Boston: Small, Maynard & Co., 1913.

With Mary Perry King. *Earth Deities: And Other Rythmic Masques.* New York: M. Kennerley, 1914.

April Airs: A Book of New England Lyrics. Boston: Small, Maynard & Co., 1916.

With Mary Perry King. *The Man of The Marne: And Other Poems.* New Canaan, CN: Ponus P, 1918.

Later Poems. Boston: Small, Maynard & Co., 1922.

With Richard Hovey. *More Songs from Vagabondia.* Illus. Tom B. Meteyard. Boston: Small, Maynard & Co., 1924.

Far Horizons. Toronto: McClelland and Stewart, 1926.

Sanctuary: Sunshine House Sonnets. Illus. Whitman Bailey. Toronto: McClelland and Stewart, 1929.

Wild Garden. Toronto: McClelland and Stewart, 1929.

Bliss Carman's Poems. New York: Dodd, Mead & Co., 1931.

Bliss Carman's Scrap-Book: A Table of Contents. Ed. Lorne Pierce. Toronto: Ryerson, 1931.

Pipes of Pan. Toronto: Ryerson, 1942.

The Selected Poems of Bliss Carman. Ed. Lorne Pierce. Toronto: McClelland and Stewart, 1954.

A Vision of Sappho. Toronto: Canadiana House, 1968.

Windflower: Poems of Bliss Carman. Ed. Raymond Souster and Douglas Lochhead. Ottawa: Tecumseh, 1985.

Vagabond Song. Tweed, ON: Bundle Buggy P, 1987.

Critical Materials

Book Length

Bentley, D.M.R. and Margaret Maciejewski, eds. *Bliss Carman's Letters To Margaret Lawrence, 1927–1929.* Post-Confederation Poetry: Texts And Contexts. London: Canadian Poetry P, 1995.

Gundy, H. Pearson, ed. *Letters of Bliss Carman.* Kingston: McGill-Queen's UP, 1981.

Hawthorne, Julian. *Bliss Carman: 1861–1929*. Palo Alto, CA: privately printed, 1929.

Lynch, Gerald, ed. *Bliss Carman: A Reappraisal*. Ottawa: U of Ottawa P, 1990.

McPherson, Hugh. "The Literary Reputation of Bliss Carman: A Study in the Development of Canadian Taste in Poetry." M.A. Thesis. U of Western Ontario, 1950.

Miller, Muriel. *Bliss Carman, A Portrait*. Toronto: Ryerson, 1935.

———. *Bliss Carman: Quest and Revolt*. St. John's, NF: Jesperson P, 1985.

Shepard, Odell. *Bliss Carman*. Toronto: McClelland and Stewart, 1923.

Stephens, Donald G. *Bliss Carman*. New York: Twain, 1966.

———. "The Influence of English Poets upon the Poetry of Bliss Carman." M.A. Thesis. U of New Brunswick, 1955.

Stewart, Margaret A. "Bliss Carman: Poet, Philosopher, Teacher." M.A. Thesis. Dalhousie U, 1976.

Articles

Nelson-McDermott, C. "Passionate Beauty: Carman's Sappho Poems." *Canadian Poetry* 27 (1990): 40–45.

Ware, Tracy, ed. "Arthur Symons' Reviews of Bliss Carman." *Canadian Poetry* 37 (1995): 100–13.

Online Resources

http://www.carman.net/bliss.htm

http://eir.library.utoronto.ca/rpo/display/poet56.html

http://digital.library.upenn.edu/women/garvin/poets/carman.html

http://www.ucalgary.ca/UofC/faculties/HUM/ENGL/canada/poet/b_carman.htm

The Secret of Art

Reprinted from *The Friendship of Art*, Toronto: Copp Clark Co., 1904, 98–106.

As in Homer's line, "Many are the tongues of mortals, but the speech of the immortals is one," so the secrets of the artist are many, but there is only one secret of art. Lacking that, we may spend lifelong toil in the pursuit of perfection; we may master a brilliant technique and compass the profoundest thought; the architecture of our work may be sound and its finish flawless; nonetheless without the secret it will be futile. We may heed every tradition, follow every hint of written or unwritten lore; yes, and we may even fling every accepted creed of our craft to the four winds, and build anew with the intuitive instinct we call originality, so that we will endure awhile, filling all eyes with wonder and every mouth with praise, and yet we will fail ultimately if the secret was not in our heart.

There is a sort of greatness about a true masterpiece that makes itself felt we hardly know how, that moves us we do not know why; just as there is a sort of greatness about some men, which compels an unreserved enthusiasm and loyalty toward them. It is the quality which endears people to us. This man may be brave and irreproachable; that one may be clever to bewilderment; yet, if they are not lovable, we meet them and part without regret. They convince us, and charm, and even win; yet a moment later we are left as cold as before. Here may be a play, or a book, or an exhibition of pictures, which is the talk of the town, and which dazzles the sense with its novel beauty; yet somehow, while drawing our utmost commendation and provoking not a single palpable criticism, it never stirs us from the centre of our being. We sit in approving calm, even with generous applause, unwarmed, unfired.

But show me, perhaps, ever so hasty a sketch of gray morning, a half-finished scrap of purple sea-beach, or a couple of stanzas like

> Under the wide and starry sky,
> Dig my grave and let me lie,

or,

> The year's at the spring,
> The day's at the morn,

and just because it has the echo of the secret in it, I shall never recall it without a quickening joy. It has entered in to be a part of me for ever; and whatever I do, whatever I say, will have in it some minute reverberation of the echo of that secret.

What quality of art can it be, so magical, so vague, so strong? You must ask first what quality it is in men. For art is no more than the universal speech of humanity; and whatever taint there is in a character will be betrayed in the voice; though only the wise know this. What quality is it in the personality that makes it most memorable to its fellows? A man to be remembered must have endeared himself to men. He will not be remembered for wealth, nor power, nor wit, unless he have used it beneficently, winning regard as he won command. So you may say love is the secret of art, as it is the secret of life.

To be inevitable (in our recent phrase), to have the inescapable magic, this is the aim of the artist. If you analyze this strange potency, it seems to resolve itself into the essence of endearment. It is, as we say, the heart of the matter; it draws our attachment, our unreasoned devotion, our love. There are, of course, works of mediocre value, which enlist the crudest affections, and yet are patently false and worthless to the better judgment; but I do not mean these watery sentimental things. I am speaking of the rare achievements of art, such as came from the hands of Blake and Corot and Wordsworth. Think, for instance, of that beautiful lyric:

> I wandered lonely as a cloud,
> That floats on high o'er vales and hills.

You would not say that it embodied a very common human sentiment; you would say it is rather a poem for the cultivated. And yet, I think, the quality in it which holds us, the indwelling spirit behind that bewitching mask of words, is the spirit of love. The heart of the man, one is sure, must have been greatly moved before he could speak so. And we, in our turn, are greatly moved under the spell of that wizard cadence. At first it might seem a mere trick of the senses, a skill in accents, the craft of melodious syllables. It is more than that. We say it is intensity or lyric ardour. But no craftsmanship, however cunning, can match that volatile charm, nor arrest the fleeting glamour of such lines. Yet surely, if the wonder worker were only a master of skill and no more, his intricacies could be studied and his secret caught. But no, strive as we may, there is no imitation of consummate art possible. You can no more make a new poem which shall be Wordsworth's, than you can make a new man out of clay.

The secret of art and the secret of nature are one—the slow, patient, absorbing, generous process of love—sustaining itself everywhere on loveliness and life, and remanifesting itself afresh in ever new forms of vitality and loveliness. It is because of this quality, and in proportion to this quality that we value every shred of art, and are at such pains to preserve it. By the simplest natural law, humanity cares for those things which ameliorate its lot, and lets go in the long run everything that hurts or retards it. If a man is mean or cruel or false or self-absorbed, his force and cleverness may still carry him far; indeed he may come to great eminence in fame and power. The deep, foolish, blind heart of good-ness in man is deluded by his display. But by and by, in the advance of thought, he will be forgotten, because his unit of influence was never for the best, was never needful for sustaining the world. In the enlargement of aspiration in man, whatever hinders that development will be aban-doned. We shall not be fooled for ever. And he only is on the winning side, who can see in the march of history a laborious trail cut through the underbrush of experience from darkened valley to sunlit crest, who can perceive whither the blind by-paths led the lost adventurers, and who will hold resolutely to that steep road—the prevailing undoubtful trend of truth.

Of nations you may say the same, and of art you may say the same. There have been unnecessary tribes that have perished in their inutility, because in the large wise scope of progress, in the preservation of the fair and the good, they had no part to play. And in art, which is only the embodiment of the hope of the world, all that was petty or self-centred has perished and is perishing from day to day. It has endured for awhile; it has pleased us by its cleverness, or beguiled us by its charm, when we have been too near to understand its tendency. With man's avidity for truth and goodness (in spite of a monstrous inertia), he is ready to follow the wildest departures which promise more light and a liberation from wrong. But as these prove unavailing, he will leave them for others. The history of art, like the history of man, is a jungle full of blind trails leading nowhither; and you will find they were abandoned because they did not lead toward goodness, toward what was good for man; because they did not make toward the spaciousness and freshness of truth.

Long ago, of course, art was more simple and unconscious than it has since become; and the devout soul of the artist dwelt in his deft fingers. It was impossible for him to do anything without conviction; he had never heard of technique; and the pride of barren skill had not been born. The man and his work were one. This is not to say that consummate care for workmanship, and untiring diligence for perfection, are wrong; it is merely to say that between the soul and the body of art there can be no divorce—that each is necessary, and neither can survive alone.

Is modern art frivolous, vapid, unmanly? Pray who made it so? Any art is just as great as the age that produced it. And for my part I do not believe that art can fail any more than I believe that speech can cease, or nature withhold her changing seasons. If we are fallen on paltry times, as some would have us believe, let us change the times. The earth is just as fair and beautiful and generous as it ever was; and we are coming to understand it better than our fathers could. Let us love it as well. Have done with falsehood and greed, and the millennium will begin tomorrow, with paradise in your own dooryard. There is no other spirit in which life can be made worthwhile, and there is no other secret of a great art.

Personal Rhythm

Reprinted from *The Friendship of Art*, Toronto: Copp Clark Co., 1904, 183–89.

There is a rhythm of poetry, and there is a rhythm of people. And these two rhythms are similar in their charm and power.

By a rhythm of people I do not mean any magnetic or magic influence generated in congregations of individuals, but rather the rhythm peculiar to each individual. In this sense rhythm is an attribute of personality, and is manifested through the person in motion and speech. Observe your friends and notice the rhythm peculiar to each; how one is slow and another quick, one deliberate and another hurried, one jerky and another graceful. I almost fancy, indeed, that you might find one was iambic and another trochaic in essential rhythm. Can you not think of the ponderous character that moves step after step, word after word, with the emphasis always delayed until the second thought, the second look, the second movement, the second words? Dons and dowagers and policemen are always iambic in their rhythm. Recall the rhythm of blank verse, the most common iambic measure in English, in the lines:

> So all day long the noise of battle rolled
> Among the mountains by the winter sea,

and you will perceive at once how settled and prosperous and conservative it is, quite aristocratic and assured. On the other hand, to quote again from Tennyson, there is the line of excellent trochees:

> In the spring a young man's fancy lightly turns to thoughts of love.

How different from the iambics! How sprightly, tripping, gay, and emotional! The rhythm of a soubrette rather than a savant. Then, again, there is the slow, uncertain, meandering rhythm of some large people who move like a hexameter:

> This is the forest primeval, the murmuring pines and
>   the hemlocks.

Undecided people are usually of this dactyllic measure; and it is a very dangerous one to handle.

Again, persons are like poems in this, that it is possible to have a bad rhythm, though every rhythm is good in itself. We may, however, destroy our rhythm or nullify its effect by misuse. If we are naturally iambic, we must be careful how we break into trochees; and, if we are trochaic, we must beware of lapsing into iambics. The result of a bad use of rhythms is always ludicrous. The strut of a bantam and the skip of an archbishop are incongruous, and, therefore, to be employed with discrimination. And with this provision any rhythm may be used at will with expressional power. The prime rule in the poetry of man is this: Stick to your own rhythm. And remember you cannot help using your own natural rhythm so long as you are simple and sincere. The moment you begin to pose, you will unconsciously use another rhythm, not your own; and every one will know it. Do not imagine for a moment that you can appear to be what you are not. You are betrayed in every gesture. Every syllable "gives you away." Occasionally a great genius may play a part which is not his own by nature; but in that case he passes by imagination into the new character, and actually is the person he plays. This is the genius of the actor, and it is the lack of just this power that is so apparent in the mediocre player.

To live according to one's rhythm is the law of common sense and common honesty. It is the first requisite of sanity, too. And it is one of the greatest evils of modern life that it tends to throw us out of rhythm. We are nearly all hurried to a point of hysteria. It is not so much that we have more than we can do, as that we allow the haste to get on our nerves. Without being aware of it in the least, we become distraught, inefficient, and flighty, simply through the hurry in which we live. You may deny it as you please, but noise and haste are maddening. Watch the average businessman, fluttering about like an agitated hen. He is divorced from his natural, legitimate power, for he has lost his own rhythm. He does everything too quickly, and he does nothing well. If he would only take time to breathe and smile and hold up his chest, he would accomplish much more, and save his soul alive at the same time. To be in a hurry is sometimes necessary. In that case, you must be prepared with the natural celerity of lightning, prompt but poised. It is never necessary to scurry. And in order to maintain this deliberation, of course, we must never let events tread on our heels. We must never dawdle, never allow our rhythm to run more slowly than is natural. That is equally a fault. But, if we always do things that are becoming to our personality in the rhythm that is our true expression, neither breathless nor lagging, we shall accomplish more than we dreamed and we shall always have time to spare. We have all the time there is; and in that time everything can be done that ought to be done. It is merely a matter of balance, of adjustment, of rhythm, of keeping the soul at poise amid the forces of circumstance and will. If we miss that fine poise, we suffer, we feel the deterioration that comes of ineffectual effort, we have wasted our power, we have depleted our fund of inertia and initiative impulse, we have hindered the delicate rhythm of personality.

Does this seem fantastic and far-fetched? It is not really so. Perhaps it is a matter that will not bear discussion. It will bear experiment, however. If you do not believe in a personal rhythm, it is only because you have never thought of it in so many words. If you consider it for a moment in the light of your own experience, you will be convinced of its truth and power.

There is in poetry a certain influence or power quite apart from its logical meaning. There resides in the lines a subtle force not given to prose. This is the genius of the measure making itself felt. In the same way our personality makes itself felt in all we do, through the influence of our peculiar rhythm. And we shall be wise to cultivate our own proper and peculiar measure of speech and movement. For there is surely a power given to each one of us, call it what you will, that is not expended in word or act, but exerts itself in the unconscious time of speech, in the unconscious time of our deeds. And just as the measure of verse influences the hearer and serves to carry an impression from the poet, so our own rhythm affects all who come into contact with us in life. It is a form of power about which a materialistic age knows little, and therefore one the more to be cultivated and preserved.

Atmosphere

Reprinted from: *The Kinship of Nature*, Boston: L.C. Page & Co., 1904, 291–98.

In its secondary sense atmosphere is a word which is only lately come into common use. The artists, I suppose, have introduced it and given it currency. Atmosphere is to fact what the bloom is to the grape,—the mark of immaculate perfection, imperceptible to the casual or careless glance, yet full of wonder and charm to the thoughtful observer. Atmosphere is the aroma of spirit, the aura or emanation of being; and he is a happy artist who has the least command of such a perishable finish for his work.

One sees so often a picture or piece of sculpture, immensely clever, apt, refined, full of dignity, graceful in proportion, restful in line, of rich and harmonious colour, the idea transferred to the very life, and yet one can say of it: "Yes, but it has no atmosphere!" And there is the fatal sentence pronounced. Again, you come upon a creation which seems upon scrutiny to be a tissue of faults. There is nothing right about it; bad colour, bad drawing, false execution, slovenly technique; yet somehow, in spite of all that, even so poor a thing as this may tug at your sympathy; it may be able to cast a glamour over you for the moment, for all its badness. It may have atmosphere. True, this is unlikely, and a touch of atmosphere alone will not save a poor creation. Yet, how welcome, how delightful it is!

In people, too, as well as in facts and objects, atmosphere counts for so much. There are many personalities, only too many, in whom it is lacking. They are excellent, even irreproachable, citizens, and exemplary friends maybe; but they are purely negative or neutral; they seem to be invested with not a particle of mysterious envelopment which lends glamour to the individual, and irradiates the character. Without atmosphere there maybe force, directness, even beauty, but the utmost reach of power will be wanting. The hard light of character needs to be somewhat diffused and tempered by an atmospheric quality in its expression. And since expression is a matter of art, one is almost tempted to say that art consists in the creation of atmosphere. Be as faithful to reality (or to romance) as you please, but surround your transcription with an atmosphere; bestow upon it the magic air and colour which are its own indeed, but which shall still convince and transport us beyond the actual.

> The little more, and how much it is;
> The little less, and what worlds away.

In matters of art it is "the little more" which is so all important; and the absolute reproduction of an incident or an object, if such a feat were possible, would mean something very like failure.

Also the painter is in danger of seeing too much. He half closes his eyes for fear of seeing things exactly as they are. He would preserve the charm of atmosphere at all costs. He must either add something of his own to the canvas, or omit the minuteness of detail in his rendering of a subject, in order to arrest the air and the illusion of nature. But at all hazards he will avoid what science would count the truth. Your line must have just sufficient indecision to betray (I should say, to reveal) the human hand that drew it. For this is the touch of living sympathy, more important than the dead accuracy of the machine. To transfer to canvas or print something of the vitality of the original is the first concern of the craftsman, the more nearly exact the better, but living at all costs. We are apt to forget that the circle and the straight line are mathematical fictions, forms of speech which have been approached but never realized in a material world. For to apprehend absolute perfection is not given to man, though he be a prince of artists; while ever to strive after that apprehension is one of his most delightful joys. The pursuit of the unattainable is the piety of art.

To create an atmosphere, to produce an illusion, having been always the artist's prime aim and most elementary need, it follows that in every art there have been evolved its own peculiar laws which facilitate and enforce that object. In poetry, for instance, versification, with all its complex beauty of rhythms and metres, helps to enshroud the theme with atmosphere. I had almost said that versification provides the atmosphere. For although it is so easy to be hopelessly banal in verse, there must still cling even to the worst poetry some of the inalienable charm of numbers. A foreigner at least might hear it with satisfaction.

So that if a man will abandon verse, and betake himself, as he fondly says, to the freedom of prose, he will find the burden of art laid upon him more than twice as heavy as before. He is cast utterly upon his own resources, and yet the obligations of his art are not diminished one jot. There is the same old tale of illusion and atmosphere to be made up, and not a shred of material in stock. One thinks of prose as the simplest, most natural means of expression, and of poetry as laboured in comparison. I fancy, however, that if we could interrogate those who have been masters of both arts, we should find the reverse to be true. "Prose is toil," they would say, "while poetry is play."

At all events, there is atmosphere in form; and it is the engrossing business of the artist to manipulate his form, to humour it, to coax it, to compel it, to woo it, so as to make it yield the greatest possible amount of atmosphere for his purpose. In all this he must take care to call to his aid every available resource of his craft. In the first place he must enlist the sympathetic help of words by using them kindly and rightly according to their nature and genius, and as they belong, and not antagonize them by misapplication. I have known writers who established a reputation for great cleverness simply by the misuse of words. Their style was called original. It was. For pure unmitigated cruelty to our tiny, long-suffering servants, these patient words, it was unmatched. Now a man who will mutilate his mother tongue merely to display his own agility is no better than a heathen. It is so needless, too. For to the generous and sedulous master, what revelations of undreamed beauty, what marvels of import, will not words impart?

I would not speak as a pedant, nor as a dilettante, on this topic, but only as a sober bystander in this great gallery of art, this lovely world which we are permitted to wander through. I see how much things are enhanced in my eyes by the atmosphere that surrounds them; I see how naked and poverty-stricken they appear without it; and I say to myself, "I love atmosphere, in art and in life. I will surround myself with it, whenever I can do so unselfishly. And if I were an artist of any sort, it is atmosphere that I should seek first of all."

The Poetry of Life

Reprinted from *The Poetry of Life*, Boston: L.C. Page & Co., 1905, 1–14.

"The poetry of life," says the book of St. Kavin, "is the poetry of beauty, sincerity, and elation." And when you think of it, it seems reasonable enough that this should be so, since these are the archangelic trio to whose keeping the very sources of life are confided. They are the dispensers of happiness, the bringers of wisdom, the guardians of mystery.

That the poetry of life should of necessity be the poetry of beauty, first of all, seems nearly self-evident. The beauty of the world so out-reaches and overcomes all its ugliness, is so much more prevalent and vital and persistent. One concludes at once and instinctively that life concerns itself with beauty—almost, at first glance, to the exclusion of everything else. What more natural, therefore, since life cares so much for beauty, than that art, life's replica, should care greatly for it also?

As for its sincerity, the poetry of life need not always be solemn, any more than life itself need always be sober. It may be gay, witty, hu-mourous, satirical, disbelieving, farcical, even broad and reckless, since life is all these, but it must never be insincere. Insincerity, which is not always one of the greatest sins in the moral universe, becomes in the world of art an offence of the first magnitude. Insincerity in life may be mean and despicable, and indicate a petty nature; but in art insincerity is death. A strong man may lie upon occasion, and make restitution and be forgiven, but for the artist who lies there is hardly any reparation pos-sible, and his forgiveness is much more difficult. Art, being the embodiment of the artist's ideal, is, truly, the corporeal substance of his spiritual self; and that there should be any falsehood in it, any deliber-ate failure to represent him faithfully, is as monstrous and unnatural as it would be for a man to disavow his own flesh and bones. Here we are every one of us going through life committed and attached to our bodies; for all that we do we are held responsible; if we misbehave, the world will take it out of our hide. But here is our friend the artist committing his spiritual energy to his art, to an embodiment outside himself, and escaping down a by-path from all the consequences. What shall be said of him? The insincere artist is as much beyond the pale of human sympathy as the murderer. Morally he is a felon.

There is no excuse for him, either. There was no call for him to make a liar of himself, other than the most sordid of reasons; the little gain, the jingling reward of gold. For no man would ever be insincere in his art, except for pay, except to cater to some other taste than his own, and to win approval and favour by his sycophancy. If he were assured of his competency in the world, and placed beyond the reach of necessitous want, how would it ever occur to him to create an insincere art? Art is so simple and spontaneous, so dependent on the disingenuous emotion, that it can never be insincere, unless violence is done to all law of nature and of spirit. Since art arises from the sacramental blending of the inward spirit with the outward form, any touch of insincerity in it assumes the nature of a horrible crime, a pitiable revolt against the order and eternity of the universe. That the conditions of modern commercialism are to blame for this unhappy possibility, may be true; but that only makes it the more sad, and gives the final selfish touch that robs it of all sympathy.

The environs of the city of art are always full of charlatans. The clever artisan or inventor who often does not even pretend to make the real article you seek, but offers you something "just as good and much cheaper," is never far from the honest marketplace. Often he has the very appearance and pose of the true artist, and his resentment of an imputation of his honesty would deceive many. He is a cheat, for all that, and in his heart he knows it.

For the books that are written, the plays that are produced, the pictures that are painted by fatuous, misdirected, incompetent, yet sincere energy, one can have nothing but compassionate respect. The sight of some poor spirit, in guileless devoted zeal, spending years and health and hope and resources in the pursuit of some quite hopeless ambition in art, is a thing to make one weep. So pure, so kindly, so praiseworthy in its intentions, and yet so futile! For such as these there must be a special reward hereafter. They do not cumber the ground, they keep it sweet; often they shame even the great ones by their singleness of purpose and sincerity of soul.

It is not necessary, as I say, for art to be solemn and wholly serious-minded in order to be sincere. Comedy is quite sincere. She is one of the most honest of the muses. Yet it is easy to usurp her name and play the fool for pennies, with never a ray of appreciation of her true character. I know a comic poet (you may not believe me, but I believe myself), a young man who has recently arisen, who seems to me to be a true artist and no pretender. Whenever I see his name I read his jingles with delight. Such amazing productivity with such unfailing irresistible mirth I have seldom heard of elsewhere. If he is not another Hood, I am mistaken. He is, so far at least, a proof of the fact that one can live in the world yet not be destroyed by the world; for though so eminently popular, he is still genuine in his wit. I always think of his work as an example of art which may be perfectly frivolous and perfectly sincere at the same time. And every day, side by side with his, I see other work masking as comedy, which is nothing but false, uninspired, and wooden, the pitiable product of cleverness without spirit, the worthless contrivance of journeymen. There seem to be plenty of fabricators of this latter sort of rhyme. They are, I suppose, they and their works, the inevitable but odious accompaniments of our times. They write to please their editors, and their reward is sure, but the comic muse disowns them for all that.

Sincerity, then, is not in the least averse to fun, it only requires that the fun shall be genuine and come from the heart, as it requires that every note of whatever sort shall be genuine and spring from the real personality of the writer. More than this, I find in the phrase, "the poetry of sincerity," a suggestion as to the function of poetry in relation to science, to truth, for our thirst for knowing what is to be known. And the aspiration, *Da mihi, Domine, scire quod sciendum est*, seems preeminently the daily prayer for a poet to make, the voice of his longing to be brought into communication with things as they are. It points to the necessity poetry is always under of supplying food for our curiosity, answers for our deepest questions, and a reasonable explanation of life. It emphasizes the fact which I have reiterated so often, that it is never enough for poetry to be stirring and entrancing, unless it is illuminating as well. The poetry of sincerity is the poetry of truth.

In the matter of elation as a requirement in the poetry of life, perhaps a little more explanation is needed. As I understand it, "the poetry of life is the poetry of beauty, sincerity, and elation," because the poetry of ugliness, falsehood, and depression would be a poetry of death. And that is something the world does not want. It has enough of death in reality, without any artificial copy or reminder of it. When poetry, poetry that is highly esteemed and widely valued, refers to death, it seeks and celebrates some trace of survival, some hint of immortality. It strives to minimize the depressing aspect of death, and bring gladness out of sorrow. There has recently been issued a selection from Whitman's poetry, entitled "The Book of Heavenly Death." It is anything but depressing, of course. It has its place assured with the poetry of elation. And so of all great sincere poetry which has proved itself of value in men's eyes, it retains its vogue and influence because of its enheartening power, its power to strengthen our hearts in courage, faith, love, gladness, serenity, wisdom, resignation, or peace. Poetry which emphasizes depression, discouragement, and defeat, and harps upon the horrors or ills or dark enigmas of life, is of no earthly use whatever to men whose whole business in life is to avoid and mitigate and overcome those sorry evils.

I have heard a writer who insisted, in season and out of season, perhaps, on the necessity of the joyous note in art, taken to task as a pagan, and accused of being indifferent to the sorrows of man, or even ignorant of them. I am sure that by the word "joy" he could not have meant any mere momentary and shallow gladness, whether of the senses or the spirit. To rejoice, is the injunction repeated again and again by an apostle of Christianity, the religion of the sorrowful. The man who has not tasted sorrow—natural, inevitable, purifying sorrow—does not know what joy means in this larger sense. There is a higher joy which includes all sorrow, just as there is a higher good which forgives all evil, though it may scarcely be within the reach of mortals. And one who should advocate the cultivation of a small, thoughtless, selfish joy, to the exclusion of all experience of sorrow and all sympathy with pain, would be foolish indeed. For such joy is less than the joy of children, being heartless and insecure.

If one asks for the note of joy in art, and demands that the quality of gladness be emphasized, this does not imply that sorrow is to be ignored. A joy without sympathy would be unnatural, if, indeed, it were possible in such a life as this. And if we are urged to rejoice and be exceeding glad, let us understand that it is to be in spite of sorrow and evil, even somehow by their means, and not regardless of their presence in life.

That is always good in poetry, as in life, which stimulates the spirit and renews its zest, its strength, its fortitude. Sorrow and the representation of sorrow may do this at times as well as happiness. There is an influence in tragedy, a nobleness of grief, which is tonic to the soul, and leaves us sobered but not dejected. It is the squalid and unrelieved depression in them, which makes so many modern tragedies hopeless failures. They emphasize the ugly evil, yet afford the soul no escape, offer it no compensation, such as there always is in life. No wonder the public will have none of them: But in classic tragedy there is always some exit for the distraught, indomitable spirit, some incentive to endurance, some consciousness of greatness or nobility. We weep at the sorrows of Lear, yet our pride is touched by the grandeur of that old kingly man, and our just indignation at the impious daughters relieves the tension of suffering. Both sentiments are kindling to the spirit, and we come away from the play bettered, if not cheered. It belongs to the poetry of elation, tragedy though it is.

Such poetry is in accord with the trend of life; life which is full of evil and horror and confusion and mischance, and which yet goes on its long, slow, persistent course, ever putting aside these monstrous drawbacks, and gathering to itself all loveliness and truth and charity. Anything which can help the spirit of man on his difficult trail, that will he gladly make use of, that only to him is good. In poetry, in the arts, whatever gives us a touch of elation, of glad encouragement, of hope, of aspiration, of solace, that do we eagerly seize and hold. It seems to us good, as well as fair and true. If you say that the poetry of sincerity is the poetry of truth, you may add, the poetry of elation is the poetry of goodness.

To incorporate truth, to arrest and make evident those facts about nature which delight and satisfy the mind; to incorporate at the same time the feelings which delight and satisfy the heart; and to give this manifestation a guise which shall allure and delight and satisfy the senses; this is the great and only business of all art, just as it appears to be the supreme concern of all life.

Life which is constantly realizing itself in nature, does so in these three ways, and offers us these three phases of itself. An art which attempts to realize itself, while still neglecting to make itself felt in any one of these three directions, must, therefore, be faulty just to that extent. And since art is a mimic creation, made in imitation of life, we see how this saying was come by, "The poetry of life is the poetry of beauty, sincerity, and elation."

The Purpose of Poetry

Reprinted from *The Poetry of Life*, Boston: L.C. Page & Co., 1905, 15–62.

Before considering any of the aims and purposes of poetry, or any of its essential characteristics, we had better first consider it in its place as one of the fine arts. If we then ask ourselves what the fine arts are to do for us, what place they are to hold in a civilized nation, we shall perhaps be able to look at poetry in a broader way than we otherwise could; we shall be able to think of it not merely as a pleasant and amusing diversion, but as one of the potent factors of history.

If we try to find a place for the fine arts among our various human activities, we might begin by making a rough classification of our subject. The most primitive and necessary occupations we engage in, such as fishing and agriculture, trading, navigating, and hunting, we call industries. These mark the earliest stage of man's career in civilization. Then he comes to other occupations, requiring more skill and ingenuity; he weaves fabrics, he makes himself houses, he fashions all sorts of implements for the household and the chase. He becomes a builder, a potter, a metal-worker, an inventor. He has added thought to work and made the work easier. And these new occupations which he has discovered for himself differ from his earlier ones chiefly in this; that they result in numerous objects of more or less permanence, cunningly contrived and aptly fitted to use. They are objects of useful or industrial art.

Now we must note two things about this step forward which man has taken toward civilization; in the first place he had to have some leisure to do these things, and in the second place the objects he has made reveal his ingenuity and forethought. They are records of his life; and it will happen that as his leisure increases, his implements will become more and more elaborate and ornate. Every workman will have his own way of fashioning them, using his own device and designs, so that they will become something more than rude relics of one historic age or another; they will tell us something of the artificer himself; they will embody some intentional expression of human life and come to have an art value. In so far as they can do this, they contain the essential quality of the fine arts. And the more freely the workman can deal with his craft, the more perfectly he can make it characteristic of himself, the finer will its artistic quality become.

The only purpose of the primitive industries was a utilitarian one. The prime object of the industrial arts is also a utilitarian one; but they have a secondary object as well, they aim at beauty, too. They not only serve the practical end for which they were intended, they serve also as a means of expression for the workman. Now just as we passed from the industries to the industrial arts, by the addition of this secondary interest, this human artistic expressional quality, so by making this quality paramount we may pass from the industrial arts to the fine arts themselves, where expression is all-important, and utility becomes less prominent. It is the distinguishing mark of the fine arts that they give us a means of expressing ourselves in terms of intelligible beauty.

I have made this distinction between the fine and the industrial arts merely for the sake of clarifying our ideas, and getting a notion of what is the essence of all art. But really the difference is not important, and, having served its turn, may be forgotten. There is an element of art, of course, in everything that we do; the manner of the doing constitutes the art. The quality of art which we should appreciate and respect may quite as truly be present in a Japanese tobacco-box as in a Greek tragedy. The Japanese, indeed, offer an instance of a people who have raised the handicrafts quite to the level of the fine arts. All those fascinating objects of beauty, which they contrive with so much skill, are often, one may guess, only as many excuses for the workman to exhibit his deftness and his taste. This black oak cabinet inlaid with pearl, or that lacquer bowl, may, perhaps, be counted,, useful objects; but I fancy that before all else they were just so many opportunities for the artist; and when he fashioned them he had in mind chiefly the creation of something beautiful, and dwelt very little upon the use to which they might be put. He was bent on giving play to his imagination, and you may be very sure that he was glad in the work of his hands, and wrought all those intricate effects with loving care. Surely the result is much more deserving of respect than a mediocre epic or a second-rate painting. It is not what we do that counts, but how well we do it. There is no saying one kind of work is art, and another kind is not art. Anything that is well done is art; anything that is badly done is rotten.

I do not wish either to confine the word "useful," in its application, to our material needs. Everything we do ought to be useful, and so it is, if it is done well. Tables and chairs are useful; but so are pictures and cathedrals and lyrics and the theatre. If we allow ourselves only what are called the necessities of life, we are only keeping alive one-third of being; the other two-thirds of our manhood may be starving to death. The mind and the soul have their necessities as well as the body. And we are to seek these things, not only for our future salvation, but for our salvation here and now, that our lives may be helpful and sound and happy.

It is often easy to see how a fine art may grow from some more necessary and commonplace undertaking. The fine art of painting, for instance, arose, of course, from the use of ornamental lines and figures, drawn on pottery, or on the walls of a skin tent, where it served only to enhance the value of the craftsman's work and please his fancy. Gradually, through stages of mural decoration, perhaps, where ever in-creasing freedom of execution was given the artist, its first ornamental purpose was forgotten, and it came to serve only as a means of expressing the artist's imaginative ideals. So, too, of sculpture and architecture, of dancing and acting. It is an easy transition from the light-hearted, superfluous skip of a child as it runs, to the more formal dance step, as the child keeps time to music and gives vent to its gaiety of spirit. It is an easy transition from gesture and sign language, employed as a necessary means of communication, to their more elaborate use in the art of acting, where they serve merely to emphasize subtle expression and to create an illusion. Similarly, too, whenever a piece of information is conveyed by word of mouth, and the teller of the tale elaborates it with zest and interest and grace, making it more memorable and vivid and beautiful, the fine art of letters is born.

Now we may notice that the quality of art begins to appear in all our occupations, as the direst stress of existence is relieved, and man's spirit begins to have free play. Art is an indication of health and happy exuber-ance of life; it is as instinctive and spontaneous in its origin as child's play. To produce it naturally the artist must be free—for the time being, at least—free from all doubt or hesitation about the truth, free from all material tortures, free from dejection and fear. The primitive industries mark the first grade in the human story, when we were barely escaping from the necessity for unremitting hand-to-hand physical struggle for life; and the second grade in our progress is marked by the appearance of the industrial arts; while we may look on the fine arts as an index of the highest development, as we pass from savagery and barbarism to civilization. And perhaps we shall not go very far astray, in our comparative estimate of nations, and their greatness on the earth, if we rank them in the order of their proficiency in the arts.

Now the fine arts, having thus had their rise in the free play of the human spirit as it went about its work in the world, and busied itself with the concerns of life, became a natural vehicle for giving expression to all men's aspirations and thoughts about life. Indeed, it was this very simple elemental need for self-expression, as a trait in human character, which helped to determine what the fine arts should be. To communicate our feelings, to transmit knowledge, to amuse ourselves by creating a mimic world with imaginative shapes of beauty, these were fundamental cravings, lurking deep in the spirit of man, and demanding satisfaction almost as imperiously as the desires of the body. If hunger and cold made us industrious, no less certainly did love of companionship and need for self-expression mould our breath into articulate speech. Since, therefore, the fine arts are so truly a creation of man, we may expect to find in them a trustworthy image of himself. Whatever is human must be there,—all our thoughts, all our emotions, all our sensations, hopes, and fears. They will reveal and embody in themselves all the traits of our complex nature. Art is that lovely corporeal body with which man endows the spirit of goodness and the thought of truth. For there are in man these three great principles: a capacity for finding out the truth and distinguishing it from, error, a capacity for perceiving goodness and knowing it from evil, and a capacity for discriminating between what is ugly and what is fair. By virtue of the first of these powers, man seeking knowledge has become the philosopher and scientist; by virtue of the second, he has evolved religions and laws, and social order and advancement; while by virtue of the third he has become an artist. Yet we must be careful not to suppose that either one of these powers ever comes alone into full play or fruition; for man has not three separate natures, but one nature with three different phases. When, therefore, man finds expression for his complete personality in the fine arts, you may always expect to find there, not only creations of beauty, but monuments of wisdom and religion as well. Art can no more exist without having a moral bearing, than a body can exist without a soul. Its influence may be for good or for bad, but it is inevitable and it is unmistakable. In the same way no art can exist without an underlying philosophy, any more than man can exist without a mind. The philosophy may be trivial or profound, but it is always present and appreciable.

Art, you see, is enlisted beyond escape, both in the service of science and in the service of religion. Great art appears wherever the heart of man has been able to manifest itself in a perfectly beautiful guise, informed by thoughts of radiant truth, and inspired by emotions of limitless goodness. Any piece of art which does not fulfil its obligations to truth and goodness, as well as to beauty, is necessarily faulty and incomplete.

At first thought perhaps you might not be quite ready to admit such a canon of criticism as this; for truth is the object of all science, and goodness is the object of all morality, and some persons have been accustomed to say that art has nothing whatever to do either with morality or science, but exists for its own sake alone, for the increase and perpetuation of pleasure. But art cannot give us complete pleasure if it only appeals to our senses, and leaves unsatisfied our natural curiosity and wonder,—our need for understanding and our need for loving. That is to say, our reason and our emotion must always be appealed to, as well as our sense of beauty.

For instance, I may be entranced by the beautiful diction and cadence of a poem, whose conception of life and the universe may be patently false and puerile; from which point of view it could not please me at all, but must disgust me. Or, showing a just estimate of life, it might be true to philosophy and science, and yet celebrate some mean or base or ignoble or cruel incident in a way that would be revolting to my spirit. While it satisfied my sense of lyric beauty, it might fail utterly to satisfy my sense of right or my desire for truth. To be worth while, the fine arts must satisfy the mind with its insatiable curiosity, and the soul with its love of justice, quite as thoroughly as they slake the needs of the senses.

To my mind the great preeminence of Browning as a poet does not rest on any profound philosophy to be found in his work, nor in his superior craftsmanship, nor yet in his generous uplifting impulse and the way with which he arouses our feelings, but rather on the fact that he possessed all these three requirements of a poet in an equally marked degree. The work of Poe or of William Morris, on the other hand, does not exhibit this fine balance of strength, intellectuality, and passion. On its sensuous side, it is wonderfully beautiful; and yet it is not wholly satisfying, since it fails to give us enough to think about. Its mentality is too slight. Neither of these poets, to judge from their poetry alone, had any large and firm grasp of the thought of the world, such as Browning possessed, and that is why the wizardry of Poe and the luring charm of Morris are not more effective. An artist must be also a thinker and a prophet, if his creations are to have the breath of life. And again poetry may easily fail by being over-laden with this same requisite of mentality. It may have more thought than it can carry. Browning himself, in several of his later books, like the "Inn Album," quite loses the poetic poise of his powers, and almost ceases to be a poet in his desire to be a philosopher.

All this is so fundamentally important that we cannot have it too clearly in mind. It is the one great central truth, which must illumine all criticism, and help our understanding of life, as well as of art.

When we say, however, that it is the business of art to give pleasure in all three of these possible ways, of course we must not suppose that the arts do not differ one from another in their ability to meet such demand. The art of music cannot satisfy my reason as completely as the art of poetry, for example, because it cannot transmit a logical statement of fact. It may please my senses more readily than poetry can; it may arouse my emotions profoundly; but it cannot appeal to my mind in the way that poetry does. On the other hand, poetry itself is less strictly rational than prose literature; it does not attempt to satisfy our curiosity as completely as prose does, though it pleases the æsthetic sense more. There need be no question of one art being greater or less than another; a sense of art equality is born of recognizing the interesting ways in which they vary, and of realizing that each has only a different proportion and arrangement of the three requirements which are necessary to them all.

To speak quite simply, then, art is concerned first of all in the creation of beauty. At the same time it is closely related to science on one side and religion on the other. But how? I suppose we may say (to speak again quite roughly) that science is all we know about things, and religion is all we feel about them. Naturally, therefore, every artistic conception to which we give expression will betray something both of our philosophy and of our morality. It cannot be otherwise. In the case of literature the human spirit is finding expression for itself through the medium of human speech; and speech is the most exact means we have for conveying definite thought and narrating facts. So that every literature contains a great body of work which is almost pure science. In De Quincey's useful phrase, "There is a literature of knowledge and a literature of power." Euclid's *Geometry*, Newton's *Principia*, Darwin's *Origin of Species*, are works of science rather than of letters. They appeal solely to our reason, and do not attempt to please our sense of the beautiful by their literary structure and the arrangement of verbal sounds, nor to work upon our emotions in any way. Euclid does not care whether you like his forty-eighth proposition or not, so long as he can convince you that it is true. Neither does Darwin care whether his theory pleases you or not. He is only interested in getting at the truth. How that truth may affect our feelings is quite another matter. It is so, too, of theological and philosophic writers, like Spinoza and Kant; they are primarily scientists and not artists. But when you pass from these austere reasoners to a work like Plato's *Dialogues*, you perceive that two new elements have entered into the making of a book. Plato is not only interested in finding out the truth, and convincing you of its reasonableness; he wishes at the same time to make the truth seem pleasant and good; he tries to enlist your feelings on his side, and also to satisfy your sense of beauty with his form of words. He has added a religious value and an art value to the theme of pure philosophy. He has made his book a piece of literature.

And as literature is related to science on one hand, it is related to religion on the other. A book of meditation or of hymns may be extremely devout in sentiment, without possessing any value as literature. Because, very often it takes a certain set of ideas for granted, without caring very much whether they are the largest and truest ideas or not; and also because it makes no effort to be fine and distinguished in its diction. It may be entirely worthy in the fervour of its sentiment, and yet be quite unworthy in an artistic way. With great religious books this is not so. Works like the Psalms, or passages of Isaiah, or the poetry of Job, or Tennyson's "Crossing the Bar," are, first of all, religious in their intention; they are meant to play upon our emotional nature; but they do not stop there; they are cast in a form of words so perfect and fresh that it arrests us at once, and satisfies our love of beauty. At the same time they accord with the most profound and fundamental ideas about life and nature that humanity has been capable of. They satisfy our mind and our æsthetic sense, as well as our spiritual need. It is because of this threefold completeness, that we class them as pieces of literature, and not merely as records of religious enthusiasm. Depth of religious feeling alone would not have been sufficient to make them literature, any more than clear thinking and accurate reason alone could have made Plato's book a piece of literature.

We must remember, too, how vapid the artistic quality is, when it exists by itself without adequate intelligence and underlying purpose. Think how much of modern art is characterized by nothing but form, how devoid it is of ideas, how lacking in anything like passionate enthusiasm. I believe this is due to some extent to our failure to realize that the three components of which I have been speaking are absolutely requisite in all art. We forget that there is laid upon art any obligation except to be beautiful; we forget that it must embody the truest thought man has been able to reach, and enshrine the noblest impulses he has entertained. This is not so much a duty for art to undertake as an inescapable destiny and natural function.

It is a sad day for a people when their art becomes divorced from the current of their life, when it comes to be looked on as something precious but unimportant, having nothing at all to do with their social structure, their education, their political ideals, their faith, or their daily vocations. But I fear that we ourselves are living in just such a time. Fine arts may be patronized even liberally, but you could not say that they have any hold on us as a people; we have no wide feeling for them, no profound conviction of their importance.

There may be many reasons for this, and it is a question with which we are not directly concerned here. One reason there is, however, it seems to me, which is too important not to be referred to. The fine arts are an outgrowth and finer development of the industrial arts. One would expect them to flourish only in a nation where the industrial arts flourish; only in such a nation would the great body of the people be infused with the popular love of beauty, and the feeling for art, which could create a stimulating, artistic atmosphere in which great artists could be born and nourished. So much will be readily admitted. Now, under modern industrial and commercial conditions, the industrial arts are dead; they have been killed by the exigencies of our business processes. The industrial artist has become the factory hand. To produce anything worthwhile, either in the fine or the industrial arts, it is necessary that the worker should not be hurried, and should have some freedom to do his work in his own way, according to his own fancy and enjoyment. The modern workman, on the contrary, is a slave to his conditions; he can only earn his bread by working with a maximum of speed and a minimum of conscientiousness. He can have neither pleasure nor pride in his work; and consequently that work can have no artistic value whatever. The result is, that not only have we almost no industrial arts, properly speaking, but the modern workman is losing all natural taste and love of beauty through being denied all exercise of that faculty. If you allow me to learn the art of a book-binder, or a potter, or a rug-maker, and to follow it for myself as best I can, my perception and love of what is beautiful will grow with my growing skill. But if you put me to work in a modern factory, where such things, or rather where hideous imitations of those things, are produced, I should not be able to exercise my creative talent at all, and whatever love of beauty I may have had will perish for lack of use. Thus it happens that the average man today has so little appreciation of beauty, so little instinctive taste, and art and letters occupy so small a place in our regard. Before we can reinstate them in that position of honour which they have always held, hitherto, among civilized nations, we shall have to find some solution for our industrial difficulties.

It may seem, at a superficial glance, that the arts are all very well as a pastime, for the enjoyment of the few, but can have no imperative call for busy men and women in active modern life. And if we should be told that, as a nation, we have no widespread love of beauty, no popular taste in artistic matters, we would not take the accusation very much to heart. We should probably admit it, and turn with pride to point to our wonderful material success, our achievements in the realm of trade and commerce, our unmatched prosperity and wealth. But that answer will not serve. You may lead me through the streets of our great cities, and fill my ears with stories of our uncounted millions of money, our unrivalled advance among the nations, but that will not divert my soul from horror at a state of society where municipal government is a venial farce, where there is little reverence for law, where mammon is a real God, and where every week there are instances of mob violence, as revolting as any that ever stained the history of the emperors of degenerate Rome. We may brag our loudest to each other and even to ourselves, but the soul is not deceived. She sits at the centre of being, judging honestly and severely our violences, our folly, and our crime. And when at last we come to our senses, and perceive to what a condition of shame we have fallen from our high estate as a freedom-loving people, we may be able to restore some of those ideals which we have sacrificed,—ideals of common honesty, of civic liberty, of simple unostentatious dignity, of social order, law, and security.

All this, of course, goes almost without saying. But the point I wish to make is, that this decay in moral standards goes hand in hand with our loss of taste. Our sense of beauty and our sense of goodness are so closely related that any injury to the one means an injury to the other. You cannot expect the nation which cares nothing at all for art to care very much for justice or righteousness. You cannot expect a man who does not care how hideous his surroundings are to care very fastidiously about his moral obligations. And we shall never reach that national position of true greatness, which many Americans have dreamed of; we shall lose entirely those personal traits of dignity, honour, and kindliness, which many old-fashioned Americans still retain, unless we recognize the vital need of moral standards and æsthetic ideals working together hand in hand, and set ourselves to secure them.

And if you ask me why America is producing for the most part only that which is mediocre in art and literature, I am forced to reply, that it is because the average man among us has so little respect for moral ideals. In a restless age we may experiment with all kinds of reform, but no permanent scheme of social betterment can dispense with personal obligation and integrity. It all comes back to the man at last. We don't need socialism, or imperialism, or free trade, or public ownership of monopolies, or state control of trusts, so much as we need honest men,—men in public life and private enterprise who have some standard of conduct higher than insatiable self-interest.

Such ideals of conduct, in the widest sense, it is the aim of art to supply, and education to inculcate. And education, like art, has its threefold object. It has to set itself not only to train our minds in a desire for the truth, but at the same time to train our spirit to love only what is good, and our bodies to take pleasure only in what is beautiful and wholesome; and the work of education, like that of art, must, while proceeding in any one of these directions, be intimately related with the workings of the other two. Emerson's wise phrase is profoundly applicable here:

> All are needed by each one,
> Nothing is fair or good alone.

An education or an art which does not quicken the conscience, and stimulate and refine all our senses and instincts, along with the growing reason, must still remain a faulty process at best.

Let me ask all who are engaged in the great occupation of teaching, and in the delightful art of writing, to consider whether this is not so. I am sure we cannot lay too much stress on this philosophic conception of man in the three aspects of his nature. I believe it is a helpful solvent of many difficulties in education, in art, in life, in social and political aims. I believe that without it all of our endeavours for advancement in civilization will be sadly hampered and retarded, if not frustrated altogether, for the simple reason that art and civilization and social order exist for man; and they must, therefore, be adapted to the three differing phases of his requirement. While his intellectual needs and capacities must be trained and provided for; his great emotional and spiritual need and powers must be no less adequately recognized and exercised, and his sensitive physical instincts wisely guided and developed.

With this notion in mind, we may turn for a few minutes to consider what tasks literature must set itself, and what it may be expected to do for a people. In the first place, it is the business of literature, as of all the arts, to create an illusion, to project upon the imagination a mimic world, true to life, as, we say, and at the same time more goodly and fair than the actual one we know. For unless the world of art be in some way more delightful than the world of our every-day experience, why should we ever visit it? We turn for sympathy to art, for recreation and refreshment, for solace and inspiration. We ask to find in it, ready to hand, these helpful and pleasant qualities which are so hard to find in real life. And the art which does not give them to us is disappointing, however clever it may be. It is this necessity for being beautiful, this necessity for providing an immediate pleasure, that makes pure realism unsatisfying in art. Realism is necessary, but not sufficient.

For instance, if you bring me a photograph of a beautiful elm-shaded street in an old New England town, it fills my eye instantly with a delightful scene. But by and by something in it begins to offend me, and I see that the telegraph-pole is too obtrusive, and spoils the composition and balance of the picture. The photograph loses its value as a pleasure-giving piece of realism. Now a painter in reproducing the same scene would probably have left out the telegraph-pole. That is the difference. And that is why photography, as usually practised, is not one of the fine arts. It is said by those who contend for realism, for the photographic in literature, that art must be true to nature, and so it must, to a certain extent; but there are other things beside the physical fact to which it must be true. Your photograph was true to nature, but it was not true to my memory of the scene. The painter's reproduction was truer to that; he preserved for me the delightful impression that I carried away on that wonderful June morning, when I visited the spot. For me his picture is more accurate than the photograph. When I was there, I probably did not see the telegraph-pole at all. It is therefore right that literature and art should attempt something more than the exact reproduction of things as they are, and should give us the vision, not the view, of a city more charming and a country more delectable to dwell in than any our feet have ever trod, and should people its world with characters varied and fascinating as in real life, but even more satisfying than any we have ever known.

There is another reason why art must be more than photographic; as time goes by and the earth grows old, man himself develops, however slowly, in nobleness and understanding. His life becomes different from what it was. He gradually brings it into conformity with certain ideals and aspirations which have occurred to him. These new ideals and aspirations have always made their first appearance in art and literature before they were realized in actual life. Imagination is our lamp upon the difficult path of progress. So that even in its outward aspect, art must differ from nature. The world is by no means perfect, but it is always tending toward perfection, and it is our business to help that tendency. As long as we are satisfied with the photograph, we are content to have the telegraph-pole. And we shall continue to be satisfied with them both until the artist comes and shows us the blemish. As soon as we perceive the fault, we begin to want the telegraph-pole removed. This is what a clever writer meant when he said that art does not follow nature, but nature follows art. We must make our lives more and more beautiful, simply because, by so doing, we make ourselves more healthy and happy. To this end, art must supply us with standards, and keep us constantly reminded of what perfection is, so that living much in the influence of good art, ugliness may become less and less possible.

I lay so much stress on this point because we have somewhat lost the conviction that literature and art must be more beautiful than life. We readily admit that they must be sincere servants of truth, and exemplars of noble sentiment, but there is an idea abroad, that, in its form and substance, art need only copy nature. This, I believe, is what our grandfathers might have called a pestilent heresy.

If art and literature are devoted to the service of beauty, no less are they dedicated to the service of beauty, truth and goodness. In the phrase which Arnold used to quote, it is their business to make reason and the will of God prevail. So that while literature must fulfil the obligations laid upon it to be delightful, to charm and entertain us with perennial pleasure, quite as scrupulously must it meet our demands for knowledge and satisfy our spiritual needs. To meet the first of these demands, of course it is not necessary for literature to treat of scientific subjects; it must, however, be enlightened by the soundest philosophy at its command, and informed with all the knowledge of its time. It may not deal directly with the thought of its age, but it must never be at variance with the truth. There can be no quarrel between science and art, for art sooner or later makes use of all knowledge, all discoveries, all new ideas. It is the business of art to assimilate new knowledge, and make it a power; for knowledge is not a power, so long as it remains mere knowledge, nor until it passes from the mind into the domain of the will.

In a scientific age like our own, when the limits of knowledge are being extended so rapidly, prose is a much more acceptable medium of expression than poetry, because it can keep nearer to science than poetry can; though poetry, in the long run, has quite as much need of accurate and wide information as prose has.

It is only that they make different use of the same material. Prose serves to bring us definite reports of science, it appeals to our reason, our curiosity. But poetry has another motive as well; it wishes to emphasize its subject so that we cannot only know it more clearly, but feel about it more deeply. Of course prose has this aim in view also, though to a less extent, and it invades the dominion of poetry whenever this aim becomes paramount. So that in literature we must never attempt to separate prose from poetry, too dogmatically.

The attempt which literature makes to deepen our feeling about a subject is the spiritual purpose of art. And this spiritual or moral influence is always present in all literature, in some degree and condition, whether apparent or not. Art has its religious value, not because it deals directly with religious themes, but because it plays upon our moral nature and influences our emotions. How intrinsically incumbent it is upon art, therefore, to stimulate our generous and kindly feelings, rather than our cruel or violent or selfish impulses.

It may often be necessary for art and literature to deal with human crime and depravity and moral obliquity, but it must never dwell upon them excessively nor unnecessarily, nor ever make them seem to prevail. For evil does not rule the world; however powerful it may seem at moments, in the long run it is overcome by good. There is a tendency in modern letters to deal with repulsive themes, and depict for us the frailty and sorry shortcomings of human nature, and to do this with an almost scientific emphasis. Some people praise this sort of thing, as being true to life; while others call it immoral, because it touches upon such subjects at all. A juster view of the matter may perhaps lead us to a different opinion. Since it is the prime duty of art to make us happy, to give us encouragement and joy, to urge and support our spirits, to ennoble and enrich our lives, surely the one way in which art can be most immoral is by leaving us depressed and sad, and uncertain of the final issue between sorrow and gladness.

I have not said much about the technic of poetry, because I wished first to indicate, if I could, a scope and destiny for poetic art more significant than we are accustomed to grant it. If we first assure ourselves of the vital importance of art to a nation, if we set ourselves resolutely to change the tenor of public sentiment in regard to it, if we turn from the absorbing and ridiculous worship of superfluous possessions, and devote ourselves generously to the cause of beauty and kindliness, the specific development of poetry may safely be left to take care of itself.

The Poet in the Commonwealth

Reprinted from *The Poetry of Life*, Boston: L.C. Page & Co., 1905, 63–77.

A discussion was started not long ago by a college professor in Chicago who declared that a man who works with his hands cannot be a poet. It is one of those definite statements that sound conclusive and have enough truth in them to arouse discussion. In one way it is true, and in another way it is exactly the reverse of the truth.

Under our present social system, or rather our antisocial system, a man who works with his hands cannot be a poet, simply because he can scarcely be a man. He cannot be his own master, and he cannot command that amount of freedom which every creator of the beautiful needs. The creation of beauty requires first of all that the artist shall have freedom to do his own work in his own way. But the modern man who works with his hands is a slave to our mercantile system. In that complex and highly organized machine called modern civilization, it is not possible for any working man to remain free.

On the other hand, abstractly speaking, it is much nearer the truth to say that a man who does not work with his hands cannot be a poet.

What do you understand by a poet? What is his office and business in life? What part does he play in the world? First, and speaking most roughly, he is a person who has something important to say about life, and has the special gift of saying it supremely well. He must be one, I think we will all admit, who has thought profoundly about existence. And yet that is not enough to make him a poet, for that is the accomplishment of philosopher or scientist. He must also feel deeply and strongly about life. And yet that is not enough to make him a poet, either, for many of us feel much more deeply and sincerely than we can say. No, he must not only be able to speak from a great fund of thought and knowledge and from a great fund of sympathy and emotion; he must be able to speak with the wonderful power of charm as well.

The one quality which makes him a poet is his faculty of expression, of course; for we can all be poets of silence. This particular gift or talent, which determines whether a man shall express himself in words or in sound or in colours, who can say by what it is in its turn determined? To say that this man is a poet, and that one a painter, is no more than to say that one has gray eyes and the other black. But the difference in character, that is another matter; and to be a poet or a painter implies being a man. The man behind the faculty, that is the important thing.

The poet must delight our senses with the inevitable beauty of his cadences, his diction, his rhythms—with what is often called technique; he must enlist our sympathy through his own strong and generous emotional nature; he must convince our minds by his own reasonableness. He appeals to our sense of beauty, but not to that sense alone; he appeals to our sense of goodness, but not to that sense alone; he appeals to our sense of truth, but not to that sense alone. His appeal is to all three, and to all three equally.

The gift of technique, with the poet as with all artists, is largely a matter of endowment. But what he has to say about life will depend on how profoundly he has thought about it, and how keenly he feels about it. And unless a man has shared in our common life in the world, I cannot see how his opinions can have any great value, or his emotional preferences any great significance. But our common life in the world implies a certain amount of work with the hands, so that the conclusion seems inevitable, "A man who does no work with his hands cannot be a poet."

The argument is so simple. How can I talk to you with any hope of a common understanding, when I only know the facts at second hand, while you have actually experienced them, and when I have no caring about them one way or the other, while to you they are matters of life and death? The idea that a poet can ever be a mere bystander, an onlooker at life, seems to me too palpably impossible to need refutation. And I cannot believe that any great prophet or poet ever trod the earth who did not know the pinch of life at first hand, its actual bleak necessity, its terrible pathos and tremendous joy, its wonderful yet elusive significance. Nor do I believe that one for whom all the necessities and comforts and luxuries of life have been gratuitously provided, from the cradle to the grave, ever can know these things.

In moments of insight, in hours of contemplation, doubtless the poet is a bystander, as we all may be at times. But he cannot be that exclusively.

A man who never halts to look upon life in questioning wonder, is no worse fitted to be an artist than one who spends his whole time in speculation and dreaming. The one has no knowledge save experience, the other no experience save in theory.

If a man has never driven a nail in his life, nor built a fire, nor turned a furrow, nor picked a barrel of apples, nor fetched home the cows, nor pulled an oar, nor reefed a sail, nor saddled a horse, nor carried home a bundle of groceries from town, nor weeded the garden, nor been lost in the woods, nor nursed a friend, nor barked his shin, nor been thankful for a free lunch, do you think it is likely he will have anything to say to you and me that will be worth listening to? I don't.

I should as soon expect a child to set a broken bone, or tunnel a mountain, or navigate a ship. Yet this is not to disparage the heavenly wisdom of inspiration, nor the strange inexplicable authority of conviction.

The compelling necessity for exertion lies upon all created things. And we ourselves can only achieve life and realize our individual existence by meeting that necessity hand to hand and overcoming it. In overcoming it we become what we are, whether we be men or whether we be chipmunks. The moment we cease to overcome and rest inactively on what we have accomplished, that moment we begin to perish.

There is only one way to be a poet, by sweat and heartbreak and bitter weariness of brain. And even then you won't be a poet, you will only be a man, unless it has pleased the powers to bestow on you the grace of words. But when a man has some faculty of expression, begotten in him by some happy circumstance, and then learns the taste of life and the touch of it at first hand, he will have some feeling about it and some opinion on it worth heeding, and poetry will come out of him as naturally as milk comes out of a coconut.

The genius of the artist secretes beauty by some natural process, as inevitably as a bee secretes honey, and gives it forth in good time for the mystification and enjoyment of the world. The process itself is hidden even from the intelligence that carries it on, but the carrying on of the process is a continual satisfaction. The creative instinct of the artist, uneasy with the possession of his unvented ideal, is akin to the procreative instinct of the world, which cannot rest until it has attempted to realize itself in ever fresher, more lovely, and more adequate forms.

There is another reason why the poet cannot be exempt from the common lot. Affluence is not good for artists for this reason; affluence is not good for anybody—perfect affluence, I mean, the amount of affluence which relieves one permanently from all need of endeavour. Great wealth, or even a little wealth, may make people sleek and self-satisfied and fat-minded, but it cannot of itself make them either beautiful or loving, nor give them openness of mind. And since artists are always people with a large and vivid capacity for sensuous enjoyment, wealth is more dangerous to them than to others. It does not hurt a miner, or a horse-thief, or a peddler to grow rich, for in nine cases out of ten he does not know how to enjoy his money when he has made it; he can only go on making more and more, and growing more desperate every day at his own incapacity, until finally he begins to give it away in millions in sheer weariness of spirit. But in nine cases out of ten, great prosperity will spoil a good artist; he begins to be so engrossed in enjoyment, and he has such a great appreciation of the easy beauty of life, that he ceases from the strenuous work of creation.

But, after all, all this is only one side of the question, and the whole argument I have made only proves that the poet, and every other artist, in fact, ought to be and must be a normal man—not an average man, but a normal man, with all the best powers and capacities of manhood in him. He must be capable of thought, capable of passion, capable of manual labour. No one lacking in these three essentials, or lacking in any one of them, can be called a normal man; nor can he have anything valuable and great to say to us about life.

On the other hand, however, modern life is very complex (and, of course, the more complex it is the more beautiful it may be made), and we all have to specialize a good deal, and it is not possible for one man to do more than one thing superlatively well. If you would be a great financier, a great mechanic, a great statesman, or a great scientist, or a great engineer, or a great cook, you must devote your life to it, you must give your mind to it, and your love and your industry. You may learn to do many things so well that the doing of them serves to enlighten and enrich your specialty; but the main issue, the focusing-point and flower of all your effort and ability, must be some one thing that you love most, know most, and do best.

Now art (and poetry is one of the most difficult of the fine arts) is just such an occupation as these. You cannot always compose a sonnet over your evening cigar. Art is not an idle amusement, it is a natural phenomenon, as significant as war, as beautiful as the northern lights, and as useful as electricity. Of all forms of human activity it is the most exacting, as it is perhaps the most delightful. And the demand which creative output makes on all the energies is just as great and just as exhausting as that made by any other worthy occupation worthily followed. If poetry were a purely artificial pastime, fit only to engage the minds of college youths and schoolgirls, certainly it would not be worth our serious discussion. But if it is what history declares it to be, the voice of revelation, the finest utterance of human wisdom, the basis of religion, and the solace of sorrowing mortals, if it teaches us how to live, how to be happy, how to love the right and appreciate the beautiful and perceive the true, if it illumines the dark problems of existence, and heartens us upon the difficult path to perfection, then surely we may well consider how best to foster it and preserve it, and make its influence prevail in the commonwealth.

If poetry, therefore, is such a serious business, and worth the attention of strong men, it cannot be cultivated as a mere avocation. It will engage all the energies of any one who follows it. So that, while it seems to me untrue to say that a man who works with his hands cannot be a poet, and while I think it nearer the truth to say that a man who does no work with his hands cannot be a poet, I think it nearest the truth (at the beginning of the twentieth century) to say that a man who earns his living with his hands cannot be a poet. He will not have time. He will not have leisure for the requisite learning and culture; he will not be able to know even the rudiments of science and philosophy and social economics; he will not have leisure to know the pleasures of æsthetic enjoyment; he cannot be a lover of nature, nor a lover of books, nor a lover of many things lovely.

Why? Because under existing social and industrial conditions he cannot be the master of his own time. And while the normal man must have enough physical work to keep him in perfect health, the average man has enough to ruin his health and sicken his soul. The whole question of art rests on the social and industrial problems. The fine arts are closely related to the industrial arts. And at present we can have no widespread national interest in the fine arts, because we have no national industrial arts. The industrial arts of a people, like the fine arts, can only be carried on by men who are free and honest and intelligent, and therefore happy. For it is quite true, as William Morris said, that art is the expression of man's pleasure in his work. But the men who engage in our industries today cannot have any pleasure in their work. For our industrial arts—or, rather, our industries and manufactures which ought to be industrial arts—are carried on by two classes of people, the workmen and the capitalists. And all workmen, under modern industrial conditions, are the slaves of their employers; while capitalists, however generous their impulses, are of necessity slave-owners. Of course the workmen do not know that they are slaves, and the capitalists do not know they are slave-owners. But that does not make the matter any better—it only plunges both in a sea of confusion, as the blind might stumble in fighting with the blind. The workman thinks he is free, because if he does not like one owner he can sell himself to another. And the capitalist thinks he is honest because he plays fairly according to the rules of the game. But the principles of the game are fundamentally rotten, since shrewdness of mind does not make right any more than might of muscle does.

The first question, however, is not whether a poet should live by the work of his hands, but whether he should live at all. And, however much we may obscure and injure the splendid significance of poetry with our incessant and ineffectual sophistries of a day, I must believe that the world's need for great and fearless poetry is perpetual, and that without its illuminating aid we shall never come near to accomplishing our destiny.

The Poet in Modern Life

Reprinted from *The Poetry of Life*, Boston: L.C. Page & Co., 1905, 78–104.

There is such incongruity between our traditional idea of the poet and our daily experience of modern life that we can hardly reconcile the two; and our conception of the poet in modern life is pretty sure, for that reason, to be either comic or tragic. He will seem to us anything but commonplace, and we cannot take him as a matter of course. The typical poet is out of date; and the poet of the times is slow to arrive, since the time itself is scarcely ripe for his appearance. If we are to think justly of the poet in modern life, however, we must be careful not to overvalue his office on the one hand, nor on the other to depreciate the worth and significance of the age. And the greater our love of poetry, our sympathy with ideals, our feeling for beauty, the more shall we be in danger of undervaluing our own day when these things are not paramount in men's minds. Let us try to look at the question quite fairly, neither embittered by the facts nor led astray by impossible fancies.

The poet, if we attempt to form a composite photograph of him from impressions gathered here and there through the pages of history, is for the most part a serious figure, nearly always aloof from the affairs of earth, somewhat shy of life and its activities, and dealing more in dreams than in realities. But to be more precise, as we think of the long list of poets whose names still survive, whose words still are alive in our ears, we shall find them dividing themselves mainly into two groups, the religious poets and the dramatic poets, those who were inspired by the moral temper of their time, and those who devoted themselves to the entertainment of their fellows. The poet is both prophet and entertainer, both priest and artist. He stands for ever the interpreter of nature to men; that is his sacerdotal office. He is also the revealer of men to themselves; that is his business as a dramatic artist.

David, Isaiah, Job, Dante, Milton, Shelley, Wordsworth, Emerson,—
these are types of the poet as prophet or priest of nature. They "saw life
steadily and saw it whole," but in their heart there burned for ever a
passion for righteousness never to be satisfied by things as they are.
They were for ever stirred by a divine unrest; the fever of God throbbed
in their veins; they could never suffer fools gladly, nor look with
equanimity upon the sorry spectacle of human weakness. They were
lean men and laughed little. Possessed continually by a consuming love
of the beautiful, the true, and the good, and beholding at the same time
how life seems to be inseparable from ugliness and evil, they could
never attain the ruddy and placid contentment of the born comedian.
The pageant of human endeavour, the interplay of human character, so
engrossing to many, was to them only the surface and appearance of
the world. They were forever haunted by a sense of the presence behind
the mask, the spirit behind the semblance. To their endless unhappi-
ness, one must believe, they were driven forward by an insuperable
curiosity for the truth about life, an unassuageable love of the beauty of
earth, and above all by a pure and impossible desire to make actual those
ideal conditions of conduct and circumstance which never yet have been
realized by man, nor will ever leave him at peace in mediocrity.

As long as the stars remain and the soul of man fleets with the breath
of his body, so long must he suffer this bitter divergence between "I
would" and "I can." To the great poets of nature this realization has
come as an overwhelming influence, a burden of knowledge almost
insupportable. They could hardly be other than grave, impressive,
unostentatious, simple, single of purpose, strenuous in endeavour, and
modest from the very abundance of their wisdom. So great must have
been their ideality, so keen their inward vision, it is little wonder if at
times they failed in joyousness and permitted a minor strain to sound
through their messages of encouragement to men. Thus it is that not all
poets have been prophets of gladness, but sorrow and uncertainty had
their messengers, too. For the life of man, which is so large a part of
the poetry of earth, must be given complete expression in beautiful
words; and the dominant note of triumphant joy must have its under-
tone of grievous doubt. Through the glad supreme assurance of large
faith and unconquerable achievement, the brokenhearted wistfulness
of failure must be heard; else were our poetry imperfect, and half of
humanity left without a voice. Moreover, those deep consolations and
counsels which it is the business of art and poetry to furnish, can

scarcely be rendered effectively without the profoundest sympathy with suffering. The royal psalmist, on whom so many thousands have leaned for spiritual support, must have tasted the bitter waters of affliction, to be able to reach the hearts of men so surely.

Now, such a conception of the poet in his capacity as interpreter of nature and the deeper moods of the mind, is evidently not the broadest one. When we think of Homer and Virgil and Chaucer and Shakespeare, and the writers of the Greek Anthology, we think of the poet in a very different character. He is no longer the seer labouring under the stress of an almost Orphic inspiration; he is the open-eyed, glad-hearted beholder and recorder of life as he sees it. The God has breathed upon him, indeed, giving him greater insight into the foibles of his fellows than most men enjoy, and yet has not wholly rapt him out of himself. He is human, comfortable, friendly, merry, and content, a lover of wine and leisure and laughter. He is a lover of beauty, indeed, but his keen satisfaction in the loveliness of nature is not marred by the ever present sense of incompleteness, which must always haunt the preeminent poet of nature. The one finds the answer to his questions in a shrewd analysis of human motives and purposes. To the questions of the other, hearkening perpetually for some hinted solution of the riddle of existence, there is no answer possible. Small wonder, then, that the type of the first should be the jovial Horace or the genial Chaucer, while the type of the second blends something of the austerity of Dante with the zeal of David.

Now human life, when all is said, is not so very different in ancient and modern days. Barbarism or civilization, city or wilderness, the conditions vary, but the prime facts of life remain, and it is with these that the poet deals.

In modern life, as in that of old time, there are the matters of love and war, friendship and hatred, joy in the senses, sorrow, bereavement, loneliness, faith, disquietude, and death; the elemental facts from which the fabric of the universe is built, and the elemental passions and cravings with which we confront them. The poetry of the Old Testament, of Homer, or of Virgil, does not seem antiquated, except in occasional detail of local colour. The lament of David for Absalom, the mighty verses of many chapters of Job and Isaiah, the pathetic parting of Hector and Andromache, Virgil's description of the bees or the shadows on the mountainside, are as fresh as if they had been written yesterday.

This perennial vigour, this power to survive the change of fashion and the flight of years, is a test of poetry which most of our modern verse would be pitifully unable to fulfil, and which the best of it will still have to face. All that is whimsical, fantastic, grotesque, of purely contemporary value, will gradually be forgotten and cut away, while a few splendid lyrics, a few noble passages, we may imagine, will be jealously preserved and handed on as part of our bequest to the future. Men will not care to perpetuate what is essentially modern in our work, but rather what is essentially human, essentially poetic, essentially beautiful. In the long run only the fair and noble survives, whether in art or life, for the reheartening and regenerating of the earth. So it happens that all great literature that has come down to us is infused with a simple dignity of spirit, a majestic and pure sincerity, which seem for the time quite beyond the reach of our own accomplishment. Yet we may be sure our ambitious attempts, with all their cleverness, all their novelty, all their exact faithfulness to nature, will be wanting in vitality, in permanent interest, if we do not succeed in giving them just these spiritual qualities.

The spirit of the world is eager but inexorable, always in need of new thought, new beauty, new funds of emotion, and yet ruthlessly discarding everything which does not help it forward on the long, arduous progress of the centuries. The ages to come will care no more for our popular airs and songs and paintings than we care for those of vanished civilizations. But whenever the human spirit, under a stress of intense feeling, and in the face of the inescapable difficulty or bitterness or joy of life, rises to impassioned utterance, that utterance, however slight, is likely to be worth saving. This rule is unalterable, and obtains for modern poetry as for the most ancient. No art can outlive its own time which does not rise above the commonplace; and any art which rises sufficiently far above the average of contemporary achievement is sure to be treasured.

This, however, is only one way of looking at the matter. There is much very excellent art and poetry produced by every people, which is not great, and which has fulfilled its function when it has been remembered for a year or two, or for a generation or two, to give pleasure and encouragement to thousands to whom any more perfect or profound work would not appeal at all. No work is to be condemned simply because it is not of the first rank. Even if we have no great artists, it is good to have an interest in art, to have a number of men giving their energy to keep alive a great tradition, until a more favourable season. And one demands of them only a modest sincerity.

It is not my aim in the present paper to attempt any inquiry into the purposes of poetry. But in considering the relation of the poet to modern life, one necessarily takes for granted certain requirements of the poetic art, consciously or not. The business of poetry among the fine arts of expression, as it appears to me, is threefold. It must offer us some delightful counterfeit likeness of life for our entertainment; it must satisfy our intellectual need for truth; and finally it must supply us with spiritual reinforcement and consolation. We look to the fine arts in general to give us a refined pleasure of the senses, to answer the questions of our restless curiosity, and to intensify and ennoble our emotional life. We demand all these things of poetry. We ask that it shall have captivating beauty of form, that it shall be consistent with the most advanced discoveries of modern thought and modern science, and that it shall supply us with adequate standards and tests of conduct.

We must ask modern poetry, therefore, what it has to say on every topic of prime importance which bears upon life. We must expect it to embody for us all the new and wonderful revelations of modern science, discarding those old conceptions of the universe, however time-honoured and picturesque, which recent knowledge has proved erroneous. It is not easy for poetry to do this all at once, yet do it it must, if the restless mind of man is to be satisfied. It is only a poet of exceptional power who can see the poetry in modern life, its inventions, its discoveries, its ceaseless and venturesome activities, and give that poetic aspect adequate expression in words. The poet, particularly the modern poet, must have the unprejudiced eye and the exuberant spirits of a child, or he will not see the world for himself, and love it as it should be loved. Unless he sees clearly, loves intensely, and reasons profoundly, his poems can take no lasting hold upon us, however ornate or daring they may be.

To produce the best results in poetry, or in any art, then, the artist must be endowed with the alert, observing eye, the questing, unswervable mind, and a temperament at once ardent, kindly, and above satiety or corruption. He must love his age and understand it, in order to represent it justly or convert it to his way. This he can hardly do, if he feels himself out of sympathy with its ideals and pursuits. On the other hand, the actual world of things as they are can never seem quite adequate to the idealist. There is no man so uninspired as to be contented all the time. There will come to him hours of divine dissatisfaction, when nothing short of perfection will seem sufficient. Out of the wistfulness and disquiet of such moments the creative impulse may arise with its passionate longing for beauty, and give vent to that longing in imperishable forms of art; and these creations in colours, in sounds, in magical words, remain to convict the actual world of its shortcomings, and stimulate it to fairer endeavour.

Having in mind the opportunity always presented to poetry, what shall we say of its condition and scope today? What of the poet in modern life? Is it a time likely to be favourable for the production of great poetry? And have we any need of the poet with his visions? Let us admit, what seems to be the truth, that there probably never was a time when poetry was held in less esteem than at present. Why is this? We have wealth, we have leisure, we have great prosperity, we have peace, we have widespread intelligence, we have freedom of thought and conscience. All these things, it has always been supposed, go to make. up a state of society in which the fine arts can flourish. Why do they not flourish here and now? Why have we no poets whose ability and influence are of national concern?

Because, with all our comforts, all our delightful luxuries, all our intellectual alertness, we are steadily losing our moral ideas, steadily suffering a spiritual deterioration. Anglo-Saxon civilization, to speak of no other, has become a humiliating and unscrupulous game. Our fathers and grandfathers cared for many ideals, for honour, for honesty, for patriotism, for culture, for high breeding, for nobility of character and unselfishness of purpose. We care for none of these things. They have gone out of fashion. We care only for wealth, and respect only those relentless and barbarous traits of character by which it is attained. That the ideal state must be established on material prosperity is quite true. But that we should permit ourselves to rest satisfied with such prosperity, and even become engrossed by it, is fatal. All that Western civilization has done in the past thousand years to make life more secure and pleasant and comfortable, has been done under the impulse of worthy ideals and humane inspirations. Now, having attained so complete a control of all the machinery of living, we seem in danger of losing what is best in life itself. Modern life, with its ambitions and triumphs, may seem a very comfortable and delightful period to be alive in, with its immense labour-saving facilities and its many diversions. One does not wonder that people give themselves so unsparingly to the securing of those diversions and luxuries. Yet, from another viewpoint, one cannot but be amazed at the short-sightedness of men which allows them to spend laborious lives in preparing to live. One cannot but recognize the shameless materialism of the age, its brutal selfishness, ignoble avarice, and utter disregard of all the generous ideals of the spirit. We have gained the whole world, but in doing it we have lost our own soul.

Here is the theme for the modern poet. He is to bring back inspiration to our unillumined days. He is to show us how to regain our spiritual manhood. He is to show us how to make use of our wealth, how to turn our immense resources to some reasonable account. He must not be a mere detractor of his time, peevish and sour. He must love his age, with all its immense folly and pitiable sordidness; and because of his love and sympathy he must desire to reestablish for it those moral ideals which it has lost.

The latter half of the past century had, in William Morris, a poet in many ways typical of the modern artist; he loved beauty and hated iniquity with so hearty a goodwill that he could see nothing good in his own age. He found nothing in it to love, and much to detest. That was his great misfortune. It drove him too far away from us. It made him little better than a medieval visitor among us. We may be keenly aware of the modern lack of ideals, but we must not forget the immeasurable service which modern science has rendered the world. In the sphere of knowledge, in the liberation of the human mind, no century has been more remarkable than the nineteenth. This is no small matter; it is a very great glory indeed. But it did not seem to be of any significance to William Morris. So far as his conception of the ideal life was concerned, we might as well have been living in the age of Pericles or Theocritus. A man who cares no more than that for the greatest achievement of his time, can hardly hope to address it with authority. His noblest ideals must always seem to it somewhat quixotic and ineffective.

Of the two great Victorians, Tennyson and Browning, the one brooded upon modern life, yet held himself aloof from participating in it; while the other loved it well and partook of its good things, without attempting to address himself directly to its needs. It was the figure of Tennyson which satisfied the popular notion of the poet in majestic calm, undistracted by temporal affairs. And to the mind of Tennyson all our spiritual difficulties and doubts appealed; all the movements of his time were reflected in his work. Browning, on the other hand, was beset by no such difficulties. His themes were uninfluenced by the tenor of his time. The problems of the human spirit which confronted him and engrossed his thought were elemental and eternal. Perhaps for that very reason he could throw himself into the enjoyment of life with such unquestioning zest.

Of the other two poets of the later Victorian period, Rossetti and Arnold, one was a recluse, and belonged to no age, while the other belonged so exclusively to his age that his time was never his own. Though Rossetti lived in our own day, there is no touch of modernity in his work. And Arnold, who comprehended his age so well, was denied the leisure which poetry demands.

The poet in modern life, if one may indulge the fancy for creating an almost impossible figure, would have some of the characteristics of all these men. He should have all of Matthew Arnold's insight into the trend of social events, all of the sympathy of William Morris, all of the large poise and self-possession of Tennyson. Most of all, perhaps, he would resemble Browning in philosophic power combined with a vigorous love of life.

Among poets more strictly contemporary than these, there are two of marked popularity and preeminent achievement, whose position entitles them to be considered more or less typical in modern life. Mr. Rudyard Kipling and Mr. James Whitcomb Riley are perhaps the only English-speaking poets of the day who can command a respectful hearing. Others may be listened to by a few hundred admirers, but these men, when they speak, address an attentive audience, commensurate with their brilliant powers. They are not only read, but beloved; and their influence is undoubted. And our ideal modern poet, when he makes his appearance, if he is to inherit some of the traits of the greater Victorians, should also possess some of the qualities of our distinguished friends who have written "The Seven Seas" and "Poems Here at Home." He should have Mr. Kipling's capacity for perceiving romance in the midst of the seemingly commonplace, and Mr. Riley's untarnished spirit of kindliness toward this great, foolish, distracted world. He would be tolerant and intensely human as they are, he would love his age, as they do, but, at the same time, if such a thing were not impossible, he would be horrified at the consuming greed which is the ruling passion in modern life, and he would be unconquerably possessed, by a love of justice and goodness nowhere paramount in the poetry of the day.

Meanwhile, our modern bard, of whom we expect so many impossible virtues, will not have a very encouraging progress toward recognition. If he have means at his disposal, he will have to face the many distractions which modern society can make so alluring; and if he have none, he will have to face the still less desirable fate of slow starvation. For no man can serve two mistresses, and the muse will not tolerate a rival near the throne. Her devotee must offer her a single-hearted service, and be content with a hod-carrier's wage. He will have a taste for good books, good pictures, good music, and all the charming refinements of the modern world, and yet he must be satisfied to enjoy them only in the homes of others. He will need all the fortitude and cheerfulness of the poor. Indeed, he will need more of those admirable qualities than the poor possess, since his appreciation of all that is beautiful and elegant in life is so much keener and more profound than theirs.

It may be contended that the finest achievements of art are born of discouragement and privation, but I must believe there is a limit to the beneficial influence of these severe conditions. A modicum of discouragement, a few years of privation, are probably wholesome and tonic to the artistic temper. A lifetime of them seems more than is necessary. And we are always in danger of having genius perish at our doors. However, perhaps it is better that one genius should perish than that a hundred mediocre sentimentalists should fill the world with babbling.

But we must not leave our subject with so discouraging and petulant a thought. In all that I have said I have had in mind only the more serious aspects of poetry; but it is for ever to be remembered that the fine arts were born from sheer exuberance of spirits, and can never flourish long in any dolorous mood. They are analogous to the play of animals and children; they indicate excess of happiness and effervescence of life; they mean always that some mortal had more joy than he could hold, and must find vent for it in expression. The fine arts are quite superfluous in any scheme of life which looks only to the maintenance of a bare subsistence; they could never spring from a condition of bleak, unmitigated slavery. There must be some elasticity of spirit, some freedom of mind and action, to support them. They must, in truth, echo the sorrows of the world; but far more must they embody its gladness, its strength, its loveliness, its confident and careless manhood.

If the modern artist cannot have a good time living, he had better go out of business; success in art is not for him. If the modern poet cannot find a way to take life gaily, resourcefully, unquerulously, he had better

quench his songs. He must be poor-spirited, indeed, if, in a time like
this, so full of generosity, of confidence, of elation, he cannot find
something to be happy about. He may have some difficulty in meeting
his obligations, but he should certainly be able to present a gentle and
cheerful manliness to the world, and manage to participate in its gaiety.
He must not be less a man than his struggling fellows, but more. He
must not be abashed or envious at any overabundance of worldly
splendour, but exhibit a keen enjoyment of beauty and elegance and
leisure, such as very few of our magnificent moderns can attain. He may
sometimes think life is difficult, and, poetry the most thankless of all
pursuits; but he must still be glad to be alive, or no one will care whether
he lives or not. Above all, he must see to it that no drop of the poison of
ennui finds its way into his work. He must be so loyal to his beautiful
art, that he will gladly keep it unimpaired by any chance misfortune of
his own. However like a failure his own career may seem to him; how-
ever utterly he may lose at times the wholesome appetite for life, the
longing for wisdom and beauty, the zest for achievement; however his
spirit and flesh may fail before the mighty and inexorable enigma, he
will still bear himself with courage before others, and look forth upon the
confused concourse of life with an uncraven mind. So doing, he will utter
no word of personal plaint, but carefully guard his poetry from the note
of dejection. For he will perceive that his art is greater than himself, and
scrupulously embody in his work only his gladsome and encouraging
experiences, letting his darker hours perish unrecorded. However bitter
existence may taste to him personally, he surely cannot help seeing that
in the long run, in the large account, life as a whole is desirable, and art
as a whole is the reflection of its goodly joy.

The Permanence of Poetry

Reprinted from *The Poetry of Life*, Boston: L.C. Page & Co., 1905, 247–58.

It is often claimed that the day for poetry is past, that we live in an age of prose, and for the future shall get along very well without the solace which poetry was wont to supply. It is a question, however, whether those who make this claim have not conceived far too narrow a scope for poetry, and been heedless in thinking what poetry really is. They have, one must believe, allowed themselves to take a very superficial and hurried view of human history, and been content to accept the current notion of the fine arts and their place in our social order.

What is that notion? How do we at the present day think of the fine arts, and of poetry in particular? And what place do we commonly assign them in our scheme of life? Is it not true that we nearly always think of them as luxurious occupations, forms of harmless amusement or innocuous pastimes, to be tolerated perhaps, but yet without any real hold on people, and without any spontaneous life in public sentiment? By the fine arts most of us understand those eccentric, if not questionable, pursuits which fill our rich houses with pictures and statues, and our opera-houses with extravagant music. We have come to think of the fine arts as foreign to our real life, as esoteric, expensive, precious, unnecessary, and, therefore, to the ordinary mind, just a trifle ridiculous.

This is not an unjust view of the fine arts as they exist among us today. They live by sufferance, not by right. We do not acknowledge their title to a place in modern civilization; we accept them as the more or less foolish accompaniments of wealth. They have no source in popular feeling; they do not spring up irresistibly from our social conditions; they command no respect save among a small highly educated class. Our people at large have no such sense of beauty, no such native good taste, as the common people of France, for instance, or of Japan.

Yet for all that, admitting the wholly anomalous and artificial character of all the ancient arts as they survive among us today, does it follow that they will always be so entirely divorced from our social and national life? May there not come a time when our debased political institutions will be purified, when our public morals will be elevated, when our industrial and commercial ethics will come to acknowledge more honourable standards? May we not look forward to a day when old-fashioned honesty will be restored to the code of American ideals? May we not hope that our present era of unmitigated commercialism, barbarity, and greed, is only a passing phase in the story of the world, and that time will renew our enthusiasm for things of the mind and the spirit? To see clearly one's own faults, or to mark the shortcomings of one's own time, is not to be a pessimist. The pessimist is one who thinks nothing could be better. Admirable, therefore, as our life may be today, it is our business as sane men to look for its flaws and strive to mend them. Perfection, not self-gratulation, is the duty of mortals.

Granted, then, that art and poetry are in a sorry plight at present, shall we conclude that their day is over? While there is even such art life as there is, is there not hope? Had we not better ask ourselves if we are quite sure what art is, and what poetry is, before we proceed to set them lightly aside in the storeroom of oblivion with other discarded lumber of time? Our creeds must change as knowledge increases, yet faith remains of paramount importance. Our conception of the universe must change with accession of science, yet love of truth only becomes more necessary. So, too, we need art in all the business of life more imperatively today than ever before. For art is a manner of doing things, not the thing that is done. Art is not the painting itself, but the loving fervour, the hard knowledge, the skilled industry, that went to make the painting. When anything is ill done, it reveals a lack of art. And this lack of art may spring from lack of sincere devotion in the artist himself, or from a lack of wisdom, or from a lack of skill.

And this question of poetry? Is poetry a task for children and idlers, a sort of Chinese puzzle in words, something to divert the mind, an employment for invalids and weaklings? I believe if we consider a moment, and recall the hold which poetry has had on men's minds, the influence it has exerted on life, we must conclude it is something far more vital and forceful than that. Poetry has been a great power in the world. If it is not a great power at the present time, that does not prove that we have outgrown it; it only means that we have forgotten it for the moment. We can no more outgrow poetry than we can outgrow gravitation. The mode of poetry may change, as the customs of nations change; we do not enjoy the same kind of poetry that our ancestors did; our own poetry must be native to us, and must express our own thoughts and sentiments, rather than those of an alien clime and a forgotten age; but the natural phenomenon which we call poetry will always be present in the world.

Why? Because poetry is nothing more than the form which human speech assumes under the stress of clear thinking and lofty aspiration, under the terms of beautiful utterance. The laws of poetry are not conventional, but natural. The first poet to use any given form of verse is rather a discoverer than an inventor. Take, for example, the phenomenon of the iambic pentameter line in English poetry. See how universally it is used from Chaucer to Tennyson; all of Shakespeare, all of the Elizabethan drama, all of "Paradise Lost," all of Pope and Dryden, all of "The Ring and the Book," all of the "Idylls of the King," indeed, a large portion of our poetic literature is done in this measure. Now how shall we account for this phenomenon? Shall we say that succeeding poets slavishly followed their distinguished predecessors in the use of the blank verse line? Did they have to study to learn the trick? Not at all. They used it spontaneously, naturally, unconsciously. They never could tell you why. And if a poet should be born in England tomorrow and reared in entire ignorance of English poetry, he would discover blank verse for himself. Its recurrence and persistence in English mean that it is a vital form of expression, which springs inevitably into use, just as a nod of the head is an instinctive motion of assent, and not merely a conventional gesture.

The study of versification, or the outward form of poetry, becomes an empirical science. We simply collate our facts and deduce our laws; for the laws, of poetry are truly laws, and not rules. There may be rules for writing sonnets, but there are no rules for writing poetry. The poet is himself always acting under laws of expression, which are far too complex and universal for him wholly to comprehend. He is only a vent for expression—a medium through which certain powers find play in harmonious accordance with their natural laws. When he permits himself to rely on intuition, when he feels instinctively for the perfect phrase, then he attains something like perfection of utterance. When he attempts to interfere with inspiration, and to write after some plan of his own devising, then he fails. When Wordsworth wrote from instinct, at the dictate of his genius, he was great. When he allowed himself to put in practice certain conclusions of his own as to how poetry should be written, he became tedious. So, too, of Whitman; when he gave free play to his genius, he spoke with the tongue of a seraph; but when he attempted to imitate himself, when he tried to put in practice certain notions of his own as to what poetry ought to be, he failed. The artist must be a student of his own art, it is true; but he must never try to practise his art according to rule. That is folly. For, as I say, there are no rules, but only laws of art. And these laws are elemental, psychic, and govern the artist himself. He is swayed by them, and it is his business to be sensitive to them and obey them. Whether he chooses to study them, and try to comprehend them or not, is a different matter. He may be a scientist as well as an artist; but in order to be the one he does not have to be the other.

The form of poetry, then, is a phenomenon determined by the laws of nature, and as such we may very well consider it a permanency. I do not mean that the forms of poetry are unchanging. They are not. Just because they are living, they will vary constantly. We shall never be able to predict the new forms poetry may take, nor should we attempt to impose conventional limits on versification. Every new poet will find his own new forms, but form of some sort, rhythm of some sort, he will have. He can no more escape those conditions than spirit can escape the influence of all the natural forces when it enters the house of clay.

The subjects of poetry, too, are permanent as well as its form. The things which poetry deals with are the perennial hopes and fears of the human heart, the phenomena of the inner, life. From these poetry has made, and will always make, the religions of the world. Nor does it disregard the facts of science. All science and all philosophy come within the scope of poetry. It is the function of poetry to assimilate the new knowledge and make use of the discoveries of science. It cannot do this immediately, however; it has to wait until these new facts become familiar to men's minds, before it can treat of them in its own heightened and impassioned way. For this reason we often hear it said that science and poetry, or science and religion, are opposed to each other. But that is absurd. The soul cannot but love what the mind sees to be true. And when that truth is expressed in terms of beauty, our senses must be delighted as our hearts are encouraged and inspired.

If all this be so, it does not very well appear how we can ever outgrow the need of poetry. It would rather seem that we shall need it more and more, under the increasing distractions and complexities of life. The more truth we know, the more we shall need some means to assimilate it and make it effective for our happiness. The more wealth we acquire, the more we shall need some wise guide to its proper use. An expansion of power, without an accompanying increase of wisdom, is a mere embarrassment, and only makes life more difficult. Poetry in its largest sense helps us to make use of our knowledge and power in ways that tend toward a happier existence and there can hardly be anything more important than that, or of more lasting interest to men.

Genius and the Artist

Reprinted from *The Making of Personality*, Boston: L.C. Page & Co., 1908, 371–75.

No more misleading definition was ever formulated than the familiar one which declares genius to be an infinite capacity for taking pains. That is the one thing that genius is not. A capacity for taking pains may be a characteristic of every conscientious worker, but is in no way an essential distinctive trait of genius.

The very essence of genius is its spontaneity, its inspiration, its power of instant and inexplicable coordination and achievement. Its processes are incomprehensible even to itself. It cannot take pains, for it is an immediate force like gravity, and works without effort or consciousness of exertion. It is indeed an infinite capacity, but it can only have been confused with patient painstaking because in the eternal course of creation infinite patience and infinite desire must be supposed to be parts of infinite wisdom. Among men genius is more often spasmodic, uncertain, fluctuating as the tide and erratic as the wind, susceptible to stimulus and amenable to suggestion and education, but intolerant of routine, impatient of restraint, and accommodating itself with difficulty to the stereotyped requirements of conventional toil in a workaday world.

The woes of genius are proverbial. And the many annoyances, misfortunes, and distresses which usually beset its most marked possessors are charged unreasoningly to the inherent character of genius itself. But this is surely an error. It is not the unfortunate man's genius that involves him in unhappiness, but his lack of a rationally ordered and well balancing education adapted to his exceptional needs. Far from being the cause of his undoing, his genius is often the only source of satisfaction and happiness he has; and its exercise and influence afford him the only refuge possible to his otherwise chaotic and ill-regulated life.

The dictates of genius are never unsound. Its tremendous urge is a veritable breath of the life-spirit, infinitely wise, benign, and powerful, making only for good, for beauty, for enlightenment in the life of the individual and in the life of the race. It can only seem chaotic or malign when perverted by faulty art, when thwarted in exercising itself, when stultified and harried by unfortunate environment or inharmonious training. Genius often seems mad only because its possessor is inadequately educated for handling his treasure, incapable of arranging any *modus vivendi* between himself and the world. Small wonder that the bungler of such a blessing should be distracted and distraught by such failure.

The precious gift of genius is not so infrequent as is said. Not all genius is in the realm of fine art or in public or famous or conspicuous activities. It may show itself in the simplest service of humanity, and all genius is richly valuable and exquisitely pleasing. The genius of motherliness, that soothes and sustains the whole weary world! The genius of merrymaking that suns out the dark places whenever it comes near! The genius of unselfishness that gilds the dullest effort! The genius of making happiness out of the unlikeliest odds and ends saved from the wreckage of our disappointments! The genius of ingenuity,— how well balanced it must be, how modestly it works its miracles ! The many-sided genius of home-making and child-rearing! The sturdy genius of dependability! Unacclaimed, unappreciated, unapprised, but never wholly unrequited, these bits of life-spirit work against unreasoning obstruction and confusion to save the world! Who has not some genius, and what might it not grow to, if it were happily educated! How better can one serve the world than through the happy bent of one's genius?

Genius is the spontaneous coordination of inspiration, aspiration, and execution, and requires for its perfect development the finest, most harmonious culture of the spirit, the intelligence, and the senses. Why not, therefore, so educate everyone in the art of living as to establish avenues through which genius could free itself and develop to the incalculable good of the world? Genius must be educated and supplied with adequate complementary capacities in order that it may be saved from torture and frustration; and the artist, that is to say, every one of us, should be so educated that genius may emerge and find an unobstructed vent for its purpose and dream.

ARCHIBALD LAMPMAN

ARCHIBALD LAMPMAN (1861–1899)

Biographical Notes

Archibald Lampman was born 17 November 1861 in Morpeth, Ontario, a village near Chatham, where his father, the Rev. Archibald Lampman, was rector of Trinity Church. Both of Lampman's grandfathers were United Empire Loyalists. When Lampman turned six, the family moved to Parrytown, near Port Hope, and in October 1867, moved again to Gore's Landing, another small parish on the shore of Rice Lake. The next seven years living in such an idyllic setting for young Archibald left a life-long impression on him.

While his surroundings were beautiful, the family was relatively poor and could not afford to keep the house well heated; as a result, Archibald fell ill with rheumatic fever during November 1868; he spent months convalescing, and was left lame for several years. Indeed, Lampman never did fully recover his health, and was quite prone to illness thereafter. Lampman was tutored at home for the first few years of his education, but later studied under the notable schoolmaster, Mr. F.W. Barron, M.A., of Cambridge, who had been Principal of Upper Canada College. Under Barron he learned Latin and Greek; at thirteen he attended the Cobourg Collegiate Institute; and in the following year enrolled in Trinity College School in nearby Port Hope, to prepare for attendance at Trinity College at the University of Toronto. A highly successful student at the school, he was able, in September 1879, to enter Trinity College, where, with the help of scholarships he had won, he completed a B.A. with honours in classics in 1882. After graduation, he taught unsuccessfully for a few months in the Orangeville High School, and then accepted permanent employment as a low-paid clerk in the Langevin Block of the Post Office Department at Ottawa, a position he retained for the rest of his life.

Around the time of his graduation from the University of Toronto, Lampman began publishing his poetry in Canadian and American periodicals. It was during this time too that, along with Wilfred Campbell and Duncan Campbell Scott, he began writing a two-year series of articles to the Toronto *Globe* under the byline "At the Mermaid's Inn" (1882–83). While these articles ranged from discussions of nature to the pleasures of smoking a pipe, several concern the topic of poetry itself, and are included here.

In 1887 Lampman married an Ottawa woman, Maud Playter, with whom he had two children. Lampman, however, was never happy in his marriage, and within two years began a love affair with a co-worker, Kate Waddell, which he maintained until his untimely death.

Lampman was influenced by the poetry of Bliss Carman, and in particular by an early poem, *Orion*, by Charles G.D. Roberts. His closest literary friend was undoubtedly Duncan Campbell Scott with whom he made frequent canoe trips and excursions into the countryside around Ottawa and the Gatineau. Scott greatly assisted Lampman in his publications, and became his literary executor and promoter of his work after Lampman's death.

Lampman published only two important volumes of poems in his lifetime: *Among the Millet and Other Poems* (Ottawa: J. Durie, 1888) and *Lyrics of Earth* (Boston: Copeland and Day, 1895). A final book, *Alcyone* (Ottawa: Ogilvy, 1899) was on the press when he was stricken by the brief illness which resulted in his death, two days later, on the 10 February 1899. It was left to his friend Duncan Campbell Scott to bring out a collected *Poems* the next year. Despite Scott's having to sell advance subscriptions to raise money for the publication, this book proved quite successful and received several reprintings. Nonetheless, quite a lot of Lampman's poems, such as "At the Long Sault: May, 1660," languished in manuscript until 1943, when Scott and the critic E.K. Brown edited them for publication under the title *At the Long Sault and Other New Poems*.

Despite his limited opus and short career, Lampman is now widely regarded as Canada's greatest nineteenth-century poet. The majority of his manuscripts are deposited at Queen's University in Kingston, Ontario. A cairn commemorating Archibald Lampman's life can be found at the village church in Morpeth, Ontario.

Publications

Among the Millet and Other Poems. Ottawa: J. Durie, 1888. Reprinted as *Among the Millet and Other Poems.* Ed. D.M.R. Bentley. Ottawa: Tecumseh, 1988.

The Meadow Sunset at Les Eboulements. [S.l.: s.n., 1890?].

Lyrics of Earth. Boston: Copeland and Day, 1895.

Alcyone. Ottawa: J. Oglivy, 1899.

The Poems of Archibald Lampman. Ed. and with a Memoir by Duncan Campbell Scott. Toronto: Morang, 1900.

Lyrics of the Earth: Sonnets and Ballads. Ed. Duncan Campbell Scott. Toronto: Musson, 1925.

At the Long Sault and Other New Poems. Foreword by Duncan Campbell Scott. Ed. E.K. Brown. Toronto: Ryerson, 1943.

Selected Poems of Archibald Lampman. Ed. Duncan Campbell Scott. Toronto: Ryerson, 1947.

The Poems of Archibald Lampman. Intro. Margaret Whitridge. Toronto: U of Toronto P, 1974.

Lampman's Kate: Late Love Poems of Archibald Lampman 1887–1897. Ed. Margaret Whitridge. Ottawa: Borealis, 1975.

Lampman's Sonnets, 1884–1899. Ed. Margaret Whitridge. Ottawa: Borealis, 1976.

Selected Poems of Archibald Lampman. Ed. Michael Gnarowski. Ottawa: Tecumseh, 1990.

Critical Materials

Book Length

Artelle, Steven. *The Last Days of Archibald Lampman: Canadian Poet, 1861–1899.* Ottawa: Historical Society of Ottawa, 2000.

Bentley, D.M.R., ed. *Essays and Reviews of Archibald Lampman.* London, ON: Canadian Poetry P, 1996.

Connor, Carl Y. *Archibald Lampman: Canadian Poet of Nature*. New York, Montreal: L. Carrier & Co., 1929.

Davies, Barrie, ed. *Archibald Lampman: Selected Prose*. Ottawa: Tecumseh, 1975.

Early, L.R. *Archibald Lampman*. Boston: Twayne, 1986.

Gnarowski, Michael, ed. *Archibald Lampman*. Toronto: Ryerson, 1970.

McMullen, Lorraine. *The Lampman Symposium. Re-Appraisals: Canadian Writers*. Ottawa: U of Ottawa P, 1976.

Wicken, George. *Archibald Lampman: An Annotated Bibliography*. Downsview, ON: ECW, 1980.

Articles

Adams, John Coldwell. "Roberts, Lampman, and Edmund Collins." Ed. Glenn Clever, *The Sir Charles G.D. Roberts Symposium*. Ottawa: U of Ottawa P, 1984: 5–13.

Arnold, Richard. "'Thoughts Grow Keen and Clear': A Look at Lampman's Revisions." *Studies in Canadian Literature/Études en Litterature Canadienne* 10.1–2 (1985): 170–176.

———. "'The Clearer Self': Lampman's Transcendental-Visionary Development." *Canadian Poetry: Studies, Documents, Reviews* 8 (1981): 33–55.

Ball, Eric. "Life 'Only Sweet': The Significance of the Sequence in Lampman's *Lyrics of Earth*, II." (Continued from *Canadian Poetry* 25 (1989): 1–20.) *Canadian Poetry: Studies, Documents, Reviews* 26 (1990): 19–42.

Bentley, D.M.R. "A Thread of Memory and the Fabric of Archibald Lampman's 'City of the End of Things.'" *World Literature Written in English* 21.1 (1982): 86–95.

———. "Watchful Dreams and Sweet Unrest: An Essay on the Visions of Archibald Lampman." *Studies in Canadian Literature/Études en Litterature Canadienne* 6.2 (1981): 188–210.

———. "Watchful Dreams and Sweet Unrest: An Essay on the Vision of Archibald Lampman, Part II." *Studies in Canadian Literature/Études en Litterature Canadienne* 7.1 (1982): 5–26.

———. "Pan and the Confederation Poets." *Canadian Literature* 81 (1979): 59–71.

———. "Archibald Lampman (1861–1899): A Checklist." *Essays on Canadian Writing* 5 (1976): 36–49.

Clever, W. Glenn. "Lampman's 'Comfort of the Fields.'" *Journal of Canadian Poetry* 3.2 (1981): 55–62.

Compton, Anne. "The Poet-Impressionist: Some Landscapes by Archibald Lampman." *Canadian Poetry: Studies, Documents, Reviews* 34 (1994): 33–56.

Davies, Barrie. "Lampman Could Tell His Frog from His Toad: A Note on Art versus Nature." *Studies in Canadian Literature* 2 (1977): 129–30.

Doyle, James. "The Confederation Poets and American Publishers." *Canadian Poetry: Studies, Documents, Reviews* 17 (1985): 59–67.

———. "Archibald Lampman and Hamlin Garland." *Canadian Poetry: Studies, Documents, Reviews* 16 (1985): 38–46. Can be found online at http://www.uwo.ca/ english/canadianpoetry/cpjrn/vol16/doyle.htm.

Early, L.R. "A Chronology of Lampman's Poems." *Canadian Poetry: Studies, Documents, Reviews* 14 (1984): 75–87.

———. "Lampman's Love Poetry." *Essays on Canadian Writing* 27 (1983–84): 116–149.

———, ed. "Twenty-Five Fugitive Poems by Archibald Lampman." *Canadian Poetry: Studies, Documents, Reviews* 12 (1983): 46–70. Can be found online at http:// www.uwo.ca/english/canadianpoetry/cpjrn/vol12/early.htm.

Fox, Justin W. (comp.) "An Annotated Bibliography of Work on and by Archibald Lampman Published Between 1979 and 1990." *Canadian Poetry: Studies, Documents, Reviews* 34 (1994): 79–98.

Grenberg, Bruce L. "'The City of the End of Things': The Significance of Lampman's Sound and Fury." Ed. W.H. New. *Inside the Poem: Essays and Poems in Honour of Donald Stephens*. Toronto: Oxford UP, 1992. 123–29.

Herbert, Karen. "'There Was One Thing He Could Not See': William Morris in the Writing of Archibald Lampman and Francis Sherman." *Canadian Poetry: Studies, Documents, Reviews* 37 (1995): 79–99.

Kennedy, Margaret. "Lampman and the Canadian Thermopylae: 'At the Long Sault: May 1660.'" *Canadian Poetry* 1 (1977): 54–59.

Mezei, Kathy. "Lampman among the Timothy." *Canadian Poetry* 5 (1979): 57–72.

Mothersill, Sue, ed. "'Style' by Archibald Lampman." *Canadian Poetry: Studies, Documents, Reviews* 7 (1980): 56–72.

Ower, John. "The Story of an Affinity: Lampman's 'The Frogs' and Tennyson's 'The Lotos-Eaters.'" *Canadian Literature* 115 (1987): 285–89.

Precosky, Don. "Seven Myths about Canadian Literature." *Studies in Canadian Literature/Études en Litterature* 11.1 (1986): 86–95.

Rudzik, Orest H. T. and Reshard Gool (commentary). "Literary Norms and Translation." *Canadian Literature Supp.* 1 (1987): 23–37.

Steele, Charles R. "The Isolate 'I' (Eye): Lampman's Persona." *Essays on Canadian Writing* 16 (1979–80): 62–69.

Online Resources

http://www.ucalgary.ca/UofC/faculties/HUM/ENGL/canada/poet/a_lampman.htm
http://eir.library.utoronto.ca/rpo/display/poet190.html
http://digital.library.upenn.edu/women/garvin/poets/lampman.html

Poetic Interpretation

Undated, circa 1884. National Archives of Canada (MG 29 D 59 vol. 1, 585–622). Reprinted from *The Essays and Reviews of Archibald Lampman*, edited by D.M.R. Bentley. London: Canadian Poetry Press, 1996, 126–41.

There is nothing in the world, whether in nature animate or inanimate, or in the phenomena of human life, which has not connected with it some sense of beauty, either in itself or in its relation to the whole of life. Only those who have been gifted in some degree with the bright instinct which we call poetic feeling, can at all times be brought to see this; and those who have received this gift in such a high degree that they cannot be at peace with themselves or find any rest in the enjoyment of life, until they have made known to mankind the beautiful things they have seen and felt; these are the men whom we call poets.

Every phenomenon in life, every emotion and every thought produces a distinct impression of its own upon the soul of the poetic observer. The impression produced by a Mayday sunrise is very different from that produced by an October sunset. The feeling left upon the soul by the contemplation of a full-blown rose is not the same as the sense which it gathers from the beauty of a bunch of sedge. The latter is perhaps not less beautiful than the former, but the essence of its beauty is different.

Every feeling thus produced has what may be called its musical accompaniment—its own peculiar harmonic value, and in every poetic soul lies hidden an answering harmony, which may be aroused either by the presence of the impression itself, or by the more potent inter-pretation of the poet. The poetic soul is like a vast musical instrument, every chord in which represents the perfect musical value of some one of these separate impressions. Most of these innumerable chords have never been sounded; but there they will lie, as long as the soul remains, awaiting the touch of emotion either from within or from the hand of the interpreting poet.

The poet's reproduction of any impression must be effected not by a vivid picture only or by a merely accurate description, but also by such a subtle arrangement of word and phrase, such a marshalling of verbal sound, as may exactly arouse, through the listening ear, the strange stirring of the soul, involved in every beautiful emotion, which we feel to be akin to the effect of music. If the poet should undertake to reproduce the impressions of the summer sunrise, the October sunset, the rose and the bunch of sedge, not only must the pictures be different, but the tones must be different too. The perfect poet would be one in whose soul should be found the perfect answering harmony to every natural or spiritual phenomenon. He would be one who should go about the world gathering the impressions of life, not with sight and thought only, but with the inner ear of the intently listening soul. In creating his pictures of life he would weave into each of them its own peculiar harmony so perfectly that we should have no doubt whatever as to its degree of truth, but we should know it instantly for what it is. This of course has never been completely done, and no man has ever been a perfect poet.

The perfect poet, it may be said, would have no set style. He would have a different one for everything he should write, a manner exactly suited to the subject, for the style involves to a certain extent what I have been speaking about, the musical accompaniment. But almost every original poet has had his own easily recognizable method of imagination and expression, that which we call his style; for almost every poet has been dominated by some one special thought, feeling or musical instinct, which has overshadowed every other, and left an unalterable mark upon his imagery and his phraseology. This would not be the case with the perfect poet. He would not consent to be permanently influenced by any single impulse, however noble, but would arrive unerringly at the perfect rendering of everything. Often the single dominating instinct, guided by the longing for truth, impels the poet invariably to a choice of subjects of a kind exactly consonant with his mood, as in the case of Poe or Ros[s]etti, or he may endeavor to apply a peculiar form of imagination and musical feeling to a variety of subjects, and in such an effort he becomes invariably untrue.

Special purposes and special instincts have produced great poets but not perfect ones. For the perfect poet would not necessar[ily] be great.

Many things beside the capacity to reproduce every beautiful impression in all its poetic truth, go to the making of a great poet. He must have noble thought, lofty purposes and great fertility, and these things in their worth and majesty far outweigh the charm[,] glorious as it is, which we sometimes find in poets of a lesser calibre as men, but gifted with a finer instinct and a more various susceptibility. Keats was not as great a poet as Wordsworth, but he was a more perfect one.

Style has generally been in the way of all poets in their efforts at exact poetic interpretation; indeed just in so far as they have subjected the ear and the imagination to the governance of settled method and tone, have they failed to render the pure and absolute impression produced by the phenomena of material nature and the movement and emotion of human life. Their work may be supremely noble and beautiful like Spenser[']s, or passionately alluring like Swinburne[']s, but not many passages can be pointed to as fair interpretations of the things which they are intended to represent.

Of all poets of the present century Keats, it seems to me, was the most perfect. He was governed by no theory and by no usurping line of thought and feeling. He was beyond all other men disposed to surrender himself completely to the impression of everything with which his brain or his senses came in contact. He died very young and before he had had time to work upon many things; but everything that his imagination handled came from it in a shape so nearly perfect, that whenever we have contemplated any one of those exquisite creations we have been almost compelled to say—this is indeed its absolute beauty and this is its absolute harmony.

Of the eight best known poems of Keats seven are almost faultless. The first and longest, *Endymion*, is the only one, in which the tones are not quite sound. But this was the work of an inexperienced and over-abundant youth, too eager to wait for the perfect musical fulfilment of its imaginings, content to set each thing down incompletely as it came, and then hurry on to the next. In "Lamia" we observe at once the advance to developement. Here he had caught and mastered before he began the full harmonic complement of his subject, with all its action, its imagery, its beauty and its emotion. He did not, as many poets have done, endeavor to apply to a new creation an already well-used style and tone, which had served for a hundred other subjects. He knew that it must have a tone of its own, and that only by yielding to the answering echo of that tone in his own heart could the reader live for a moment with him in the full and beautiful reallity [sic] of the things he had created. His theme was a semi-mythological tale of Corinth, and he told it like an inspired Corinthian. The painting is Greek. The harmony is Greek; and our imaginations involuntarily assume the Greek pose as we follow the flow of the story, watching the beautiful Lamia turning into the beautiful woman, passing from the bright and noisy stream of traffic between Cenchreae [sic] and Corinth to observe the meeting of Lamia and Lycius, threading the streets of the twi-light city with their joyous activity, their luxurious plenty, and the murmur of their soft and fluent tongue, dwelling in that mysterious marble palace of languor and delight, holding a place at Lycius['] bridal banquet with its sparkling merriment and teeming luxury, till in the end we are chilled to the heart by the gathered horror of the piteous catastrophe. All these things we feel as beautiful reallities [sic], not through the action and the imagery alone, but through the subtle music of the verse. The tone of that joyous Corinth is everywhere woven into it, but over all hangs the terrible fate of the story, the shadow of the cynic Apollonius, austere and saturnine. This too runs in an undercurrent through the melody, giving to the complete poem a tone, which could be assumed by nothing else, and without which the thing would be a body without a soul or a body but half alive.

So much for "Lamia"; then consider the complete change of tone in *Hyperion*. No other English poet ever had such an ear as Keats. He seems to be intently listening as he writes, listening at the heart of his subject, transcribing rather than creating his song. In *Hyperion* again the subject is Greek, but it is of the older mythology. We are among the elder Gods, discomfited and dethroned, gigantic primeval shapes, huddled together, or wandering in impotent gloom and desolation. The soft luxurious music of "Lamia" with its undersong of tragic anticipation would never do for this. Nothing would do for it but what the poet found—a tone that was deep and full and solemn, with a sound in it sometimes huge, hollow, Cyclopean[,] almost ponderous. The syllables fall at times like the footsteps of Enceladus, and even the timid complaining of Clymene is deeper and fuller, and bears in it a huger gloom, than the laments of earthly women. Listen to this from the description of Thea, the "tender spouse of gold Hyperion," who comes to the aged Saturn in his bowed despair, touches his wide shoulders and speaks to him—

> But Oh! how unlike marble was that face:
> How beautiful if sorrow had not made

Sorrow more beautiful than beauty's self.
There was a listening fear in her regard,
As if calamity had but begun;
As if the vanward clouds of evil days
Had spent their malice, and the sullen rear
Was with its storèd thunder laboring up.

That is the tone—surely worthy of the Titan Gods! so large and solemn.
The poet thus describes the place where the followers of Saturn meet in
gloomy consultation.

It was a den where no insulting light
Could glimmer on their tears; where their own groans
They felt, but heard not, for the solid roar
Of thunderous waterfalls and torrents hoarse,
Pouring a constant bulk, uncertain where.
Crag jutting forth to crag, and rocks that seemed
Ever as if just rising from a sleep,
Forehead to forehead held their monstrous horns;
And thus in thousand hugest phantasies
Made a fit roofing to this nest of woe.

Listen to the tremendous fall of the syllables in those wonderful lines
describing how Enceladus broke in upon the trembling lamentation of
Clymene.

So far her voice flowed on, like timorous brook
That, lingering along a pebbled coast,
Doth fear to meet the sea: but sea it met,
And shuddered; for the overwhelming voice
Of huge, Enceladus swallowed it in wrath:
The ponderous syllables, like sullen waves
In the half-glutted hollows of reef-rocks,
Came booming thus, while still upon his arm
He leaned; not rising, from supreme contempt.

At last Enceladus arouses the wrath and courage of the Gods; and as the
final words of that vast utterance fall from his lips, a light gleams in
upon the faces around him. It is the pallid splendor of Hyperion, the
only one of the primeval deities still left in the possession of his sover-
eignty. Thus his coming is described[:]

> Suddenly a splendor like the morn
> Pervaded all the beetling gloomy steeps,
> All the sad places of oblivion
> And every gulf, and every chasm old,
> And every height, and every sullen depth,
> Voiceless, or hoarse with loud-tormented streams:
> And all the everlasting cataracts,
> And all the headlong torrents far and near,
> Mantled before in darkness and huge shade,
> Now saw the light and made it terrible.
> It was Hyperion.

The poet is painting Titans and his harmony is Titanic. Sentence after sentence it falls upon the ear and satisfies us. It is the poetic truth. It satisfies us not by the grouping[,] the action, the imagery, the thought[,] alone, but by the melody which is to these things as the living soul. Consider again these marvellous lines[:]

> There was a listening fear in her regard,
> As if calamity had but begun;
> As if the vanward clouds of evil days
> Had spent their malice, and the sullen rear
> Was with its storèd thunder laboring up[.]

All these lines might be changed, or a single pause might be removed. The thought, the image would perhaps be the same; but the harmony would no longer belong to the idea, and the beautiful truth would be destroyed or mutilated. A perfect poetic utterance is like a human body of perfect physical beauty showing the life of the beautiful soul within in the movement of every feature, every limb, every muscle, every nerve. If a simple finger be paralysed or shrunken, the splendid harmony is disturbed, and the expression of the soul is made incomplete. So it is with the perfect poetic utterance. If a single living word is changed for a dead one—one that is dead in its place—the harmony is shattered; the musical soul no longer perfectly expresses itself. Let us take a few more examples from Keats, for even his small bulk of work is a storehouse of poetic perfections. "The Eve of St. Agnes," for instance; that wondrous poem that weaves about us irresistibly the strange ringing charm of mediæval phantasy, touching the ear in every syllable with the imaginative flavor of things old and long bygone—the story of a lover who met his mistress once by a quaint device on a wintery St. Agnes

Eve, when there was wind and sleet without and revelry within and enemies on every hand—wooed and won her and carried her away with him into the storm and the night. The music and imagery of the very first lines are enough to make one shiver. They are the musical expression of the thought of numbing cold, combined with the mediaeval [sic] of the theme[.]

> St. Agnes' Eve— Ah, bitter chill it was!
> The owl, for all his feathers, was acold;
> The hare limped trembling through the frozen grass,
> And silent was the flock in woolly fold:
> Numb were the beadsman's fingers while he told
> His rosary, and while his frosted breath,
> Like pious incense from a censor old,
> Seemed taking flight for heaven without a death,
> Past the sweet Virgin's picture, while his prayer he saith.

The vivid harmony of these other lines, when the lovers make their way down the darkling stairway—

> In all the house was heard no human sound
> A chain-drooped lamp was flickering by each door;
> The arras, rich with horseman, hawk and hound,
> Fluttered in the besieging wind's uproar;
> And the long carpets rose along the gusty floor[.]

And the last stanza with its tone of ancientness and of lives and dreams that have been ages buried in the tomb.

> And they are gone; aye, ages long ago,
> These lovers fled away into the storm.
> That night the baron dreamt of many a woe,
> And all his warrior guests, with shade and form
> Of witch, and demon, and large coffin-worm,
> Were long be-nightmared. Angela the old
> Died palsy-twitched, with meagre face deform;
> The beadsman, after thousand aves told,
> For aye unsought-for slept among his ashes cold.

Turn then to the "Ode to a Nightingale." Read it over and over. Gather into the ear the whole of its sad deep yearning tone—the pure out-pouring of that mood of melancholy, so strange an interweaving of joy and sorrow, when the poetic soul flags and falls from its dream, for a moment well-nigh broken and sore wearied with the iron necessities of this earthly life, yet finding in the very strength of its glorious desire a kind of shadowy joy, a mournful delight, whereby even the bitterness of its situation is transfigured and made to wear the semblance of something grand and poetic. The poet wishes that he might become like the nightingale, and with her "Fade away into the forest dim":

> Fade far away, dissolve, and quite forget
>> What thou among the leaves hast never known,
> The weariness, the fever, and the fret
>> Here, where men sit and hear each other groan;
> Where palsy shakes a few, sad, last grey hairs,
>> Where youth grows pale, and spectre-thin and dies;
>>> Where but to think is to be full of sorrow
>>> And leaden-eyed despairs;
> Where Beauty cannot keep her lustrous eyes,
>> Or new love pine at them beyond to-morrow.

The tone of this stanza is the tone of the whole. The poet describes such things as might breed despair, but there is none of the strident accent of despair. They should not make men fail, but they are nevertheless mournful. He has therefore found for his thoughts their own proper music—a music that is deep and sorrowful, but too beautiful to be desperate.

In the "Ode to [sic] a Grecian Urn" we find another complete change in the harmony. It is the expression of the attitude to the poet's mind in the intense contemplation of some work of antique art, something calmly and perfectly beautiful; and the tone of the verse, so quiet and at the same time so ecstatic, is the pure musical expression of wrapt and enchanted reverie[.]

> Oh Attic shape! Fair attitude! with brede
>> Of marble men and maidens overwrought,
> With forest branches and the trodden weed;
>> Thou silent form! dost tease us out of thought
> As doth eternity: Cold Pastoral!
>> When old age shall this generation waste,
>> Thou shalt remain, in midst of other woe
> Than ours, a friend to man, to whom thou say'st,

> "Beauty is truth, truth beauty"—that is all
>> Ye know on earth, and all ye need to know.

"Dost tease us out of thought as doth eternity." There is in that the tone of the whole poem. It is a beautiful commentary on those other well-known words of Keats "A thing of beauty is a joy for ever." The smallest thing that is perfectly beautiful in form and hue, may seem at first glance to satisfy us, but in a little while, we find that we can never fill our souls with the entire sense of its beauty and perfection. It is something that is eternal and illimitable. Our finite mind cannot contain it. Lift and expand as it may, it is still conscious that there are breadths and heights even in this little thing that it can never reach. It will "tease us out of thought as doth eternity."

> Oh Attic shape! Fair attitude! with brede
>> Of marble men and maidens overwrought.

Can we not hear in every syllable of these two blameless lines the clear yet dreamy utterance of the purest surrenderment to the spirit of serene beauty, that mood of contemplation, which is so still, so passionless and yet so strangely full—the emotion of perfect rest.

I have illustrated my subject so abundantly from Keats, because he seems to me to have been the most perfect of later poets. His work is a storehouse of musical perfections. Next to Keats in the truth of poetic interpretation stands Wordsworth, who in his moods of inspiration was the most spontaneous of all our later poets, and in the loftiness of his nature was the greatest. Wordsworth's subjects, especially those in which he was successful, were humble. Very young people do not care for them. He never flatters or allures the imagination; and it is his glory that he has rendered the quiet musical feeling of very homely things with such a touching truth, that they grow in favour with us as we grow in years and in the knowledge of life. Often when we weary of the flowerier utterances of those who deal with more splendid scenes and more romantic passions, we turn the work of this wise poet, with an ineffable sense of health and rest.

Wordsworth's work is very uneven; but it seems to me that the very fact that a few of his poems stand out in such fine and glorious contrast to the rest, is the strongest evidence of the genuine spontaneity of his gift. A great lyric poem is a thing which is written if one may so speak it in a dream. The emotion comes upon the poet and almost before he is conscious of it, the thing stands there on paper before him. It is done and he knows not how it was done. It has passed from him as the perfume from a flower. Wordsworth must have been hardly conscious of the great disparity of his work. He wrote steadily and serenely[.] Sometimes the great passion came over him, and he created things that were rarely beautiful, thrilled with the brightest life and tuned with the most accurate music. But he did not wait for these moments. He had a theory by the light of which he labored on incessantly, believing that every thought, that entered his mind, and was dear to him, might be run out into lines and stanzas, and so made to stand for a poem. His theory however was noble, and to aim at the highest level, with a partial failure is greater than to attain to an absolute perfection in a lower one. Wordsworth aimed at the loftiest, now and then he succeeded, and in his success he was the noblest of later English poets. Yet even in his best passages the rendering of the subtle melody of his idea is never perfect. He had not the imperious ear of Keats, who could not have rest[ed] till he had caught and mastered the fullness of every harmony. Wordsworth's finest utterances are always a little broken. They weaken and fall somewhere; but there is enough of them in every case to make us feel most vividly the beauty and truth of the conception[.] They awaken without doubt the answering harmony in our own souls. Such poems as "Michael," "The Leech-gatherer," "Ruth," seem to him who reads them for the first time quite unmusical; only after long acquaintance do we learn that they not only have a harmony but that it is exquisitely true. After having once learned to take delight in the quiet tones of Wordsworth, we begin to value at their true worth many things which had before so unreasonably mastered us.

One of Wordsworth's finest poems is "The Leech-gatherer," or as it is otherwise entitled "Resolution and Independence." The opening stanzas convey very perfectly the poetic impression of a blithe bright morning after a night loud with rain and storm[.]

> There was a roaring in the wind all night;
>> The rain came heavily and fell in floods;
> But now the sun is rising calm and bright;
>> The birds are singing in the distant woods;
>>> Over his own sweet voice the stock-dove broods;
> The jay makes answer as the magpie chatters
> And all the air is filled with pleasant noise of waters.
>
> All things that love the sun are out of doors;

The sky rejoices in the morning's birth;
The grass is bright with rain-drops; on the moors
The hare is running races in her mirth.

"And all the air is filled with pleasant noise of waters." How simple and
how perfect? Have we not a hundred times felt those words, though we
have never expressed them? In the description of the aged and lonely
leech-gatherer, wandering about the moors, there are several examples
of the *curiosa felicitas* of expression noted by Coleridge, and of the most
faithful and delicate musical interpretation[.]

I saw a man before me unawares
The oldest man he seemed that ever wore grey hairs[.]

... Not all alive nor dead,
Nor all asleep, in his extreme old age:
His body was bent double, feet and head
Coming together in their* pilgrimage,
As if some dire constraint of pain, or rage
Of sickness felt by him in times long past,
A more than human weight upon his frame had cast.

Himself he propp'd, his body, limbs, and face,
Upon a long grey staff of shaven wood;
And still as I drew near with gentle pace,
Beside the little pond or** moorish flood,
Motionless as a cloud the old man stood;
That heareth not the loud winds when they call,
And moveth altogether, if it move at all.

There is something, not in the ideas alone, but in the very choice and
grouping of the syllables, in these strange lines, which causes us to feel
irresistibly that we are in very truth face to face with an object of extreme
feebleness, bent with the burden of an almost lifeless old age. They have
a keen, strange force together with a curious dragging effect in the tone,
that is altogether unique and lingers in the ear with a growing assertion
of its mysterious truth.

---

*   Wordsworth had written: "life's."
**   Wordsworth had written: "Upon the margin of that."

As a total change we may turn to the little poems on the "Small Celandine."* A little flower is no doubt a small subject for great poetry; yet is not the frailest thing that is sweetly beautiful worthy of a song? At any rate Wordsworth thought so, and honored the Small Celandine with two of the most charming efforts of his genius. Indeed after wandering through the loose and redundant verbiage of such poems as "The Thorn" and "Goody Blake," so extravagant in their homeliness, we are almost startled by the musical sweetness and compact cutting of these rare stanzas. They express, with a delicate brightness, and loving sincerity of music, the poet's happy contemplation of a little starlike blossom, which was to him not only a harbinger of spring, but the emblem of many humble things that are of more value than their gaudier neighbors[.]

> E'er a leaf is on a bush,
> In the time before the thrush
> Has a thought about its nest,
> Thou wilt come with half a call,
> Spreading out thy glossy breast
> Like a careless prodigal;
> Telling tales about the sun,
> When we've little warmth or none[.]
> [...]

> Prophet of delight and mirth,
> Scorned and slighted upon Earth!
> Herald of a mighty band,
> Of a joyous train ensuing,
> Singing at my heart's command,
> In the lanes my thoughts pursuing,
> I will sing, as doth behove,
> Hymns in praise of what I love!

> ...

> Soon as gentle breezes bring
> News of winter's vanishing,
> And the children build their bowers,

---

* These are two poems, actually. The first is titled "To the Small Celandine," and has eight stanzas; the second is called "To the Same Flower," and contains six stanzas. "Soon as gentle breezes bring" begins the third stanza of the second poem.

Sticking kerchief plots of mould
All about with full-blown flowers,
Thick as sheep in shepherd's fold!
With the proudest thou art there,
Mantling in the tiny square[.]

These are only three stanzas out of fourteen, all of them exquisite; but they perfectly represent the tone.

As an example of an unsuccessful attempt at poetic interpretation. I may quote from Wordsworth's "Thorn."

Like rock or stone, it is o'ergrown
    With lichens to the very top,
And hung with heavy tufts of moss,
    A melancholy crop:
Up from the earth these mosses creep
And this poor Thorn they clasp it round
So close, you'd say that they were bent
With plain and manifest intent
    To drag it to the ground;
And all had joined in one endeavor
To bury this poor thorn forever[.]

The picture intended to be painted in these lines is a strong one, but the ear at once informs us that the attempt has failed. It awakens no answering harmony in the soul. It has in fact no harmony at all, either true or false. The best examples of false harmonies are to be found in Byron, whose musical range was very narrow. The opening lines of the third canto of *The Corsair*, so magnificent and stately, but so untrue and so really unsympathetic, are a striking example.

One of the most interesting of Wordsworth's poems is that which begins "She was a phantom of delight." Its lofty masculine tone of noble praise, its serious, rapid, concise descriptive movement remind us wonderfully of Tennyson—so much so that one is led to imagine that Tennyson might have caught the keynote of his style from the reading of this poem. There are the lines in "Isabel"[*] which seem like a richer echo of the music of Wordsworth's grander and simpler ones. The final stanza[**] will be enough to quote.

---

[*]   "Isabel" by Tennyson, 1830.
[**] i.e. of Wordsworth's "She Was a Phantom of Delight."

And now I see with eye serene
The very pulse of the machine;
A being breathing thoughtful breath,
A traveller betwixt life and death;
The reason firm, the temperate will,
Endurance, foresight, strength and skill;
A perfect woman, nobly planned,
To warn, to comfort, and command;
And yet a spirit still, and bright
With something of an angel light.

Turn then to that other poem, also without a title, beginning "Three years she grew in sun and shower." This is the musical expression of sympathy with a more impassioned spirit. He is describing not the calm-minded noble woman of the former poem, but a figure glowing with the spirit of poetry, the light of a mind akin to his own. The measure is therefore no longer keen cut and stately, but swift and vehement[,] ringing with a sweeter and wilder intonation. This is the musical difference in the poet[']s interpretation of the two characters. Listen to the passionate melody, the flash of imagination in these lines—*

"The stars of midnight shall be dear
To her; and she shall lean her ear
        In many a secret place,
Where rivulets dance their wayward round,
And beauty born of murmuring sound
        Shall pass into her face[.]"

In "Michael" and a great many parts of the *Prelude* and the *Excursion* we find a tone, which is the purest rendering imaginable of whatever musical sense attaches to those pictures and emotions of homely rustic life, which were dearer to Wordsworth's heart than any more complex development of human society could ever be. In his best treatment of these simple things he indulges in no pomp. His lines are direct and homely in their music; but there is in them a noble dignity which is due to all nature in her simple elements. What a sense of healthful content

---

* The quotes indicate that Nature is speaking.

and rustic industry there is the following lines from the description of Michael[']s cottage[.]

> Down from the ceiling, by the chimney's edge,
> Which in our ancient uncouth country style,
> Did with a huge projection overbrow
> Large space beneath, as duly as the light
> Of day grew dim, the housewife hung a lamp,
> An aged utensil which had performed
> Service beyond all others of its kind.
> Early at evening did it burn and late,
> Surviving comrade of uncounted hours,
> Which, going by from year to year, had found
> And left the couple neither gay, perhaps,
> Nor cheerful, yet with objects, and with hopes,
> Living a life of eager industry.
> And now when Luke was in his eighteenth year,
> There by the light of this old lamp they sat,
> Father and son, while late into the night
> The housewife plied her own peculiar work,
> *Making the cottage through the silent hours*
> *Murmur as with the sound of summer flies*[.]

Some very noble examples of poetic interpretation are to be found in Wordsworth's sonnets. It seems strange at first thought that a poet whose utterance was often so loose and irregular, at times even garrulous, should have succeeded so well in a species of verse, requiring in the highest degree the artistic instinct for beautiful form, and the musical instinct for the most delicate and at the same time the largest harmonies; yet this looseness and irregularity in his methods was to a great extent a matter of principle with him, not of feeling, and it was no doubt often with a sense of fine comfort that he betook himself in easier hours to the sonnet, humouring the bright artistic instinct, which was certainly his, and which must have been always hungering within him. Some of his sonnets are the best in the English language. They are rhythmically finer than Shakespeare's or Milton's. His prefatory sonnet on the sonnet is perhaps from an artistic point of view the most perfect work of the kind ever written in our tongue. It could hardly be improved. It is so well known that I need not quote it. Let me rather draw attention to one of the beautiful sonnets on sleep.* I will give it in full. The sense and melody of the first lines are curiously interpretive of that strange uncertain condition between sleep and waking, when we lie for hours haunted by innumerable images that pass before the mind in blind unreasoning succession, persuading us to the sleep, that is ever upon us, but never comes.

> A flock of sheep that leisurely pass by,
> One after one; the sound of rain, and bees
> Murmuring; the fall of rivers, winds, and seas,
> Smooth fields, white sheets of water, and pure sky,
> I've thought of all by turns; and still I lie
> Sleepless; and soon the small birds' melodies
> Must hear, first uttered from my orchard trees;
> And the first cuckoo's melancholy cry.
> Even thus last night, and two nights more, I lay,
> And could not win thee, Sleep! by any stealth:
> So do not let me wear to-night away:
> Without thee what is all the morning's wealth?
> Come, blessed barrier betwixt day and day,
> Dear mother of fresh thoughts and joyous health!

I have illustrated my subject altogether from Keats and Wordsworth because they furnish the most perfect and most abundant examples. No other of our later poets has had such an exquisite ear for all delicate harmonics as Keats, and no other has had such an eager and loving one for the sweet and simple harmonics of free healthy nature as Wordsworth. Next to these, I believe, comes Matthew Arnold. His "Forsaken Merman" with its strange haunting pathos, the grand endings of "Mercerinus" and "Sohrab and Rustum," many passages in "Empedocles on Etna" and various other poems are matchless interpretations of things that echo with a pure and solemn music. Tennyson though a splendid poet and a noble nature is by no means so faithful a poetic interpretor [sic]. Through all his work there is the grasp of a settled system of phrase and melody. The style is powerful and noble, but it does not always accurately interpret. The poet's ear is not sufficiently simple and ingenuous. Shelley failed often for a somewhat similar rea-

---

*   "To Sleep," 1806.

son. Into every picture that he drew, into every thought that he expressed, he wrought the strange unreal color and the wild spiritual music, natural to his own beautiful but fantastic imagination. It is not actual nature that he interprets, but Shelley[']s wonderful re-creation of it. In all such pictures of life as are vehement, intense, passionately imaginative and tender, Robert Browning is a wonderful master; but he is to[o] rapid, too rough, and has too much of a fixed way of talking about things to have a complete musical range. He is not one of the patient listeners for all of nature's secret harmonies. Rossetti interpreted some things, that were in consonance with his own life-long mood, strangely well. Coleridge succeeded perfectly in two poems, "Christobel [sic]" and the "Rhyme [sic] of the Ancient Mariner" but in the rest of his work he seems to have been laboring in the dark, far away from his natural bent.

Byron expressed admirably enough one of his own moods, that of romantic and melancholy self-contemplation. Swinburne is without varie[ty][,] being absorbed and carried away by a single strain of riotous melody which he applies to everything. Such things as can be expressed in his manner he has interpreted as no other man has ever interpreted them, or ever will[.]

Perhaps the world shall some day have a poet who will interpret tenderly passionat[e] dreams like Keats, simple and lofty ones like Wordsworth, strong and passionate pictures of life like Browning, etherial imaginings like Shelley, grave and manly thought like Tennyson, and everything else with the best truth of the special poet who has handled it best. But we shall not look for such a poet for many a long [age][.]

The Modern School of Poetry in England

Composed circa January–February 1885. Undated, unsigned, National Archives of Canada (MG 29 D59 vol. 2, 680–93). *The Essays and Reviews of Archibald Lampman*, edited by D.M.R. Bentley. London: Canadian Poetry Press, 1996, 58–69. Reprinted from http://www.canadianpoetry.ca/confederation/Archibald%20Lampman/essays_reviews/the_modern_school_of_poetry_in_england.htm.

There have been many definitions of poetry[,] chiefly two. It has been defined by one to be the "Interpretation of the Invisible" by another the "Criticism of Life." But poetry is not altogether the interpretation of the invisible and it is more than the criticism of life. As religion is called by Mr. Matthew Arnold "Morality touched with emotion" so poetry is the criticism of life, touched with emotion and something besides. The best naming of it that I have ever seen is that of Mr. Alfred Austin in a paper on "Old and New Canons of Criticism" in *Nineteenth Century Review*. He calls it "The Transfiguration of Life," meaning Life with the halo of the imagination thrown over it[.] That is, it seems to me, the nearest definition that can be got in a single phrase.

If then poetry is the transfiguration of life, in order to establish the value of the poet's work, it is necessary to consider whether the life which he has transfigured is the true life, whether the transfiguration is real[—]that is whether he has thrown the true light of the imagination over it, and finally how much of the true life his work of transfiguration has covered. It seems almost impossible that one living in the same generation with the poet should be able to decide upon any of these things with certainty. It is only after the change of many years, when the irresistible bias of schools and the haunting flavour of mannerisms are forgotten, that the permanent worth of any man's work is finally laid bare, and then it is not the critics, who discover it, but the universal heart of man.

It seems to me however, that there is one thing concerning the true life which may be laid down as a guide in criticism. It is this. Life is not a dreary thing. Human beings are not mere hopeless play things in the hands of chance, utter[ly] governed by a multitude of passions, that must mar and twist them, befoul them or beautify them as they will. Human nature may be represented by the ancient Pan—half human and half beast—but the human is the mightier part, and the whole is ever striving to be divine. The main current of the human spirit through many changes, and many falls[,] is setting eternally toward a condition of order and divine beauty and peace. A poet may never have uttered this thought, may never perhaps have been even conscious of it, but unless the general body of his work is in some way accordant with it, unless his transfiguration of life has in some way tended to strengthen and glorify the universal yearning for order and beauty and peace, the heart of man will keep no hold of it. A dilettante class, and such as are lovers of powerful creation and passionate utterance for genius['] sake, may preserve it as a monument of strength and fire, but the succeeding time must surely cast it off, along with any other empty dream or custom as something unessential to the perfecting movement of its spirit. The greatest poets have taught us that a life of nobility and purity may be made happy, and that only such a life is worth the living. Those who have not taught this, either directly or indirectly, have never been called great. The sympathy with this main truth is what strikes as being conspicuously absent from the dreary and monotonous realism of almost all our present literature.

Moreover it seems to me that in endeavouring to reach approximately the worth of a living poet, there are two qualities to be specially looked for as indications of the genuineness of his transfiguration, and of the liberality with which he has entered into the fullness of the true life. These are variety or versatility, and geniality. The work of all the greatest poets has been very varied, and it has been very genial. Looking with a wide and hearty and sympathetic eye upon all life, they have touched innumerable notes, and have absorbed themselves readily into every phase of its humour or pathos. They have laughed and wept with living men and women; and in their laughter is the kindliness of a large heart, in their sadness the sweetness of brotherly sympathy. Two especially in the present century may be cited as examples of these qualities—Keats and Tennyson. Keats' life was cut short of twenty-six yet in his brief writing season he produced eight noble poems[.] Not one of these is like another; each has a peculiar flavour: for his genius was easy and versatile. He was able to immerse his imagination totally in the spirit of the most different themes. As instances—the "Ode to [sic] a Grecian Urn" is quiet, reflective and antique; each phrase like a curve in the marble— but the "Eve of St. Agnes" is rich and mediæval, having the flavour of stained windows, storm and old time phantasy. No doubt if Keats had lived, a wider contact with individual human life, would have given him also the spirit of geniality—indeed he even had somewhat of it in his own delicate and romantic way. So Tennyson has written for instance three poems, among many others, which but for a certain mannerism might be deemed the product of different hands—the "Lady of Shallott [sic]," mystic and Armorican, "The Lotos-Eaters" with its southern glamour and lazy cadence—lastly the "Talking Oak," with its sweet humour and flavour of parks and minster-bells[.] It was when Tennyson had come to write the "Talking Oak," that time and the working of human experience had mellowed his hand and made it genial.

It is these men who were the masters; for their eyes were not forever fixed upon one usurping corner of life, till it became vast and lurid, but they sang out of the midst of the inner spirit of many conditions of man's happiness and pain. They sang not for themselves only; but in the person of every living creature[.] Moreover they held that life for all its woes and perplexities might be a cheery thing, and that the centre of man's heart was bright and pure. Hardly any of the famous poetry of the present day is like this. For the most part it is not the transfiguration of life. It is little more than the restless utterance of refined selfishness, the transfiguration of personal chimæras. For that reason it has no variety and very little geniality[.] It is not versatile, for it has one uniform coloring for everything, wonderfully beautiful colouring to be sure, but wearisome for lack of change. It is not genial; for it is limited in sympathy and has failed to find beauty in some of the purest and most sacred of human yearnings. If we search the poets of the Preraphaelite school from end to end, we shall find not one thing that may remind us of the lovely cheerfulness of Milton's "L'Allegro" or the delicate bonhomie of the "Talking Oak."

In fine these men* have transfigured very little of life and what they have dealt with lacks much of being the true. Their chief merit lies in the manner of the transfiguration. They have taught the world how

* i.e. The Pre-Raphaelites, and probably Swineburne.

verses should be made. It is reserved for a future generation of poets to show how the lesson, so taught, should be used. They have wrought for us the loveliest garments of poetry, but have given it no pure body or soul. They are cunning painters and musicians, but not great poets; for the great poet must be a broad and noble thinker. They have written much that will charm the world's sense for a moment with its strength of vision and music, not one thing that will hearten it in its journey toward order and divine beauty and peace. They have forgotten that human nature is something more than mere primal nature[.] One of them* in especial seems to have cast off all regard for the spiritual garment of law that time is weaving eternally for the covering of our baser instincts. He has painted the soul[']s existence as little more than a brief delirium, a hopeless texture of strange delights and miseries, springing from the darkness of birth and passing into the darkness of death. Such work can be of no avail. Man is to be taught self-government and hope. Only such teaching will he ultimately accept. The poet who has nothing to show to him, but such phantasmal pictures, [as] some of these men have drawn, no lesson to teach him but such madly confused ones as these men have taught, is only setting his shoulder unconsciously against the pure current of civilization, and all his gifts, how great soever, will hardly help him to be long remembered. Longfellow with his gentle sweetness and occasional insipidity will be remembered, when Poe, for all his strange and fascinating power will be forgotten. Matthew Arnold's "Forsaken Merman" will live, when all the beautiful insanity of Swinburne is spoken of no longer.

II

The greatest of the Preraphaelite school was Dante Gabriel Ros[s]etti[,] painter and poet. He was a secluded artist, brooding acutely upon certain strange things of life, one of those upon whom routine obtained no hold. Of a morbid and impressionable disposition, every object in

---

*   Likely Swineburne mentioned below..

inanimate nature, every hour of time, every thought and emotion was marked by him as having an inner feeling and a mystic worth. In several attributes of the poet he was great, and his work was distinctly original. He had a quick and sensitive imagination, a piercing insight into some sombre and wayward shades of feeling, and a rich gift of music. Although the ideas and emotions, with which he deals are often subtle and occult, his style is wonderfully plain and direct. In this he is different and superior to the rest of his school. He seldom makes an elaborate description of outward things,—indeed he had not the healthy delight in them, which leads men to do so—but rather he is a sketcher in brief and magical phrases, which sometimes strike upon the imagination with the effect of astonishment. He was fond of giving material shape to the inmost motions of the heart and soul, using a system of mystic imagery, which is the most singular and poetic characteristic of his genius. Thought and imagination with him were inseparable in their working, every idea became a bodily tangible thing.

He wrote little. His poems like his paintings were the result of peculiar moods fashioned with long brooding thought, and subject to perpetual change. They will have little hold upon mankind at large, of whose needs and aspirations he studied for the most part only a few unusual phases. They are rather food for poets, and the searchers in the by-ways of emotion. But Ros[s]etti made at least one poem, which has already caught the general heart and is likely to hold it. That is "The Blessed Damosel [sic]"; for though a purely visionary thing the idea at the bottom of it is beautiful, like something that Charles Kingsley holds in one of his letters. The love of men and women was ever present to Ros[s]etti's mind as an infinitely wonderful and strange thing. To him it could not be earthly only, wholly mortal and ephemeral. It was more than that. It was spiritual and eternal. The perfect union on earth was but the prelude to a beautiful and mystic condition hereafter that should have no end forever. In "Love[']s Nocturn" too and the "Stream," and the beautiful lyric called "Love-Lily," we find representations of the same delicate and intense spirituality woven into the speech of earthly passion. But "The Blessed Damosel [sic]" is the succinct expression of it. In this poem also, written at the age of eighteen, we find some of the finest instances of his disposition to give to every mental and emotional thing a material shape—as an instance the words of the Blessed Damosel [sic]:

> We two shall stand beside the shrine,
>> Occult, withheld, untrod,

> Whose lamps are stirred continually
> > With prayers sent up to God,
> And see our old prayers, granted, melt,
> > Each like a little cloud.

With Ros[s]etti every material thing was but the expression of something inward and spiritual, and whatever spiritual thing had no outward shape in nature, must have an exact one somewhere in the realm of thought and emotion.

If all Ros[s]etti's poems had been like these it would have been better. He has unfortunately written others of a very different character and worth. The best known of these is the one called "Jenny." It embodies a criticism of life to be sure, of a very strange and hideous condition of life; but is chiefly noteworthy as being a representative work of the whole school and of the later literature generally, bare, realistic and hopeless—one of the several entirely unpleasant things that Ros[s]etti wrote. It is a picture of dark life, bare and simple, without any help or lesson in it whatever, with very little light of the imagination, and not a vestige of emotion. Whatever bad thing a master has done, the pupils are most ready to follow. The imitators of Ros[s]etti have caught little of his truth and beauty, but such work as "Jenny" has been abundantly and drearily imitated. Another poem, realistic also, but of somewhat greater worth is the "Last Confession," the narrative of one who has loved with Italian fervour and revenged desertion by striking a dagger into the heart of his mistress. The manner of it is intensely quiet and vivid. There are passages of enormous pathos, with a subtle and terrible insight into the darker workings of passion. It is put together with consummate talent, but is, of course, in its nature, painful and disagreeable.

Ros[s]etti is perhaps best known as a fine sonneteer. The sonnet was a form exquisitely adapted to his exact and acutely brooding genius. In one or two of his sonnets he has given new form to some old lessons that can never be too often spoken for mankind—for instance the one on the value of time, and how some good thing should be done in every day that we live.

Most of these poems were unknown to the world, until the year 1870 when the first volume was published. The second and last of ballads and sonnets was issued in 1881. Some of them have a modern groundwork. The most are quaint and mediæval, for Ros[s]etti loved to get back into simpler days. Modern life is vast and complex, and the poet often finds that such primary feelings as belong to all ages and places may be dealt with more freely and with a sharper accentuation, when they are wrought upon a background of ruder and simpler custom. But as Ros[s]etti's mind was moody and personal, so his range was narrow. He dealt with little of life and, though what he worked upon is strikingly done,—for he was serious and sincere—yet he cannot be called a great poet. He had not the large mobile heart, that can throw itself into every variety of life, laughing and weeping with every condition in turn. He has not the cheery manfulness, that is for all of us like the sign and seal of the genuine mastership in verse. His work is in spirit sombre and disturbing. He is confined in art and has no variety of flavour. He is not broadly human in thought and has little geniality. Though he has taught the world some very beautiful things, for which he can never be quite forgotten, he has not cheered its main heart much.

The next of this school[,] as it seems to me, in order of greatness is Charles Algernon Swinburne. Mr. Swinburne is a wonderful musician. One might imagine that he had fallen by mistake into poetry. Everything in his hands turns to enchanting sound[.] In the beautiful management of words, cadences, and forms of metre and stanza, he has reached, it would almost seem, the highest development of art. In the *Songs before Sunrise*, at best they are so many harpings upon one cracked string; he has sometimes held for stanzas together to strain[s] of sonorous sublimity, that might remind us, but for the hollowness of the subject, of some utterance of the old Testament prophets. His lyrics are full of riotous melody. He claims, justly enough, the sea-wind and the sea for the makers of his spirit[:]

> Yours was I born, and ye,
> The seawind and the sea,
> Made all my soul in me
>   A song forever,
>
> A harp to string, and smite,
> For love's sake of the bright
> Wind and the sea's delight
>   To fail them never.

Yet beneath this lovely mastery of expression there is much wanting when we come to look into it. His vocabulary is not large, his range of imagery astonishingly narrow. He has certain set images—day and night, light and darkness, sunrise and sundown, snow and sleep and the like, the use of which is perpetually recurring with the effect of monotony in every thing he has written. We find stanza upon stanza, wrought almost entirely of such things as these, woven and rewoven in glamorous and bewildering confusion. The matter of his verse is generally impalpable, misty, illusive, running on from line to line, in such manner that when we have reached the end, we find ourselves in contact with no thought but merely rolling in a musical ecstacy. The practical value of a writer's work may almost be determined by its adaptability to quotation. There is hardly a line of Swinburne's that any man will ever quote for any purpose, but to show the astonishing gift of the composer. He has uttered no lesson, directly or indirectly, or given striking expression to any truth old or new. His is not the transfiguration of life but[,] as it seems to me, a strange transfiguration of only two things—political and social anarchy. His *Songs before Sunrise* are mere vague communistic chants, mad glorifications of liberty, defining nothing and teaching nothing. At the bottom of them is no idea whatever save that of blind confusion. In the "Last Oracle," one of his later poems and the completest expression of himself, he hails the Greek Apollo, the ruler of light, "strong to help and heal, to lighten and to slay," and invokes the return of Hellenic beauty and freedom[.] The age of Christianity, with the lessons, that she has taught us of nobility and purity, is only darkness to him or the twilight of the Gods[.] For thus he calls upon Apollo[:]

> Age on age thy mouth was mute, thy face was hidden,
> And the lips and eyes that loved thee blind and dumb
> Song forsook their lips that held thy name forbidden,
> Light their eyes that saw the strange God's kingdom come[.]
> Fire for light and hell for heaven, and psalms for paeans
> Filled the clearest eyes and lips most sweet of song
> When for chant of Greeks, the wail of Galilaeans
> Made the whole world moan with hymns of wrath and wrong [.]

Again in another part of this marvelous pagan song he cries

> Yet it may be, Lord and Father, could we know it,
> We, that love thee, for our darkness shall have light.

"Light." It is a favorite word with him; but he has nowhere told us what it means. From the *Songs before Sunrise*, as I have said before, we gather that in politics it means anarchy—or the rule of Cleon and the rabble. From the rest of his poetry we find that socially it means license. In morality Mr Swinburne is the singer of unfettered passion. Reason and order have nothing to do in the matter. In the "Laus Veneris," the praise of Venus, to him the goddess simply of libertinism, he cries

> Thy ways, Lord Christ, are very fair;
> But, lo, her wonderfully woven hair.

The ways of Christ, that did most to give to us the idea of the beauty and whiteness of innocence, are very fair to be sure; but they are nothing to him and to those, who are of art and earnest looking toward the light.

Mr. Swinburne even as an artist, is utterly without restraint. He has nothing of the depth and calm of the master, and for all his impassioned music, has no dignity, and reasonably so, for he has very little that is noble and true to say. He is quite destitute of dramatic or narrative power. In his lyrics, however unwholesome the spirit of most of them is, he is irresistibly fascinating. One is completely carried away with the supreme loveliness of word and form and rhythm. His dramatic work on the contrary is almost unreadable. The movement is heavy, the range of action and feeling circumscribed and gloomy. Even the manner of expression is intricate and lifeless. His *C[h]astelard and Bothwell* can hardly seem otherwise than monuments of misdirected labour. His *Tristram of Lyonesse*, a narrative poem on the story of Tristram and Queen Iseulte, has the same defects. The movement is utterly heavy. The style, the imagery and description are glamorous and intricate, without life or interest[.] The first fifty lines of the poem are enough to frighten any reader away from it. Moreover the treatment of the subject is over sensuous and unhealthy, and wherever it was possible to give any morally hideous colouring to the original tale, he has done so to the full. There is surely nothing in this work to be remembered and everything that it were well to forget. All such poetry of Mr. Swinburne[']s and a great deal of his lyric writing too, will last, I think, but a little time in the world's memory: for as it has been said, the core of the world's heart—and it is that that always settles the value of these things in the end—is working for peace and purity—and it will not bear to be contaminated. Instead of helping man in his labour for order and divine beauty and peace, he has given his whole strength to disturb him. The soul of Mr. Swinburne's work is shere [sic] recklessness—a mad self-abandonment to the rush of music and sensuous vision. For this reason his glorious gift of expression will only serve as matter of study to those who may know better how to use it. He has never meditated genially and sympathetically upon the homely things of life. He has not entered heartily in the stir of human nature, and many of its most sacred instincts he is incapable of understanding. His spirit is certainly unhealthy and destructive. His poetry looks like a beautiful ignis fatuus—and when we have followed it to its goal we find that we have only wandered into a lurid and miasmatic wilderness, wherein is no happiness at all, but only delight that is sapped with pain and pain that has no guide of truth whatever in the soul to help or save.

Of all this poet's enormous bulk of writing the only parts which seem likely to live are a few of his lyrics, such rare ones as have dealt with inanimate nature, sweetened with simple human reflection—and especially those that [are] written with much tenderness and geniallity [sic] about children and childhood. Perhaps also men will not quite forget the *Atalanta in Calydon* which though one of the earliest is strangely enough the sanest and soberest of his longer works.

The third and last poet of consequence in the Preraphaelite school is William Morris, who like Swinburne has written a great deal too much. His greatest work is the *Earthly Paradise*, written somewhat in imitation of Chaucer, but without Chaucer's blithe geniallity [sic] and practical wisdom. A ship full of Norwegians set sail in the fourteenth century to search for a fabled country in the West, where there is no death or pain. After many adventures and many miseries they came, when they were worn and old, to an unknown island and found there certain Greeks, whose ancestors had emigrated long ago from the mother land, bringing with them their customs and legends. The Greeks made homes for the Norwegians, and in their hours of idleness they amused one another by telling stories alternately from the Greek Mythology and the northern sagas. These tales are very sweetly told; but they have no strength or variety. One cannot read many of them without weariness. They have no genuine hearty sympathy with the movement of life—no humour or real pathos—no dramatic or narrative force[.] Beautiful as they are, one cannot long follow without a sense of monotony an idle story, which has nothing to recommend it but the easy flow of a sensuous imagination, sometimes gar[r]ulous[,] and an indolent murmuring versification. *The Life and Death of Jason* is more unreadable; for it is long and equally purposeless and the idea at the bottom of it dark and cheerless. *The Story of Sigurd the Volsung* [is] most unreadable of all. How any man could have undertaken to reconstruct the whole Nibelung legend in English ballad verse, would be incomprehensible, if we had not already had a specimen of William Morris' marvelous diligence in the *Life and Death of Jason*. All these poems, besides their universal monotony and want of hearty life, are rendered of no avail by the prevailing curse of the whole modern school—a morbid unhealthiness of the soul. This man, like the rest, has no true and vital principle, upon which to base his work. His whole stock for thought seems to be, the power and blind prevalence of material passion and the dreariness of death and old age. The world has been told already too much about these things, and she will welcome most readily him who will teach her to forget them[.] William Morris has done nothing to help the cause of order and divine beauty and peace, and his work can therefore hardly be of much lasting interest to mankind.

To repeat and conclude, the modern men have taught us many things in the graces of art. They have taught us much about the magic of colour and much about beauty in form. We find in them a more *glowing* delight in nature than in most of our elder poets. They have taught us also many secrets in the use of words and metres—the sweetest mysteries of sound. The artistic failings of the school are the failings of the age— restlessness and want of restraint. It has neglected the grandest attribute of genius, patience. Most of its members have written too much and too unevenly. But their most serious fault is a moral one—and that is want of innocence. It seems to me that the Preraphaelite poets have forgotten this. That original nature is not precisely human nature. Those things which are the laws of original nature they have mistaken to be the laws also of human nature. They have forgotten that society, for its own happiness and peace, has formed for itself age by age and change by change a system of order and law, which has now come to be as much a part of human nature as our primal instincts are. This they have forgotten and in forgetting have been led almost to glorify and treat as things divine some of the very passions, which it has been the aim of social progress to soften and command. They have forgotten also an- other thing. That all true art must rest upon a sense of wonder,—a sense of the invisible that is around everything,—and that this sense of won- der can only dwell in its purity in a perfectly simple and innocent mind—true art must be naive.* Now a mind which is not in accord with

---

*　　Lampman's note: "Tennyson says of the poet's mind
　　'Clear and bright it should be ever
　　Flowing like a crystal river
　　Bright as light and clear as wind.'"

those main social laws which are become instincts, is not simple and in-nocent,—and its sense of wonder is overshadowed and distorted. Con-tact with uninnocent emotion has unsettled it, till it is no longer capable of the clearest poetry: [t]hat is the reason why so much of our modern verse is gifted with innumerable attributes of poetry, but is at the soul, feverish and unmanly. It is the utterance of minds that are longing for the true happiness and have mistaken the way to find it. They have sung for us the extremes of human joy and pain, but never anything of man-ful trust or hearty endurance—or if they have ever preached to us, re-straint and endurance, it has been a hang-dog stoacism [sic], wearing the yoke about its neck. All this is very useless to us, and it seems to me that the modern school cannot have much permanent influence upon taste, for the one grand reason that they have done nothing to help mankind in the gradual and eternal movement toward order and divine beauty and peace.

From the Globe
13 February 1892

Reprinted from *At the Mermaid Inn: Wilfred Campbell, Archibald Lampman, Duncan Campbell Scott in The Globe 1892–93*, intro. by Barrie Davies, Toronto: U of Toronto P, 1979, 10.

There is no limit to the making of fanciful classifications in literature, yet after the manner of men I must needs put forward a little one of my own. Poetry of the imaginative and essentially lyrical sort may, as it seems to me, be divided into three classes: poetry of imaginative inspiration, poetry of impassioned reflection, and poetry of eloquence. The most eloquent of poets was Shakespeare, the most inspired was Shelley, and the most intensely reflective, Rossetti. Shelley's "Alastor" and Coleridge's "Ancient Mariner" are perfect examples of the poetry of imaginative inspiration; Rossetti's "Blessed Damosel" [sic] and "Bride's Prelude" of the poetry of impassioned reflection, and I can think of no finer example of the eloquent in verse than Tennyson's "Revenge." The poetry of eloquence lends itself most readily to vocal rendition; that of reflection is the most difficult to interpret to an average audience. Swinburne is also, I think, one of the poets of eloquence. How magnificently readable is "The Lost Oracle." Contrast with this the "Bride's Prelude" of Rossetti, a poem to be held and brooded on, its intense and restrained passion, its subtle and vivid touches only to be thoroughly apprehended upon repeated reading, and not to be successfully interpreted save by a spirit and tongue exceptionally rich in resource and utterly in accord with the bent of the poet.

From the Globe
2 April 1892

Reprinted from *At The Mermaid Inn: Wilfred Campbell, Archibald Lampman, Duncan Campbell Scott in The Globe 1892–93*, intro. by Barrie Davies, Toronto: U of Toronto P, 1979, 44–45.

A great many people have the idea that a poet, or, indeed, any kind of literary artist, must be a sort of monstrosity, a person whose dress, language, and habits are quite out of the line of their ordinary experience. They expect to find him a being wrapped in fiery abstractions, of frenzied glance and disordered locks, forever impelled by the most gorgeous sentiments, and getting off impassioned remarks, full of unintelligible profundity. And how astonished they are to find the poet so wonderfully like other sensible men, the chief difference being that he is possessed in a much higher degree of that quality which they least looked for, namely, common sense; for the faculty of genius is nothing more than clear, plain common sense, carried to a high degree and kindled with imagination. The poet differs from the ordinary man of affairs in that he applies the quality of common sense to all the relations and activities of life; the man of affairs merely applies it in a limited way to things as they are related to certain accepted ideas, which he has been taught to regard as the sum of existence. The hardheaded man of the world always distrusts the poet as a dreamer or unpractical person. It is a curious thing to reflect that the very reverse is the fact. The businessman, for instance, who with ingenuity and labour accumulates a fortune, spends his whole life in the pursuit of a dream, which in the end is the most empty and futile imaginable; a dream which to the unsparing eye of the poet is not only despicable for its narrowness but possesses in a gigantic degree all the elements of the ludicrous. The poet attaches himself to no dream. He endeavours to see life simply as it is, and to estimate everything at its true value in relation to the universal and the infinite. But the man of affairs still calls the poet a dreamer. There are also a very great number of people, especially, I believe, in this country, who regard the word "poet" as simply and completely synonymous with the word "fool." They expect to find in the poet a very erratic person, with weak eyes, a flabby complexion, an effeminate drawl, and an alarming tendency to be affected to tears on slight provocation. What is their astonishment when he proves to be the wisest, the manliest, the most self-contained, and sometimes even the austerest and apparently most unimpassionable of all men. Let us instance a few of the great names: Aeschylus, Sophocles, Dante, Shakespeare, Milton, Goethe, Wordsworth, Tennyson. Are there in the annals of statecraft or business or philanthropy any goodlier or wholesomer figures of men than these?

From the Globe
25 June 1892

Reprinted from *At The Mermaid Inn: Wilfred Campbell, Archibald Lampman, Duncan Campbell Scott in The Globe 1892–93*, intro. by Barrie Davies, Toronto: U of Toronto P, 1979, 97–98.

It is not the brilliancy, the versatility, the fecundity, or the ingenuity of a poet that makes him 'great'; it is the plane upon which his imagination moves, the height from which he looks down, the magnitude of his ideas. This largeness of vision is often accompanied by extreme simplicity in the literary faculty, and it is on this account mainly that the really great poet is often partly obscured from public recognition by the greater brilliancy and fertility of some of his contemporaries. We are too apt to measure the greatness of a writer by the degree to which he astonishes us or interests us, rather than by the actual spiritual benefit and enlargement of ideas which he confers. There was a time when Dryden was considered a greater poet than Milton. Dryden was a writer of great intellectual power, great literary activity, and an admirable range of accomplishment; but we know now that that obscure old man, who did not write so very much in all his life, and who but for his obscurity and his blindness might never have written our grand epic at all, was so far greater than the renowned Dryden by the grandeur and breadth of his imagination that the latter sinks altogether into a lower rank in the record of literature. So, too, in more recent times, Lord Byron, with his dash and daring and his immense cleverness and gift of verse, over-clouded all the reputations of his age, but I think that we are now nearly all of us agreed that three at least of his contemporaries dwell upon an intellectual level far loftier and purer than his, and were, therefore, essentially greater poets than he.

In our own time I think we allow ourselves to be a little too much dazzled by the supreme literary gift and magnificent versification of Tennyson, and the insight, vigour, and extraordinary versatility of

Browning. We are apt almost to pass by a poet who in this last age occupies the clearest and noblest plane of all. I mean Matthew Arnold. Arnold is not so triumphantly the poet as Tennyson, nor is he so various or so clever as Browning, but he looks from a grander height than either, his imagination has its natural abode in a diviner atmosphere. The whole range of life, time, and eternity, the mysteries and beauties of existence and its deepest spiritual problems are continually present to his mind. In his genius is that rare combination of philosophy and the poetic impulse in the highest degree, which has given us our few solitary poets. The only test by which we can measure the greatness of a verse writer is the quality of the effect which he produces upon the mind of the reader. He who has been reading Browning till his head spins with the multitude of subtleties and splendid tours de force, or he who is even weary, if such a thing may be, of the rounded perfections of Tennyson, betakes himself to Matthew Arnold, and then he seems to have reached the hills. With a mind blown clear as by the free wind of heaven he surveys the extent of life. He passes through an atmosphere where only the noblest emotions, life, beauty, and thought, possess him. He becomes gentle and majestic as the mind of the master who commands him.

I believe that the time will come when Matthew Arnold will be accounted the greatest poet of his generation, and one of the three or four noblest that England has produced.

From the Globe
6 *August 1892*

Reprinted from *At the Mermaid Inn: Wilfred Campbell, Archibald Lampman, Duncan Campbell Scott in The Globe 1892–93,* intro. by Barrie Davies, Toronto: U of Toronto P, 1979, 125–26.

When Keats said, "Beauty is truth; truth beauty; that is all ye know and all ye need to know," he might have added, if he had been writing prose, that goodness is another synonym for both truth and beauty. The love of beauty is the love of truth and goodness. By the love of beauty I do not mean the artistic instinct, of which it is only a branch. Art is not necessarily true or good. Perfectly genuine art may be neither beautiful nor true nor good. Art is a non-moral thing, and may be good or bad, according to the nature of him who uses it. The man of fine and noble instincts is all the finer and nobler for being an artist, but the man whose instincts are originally weak and base becomes all the weaker and baser in the atmosphere of art. It is not thus at all with the sense of beauty. This can only be of truth and goodness. Art may disturb, but beauty can only bring rest. Beauty expands the soul and raises it to quiet heights. Everything that is mean or cruel or impure shrinks from the sense of beauty as a disease shrinks from the mountain air. Beauty is the essence of harmony. The moment the soul is shaken by any unworthy passion, any distress or bitter remorse, the sense of beauty is undone. Only with those who live nobly can the spirit of beauty dwell secure. So absolutely true is it that "beauty is truth" that this is the perfect justification of many things in art that are condemned by the rigid realist. That art, which is the accurate transcription of nature, since it is true, is beautiful, but there is also the art of creation which is not contrary to nature, but parallel with it. The painter may paint us a flower different from any flower that exists upon earth, and yet he may paint it under so clear an impulse of creation that it may be actually as beautiful and true a thing, and as fully entitled to existence, as anything we have seen with our eyes. He has made no unreal thing. He has simply been active under the influence of the same eternal spirit that moulded and constructed the universe. A great poem may be built up of images utterly unreal, and yet its beauty and imaginative fitness may be so convincing that we feel that nature herself might have fashioned it in some such manner had she not followed another vein. The poem, therefore, is artistically true. The novelist may paint us a character such as we never actually met with, nor believe to be anywhere existent in life, and yet it may be so life-like, so in touch with the warm human impulses within us, that it becomes real to our imaginations, as genuine a human being as any whom we cannot hear or see in the flesh. Such a character, no matter what the extreme realists may say, is true. There is scientific truth, and there is also artistic truth, and the latter is of almost as much value in the economy of intellect as the former.

From the Globe
17 September 1892

Reprinted from *At the Mermaid Inn: Wilfred Campbell, Archibald Lampman, Duncan Campbell Scott in The Globe 1892–93*, intro. by Barrie Davies, Toronto: U of Toronto P, 1979, 152–53.

Sonnet writing is fascinating exercise. Every man who writes verse at all must write a sonnet. The form has been abundantly cultivated in America. Our magazines and journals are full of sonnets, many of them revealing an excellent gift of versification and true thought and feeling; yet America has not produced any poet who has been a really eminent sonnet writer, and she has produced very few sonnets of a very high order, perhaps none of the highest. It may be that the unsettled social atmosphere of this continent is not fitted to develop that particular union of austere dignity and lyric fervour which makes the fine sonnet writer. The sweetest sonnets and the most beautiful in all the American collections are undoubtedly Longfellow's. His "Nature'" "Sound of the Sea," "Milton," "Tides," and "Chimes" are very lovely little poems and only need a little strengthening, a slight access of ruggedness, to make them sonnets of the highest order. The cleverest sonnets we have are those of Mr Edgar Fawcett. They are the cleverest, the strongest, the most ingenious, and the least touching. Like all Mr Fawcett's work, they are the product of a powerful artistic genius, devoted to a sort of subtle imitation of passion and equipped with an unusual faculty of invention. Some of them are splendid as bits of versification—"Sleep," for instance—others are simply horrible, the more so for being able, and not one of them has the accent of real tenderness or moves with the freedom of the noblest beauty. Edgar Allan Poe came nearest to writing the grand sonnet of this continent in "Silence." Bryant nearly succeeded in "October," and so did Lowell in some of his sonnets addressed to persons, in which he seems to have been moved by a specially lofty and musical spirit. Mr Aldrich has written some exceedingly able and grandly sounding sonnets, but he has generally erred, as Americans are so apt to do, on the side of cleverness. Many of his pieces are marred by a line or two of much too evident effort at fine writing. He has not often the patient ear and majestic self-restraint of the true sonneteer. Sydney Lanier injured the character of his sonnets not only as sonnets but even as poems by weaving them full of careful subtleties of phrase and meaning and weighting them too heavily with intricate imagery; for the sonnet — most particularly among all kinds of poetry—should be simple. Mr Gilder, who also came very near the ideal American sonnet in "The Life-Mask of Abraham Lincoln," has written a number of other beautiful ones—"The River" and "The Holy Land," especially. His sonnet on the sonnet, which is much extolled, seems to me rather a spasmodic little production, a sort of task momentarily imposed, and done by tour de force, but very cleverly. Some of James Whitcomb Riley's sonnets are exquisite in their almost impish cleverness and their dainty and whimsical beauty. For with him the sonnet has put off her fair and majestic robes of wisdom and has donned not exactly the cap and bells, but certainly some sort of gay and rather impudent apparel. The sonnets of Emma Lazarus are the finest of those written by American women. One or two of them—"Success," for instance, and "The Venus of the Louvre"—are strong, and bite keenly into the memory. A certain looseness, however—the flagging of a line here and there— prevents them from ranking with the very best work of their kind. Our own poet, Chas. G.D. Roberts, has written at least one sonnet of a high order, "Reckoning," and several others of marked and individual excellence. Among the poems of Mrs Moulton, Helen Gray Cone, Mrs Jackson, Clinton Scollard, Charles H. Luders, Bayard Taylor, and R.H. Stoddard are scattered sonnets of considerable beauty, but not often with the genuine sonnet ring.

From the Globe
29 October 1892

Reprinted from *At the Mermaid Inn: Wilfred Campbell, Archibald Lampman, Duncan Campbell Scott in The Globe 1892–93*, intro. by Barrie Davies, Toronto: U of Toronto P, 1979: 180–82.

No man is more sincere than the poet; yet no man is more given to expressing under different circumstances the most opposite sentiments. Let none quarrel with the poet for this variableness of mood; in fact it is his chiefest charm; it is that which brings him into the most tender and intimate relation with the general soul of humanity. The listener, as he is touched in turn by so many rapid and equally passionate alternations of hope and sorrow, anger or despair, perceives that he is in contact with one who knows the most secret impulses of his heart, and whose spirit, through quickness of sympathy, is in the closest friendliness with his own. I have a friend—a lyric poet—whose mind is, as a general rule, more stolid and less violent in its changes of colour than is the case with many of his kind; yet he has just furnished me with a very pretty example of this fine fickleness of thought. It had been an unfortunate day for my friend. Unpleasant sensations had followed closely one upon another. He had been worried by some small monetary difficulty, a thing that to another man would have been a very trifle, but to him was like the breaking of the Bank of England. He had been in contact with businessmen, men who deal in money, and their cold brutality and callousness of heart had affected his spirit with a kind of gloomy horror. When night came he was sad and weary, and enveloped in a cloud of portentous darkness. Yet it was not long before, the old and ever-active remedy began to insinuate itself and work among his distracted thoughts. As by some happy accident, a touch of song kindled his thoughts. with a sudden illumination, and after meditating a little while he composed with little effort a sonnet which he has called the "Cup of Life," and here I give it just as he read it to me a few days later:

One after one the high emotions fade,
Life's wheeling measure empties and refills
Year after year. We seek no more the hills
That lured our youth divine and unafraid,
But, swarming on some common highway, made
Beaten and smooth, plod onward with blind feet,
And only where the crowded crossways meet
We halt and question, anxious and dismayed.
Yet can we not escape it. Some we know
Have angered and grown mad, some scornfully laughed,
Yet surely to each lip—to mine, to thine—
Comes with strange scent and acrid, poisonous glow
The cup of life—that dull Circean draught—
That taints us all, and turns the half to swine!*

The following morning seemed to usher in a complete change of destiny for the poet. As he passed the threshold, the sunshine greeted him with an unusual heartiness of warmth, and the great elm before his door, whose vast level fleece and pendent draperies seemed afloat upon the air, invited his eyes coolly and alluringly into its shadowy recesses. The birds sang in their gayest and happiest humour. A few paces on a friend met him with good news. When the long day's toil was over, still under the influence of the morning's first joyous impressions, he made his way into the fields, and as he returned homeward after an hour of easy accord with nature, at peace with all mankind, the following verses formed themselves naturally and almost unconsciously in his mind. I give them exactly as he set them upon paper** at the moment of his return:

I love the warm bare earth and all
    That works and dreams thereon;
I love the seasons yet to fall;
    I love the moments gone.

The valleys with the sheaved grain,
    The river smiling bright,

*   *The Poems of Archibald Lampman*, Toronto: Morang, 1900, 280.
** This version of "Amor Vitae" is quite different from that which appears in *The Poems of Archibald Lampman*, 250–51. If, as implied, this is a first draft of the poem, it is remarkably good, and to my mind superior to the collected version.

The merry wind, the rustling rain,
    The vastness of the night.
I love the morning's flame, the steep
    Where down the vapour clings;
I love the clouds that float and sleep,
    And every bird that sings.

I love the masted pines that soar
    Above the mountain villas;
I love the silent wood whose floor
    Is spread with golden lilies.

I love the heaven's azure span,
    The grass beneath my feet;
I love the face of every man
    Whose thought is swift and sweet.

I let the merry world go by,
    And like an idle breath
Its phantoms and its echoes fly;
    I have no dread of death.

I hear the jar of right and wrong;
    Yet both are things that seem;
Each hour is but a fluted song,
    And life a lofty dream!

Assuredly one may say that these verses are light, and inconsiderable in texture, and ethically of little value; yet I give them as the happy and sincere expression of a wonderful change of mood and of all the relations of the poet's mind. Under what different aspects indeed did this life present itself to the poet when he composed these two diverse poems, yet they are both equally sincere.

Happiness:
A Preachment by Archibald Lampman

First published in *Harper's New Monthly Magazine* 18 (July 1896): 309–12. Reprinted from Arthur S. Bourinot, ed. *Archibald Lampman's Letters to Edward William Thomson*, Ottawa: Privately published, 1956.

To each man, emerging from the period of childhood, the thoroughfare of life branches into three ways—one to the right, one to the left, and the third, the broadest, straight ahead. The portal to the right is lofty but narrow, and, over it is hung the aegis of Pallas Athene. Within stand the attendants of the goddess, an innumerable throng, infinitely various in face, figure, and attribute. Some one of these advances to the greeting of every man as he comes up from the open meadows of youth. This is his good genius; in other words, the radical gift through which he is intended by nature to be operative and fruitful among men. If he yield to her, she will take him by the hand, and thenceforth become his guide. He will journey by upward and difficult paths, often losing his way, often retracing his steps; sometimes piercing the unbroken wild, uncertain as to the immediate goal, for even the appointed guide rarely sees with unerring instinct. But the sense of health, of general rightness, of gratified individuality, will continue to be with him. In the end he will reach high table-lands, from which he will survey the world and mankind, and perceive that even the cloudiest tracts are overarched by the interminable blue, and dreamed upon by inexhaustible sunshine. This is the road of happiness—such happiness as can be commonly attained by man.

The pathway to the left opens through a portal festooned with vines and heavy with the scent of roses. From it issue sounds of music and mysterious revelry. Near the threshold, beautiful and alluring, stands Circe with her cup, a figure endlessly changing, fitting herself to every man's desire. This is the road of mere delight, of emotional inclination, of aimless excitement. We need not follow its windings, till it ends at last in that gloomy lake, full of the nameless outcries of creatures abject and deformed, writhing under the final incantations of the dreadful goddess, now horribly revealed and stripped of all her beauty.

The third portal is broad and obvious and unattended. No goddess stands there, for it is an entrance abhorred and shunned by all the immortals. This is the way of the commonplace, the path of routine. Into it drift the majority of men, blindly and aimlessly, not having fire enough in their blood to choose the wrong road, nor sufficient consciousness of soul to choose the right. Here there can be no true happiness; for the pale multitudes that infest it live no life, are stirred by no inspiration, yield to no movement of individual purpose. The most that they do is to blunder into some pleasant land of Cockagne, where puddings grow upon stalks like cabbages, and roasted pigs run about under the trees.

There appear to be certain rare temperaments to which a sort of happiness is attached as a gift of nature. The complete egoist, absorbed in the exploitation of the powers and impulses of his own nature, provided he has little imagination and is gifted with faculty to attain his ends, may be happy with a sort of solitary and arid happiness. The perfect altruist also, that rare spirit that devotes itself wholly and willingly to the profit and pleasure of others, may be happy with a happiness beneficent and sublime. Between these lies the vast range of temperament in which the alter and the ego are in every degree in conflict. Here there are broken lights and shadows, storm and stress, aspiration and despair, and all the tragical battles of desire and conscience. Only a few blessed souls stand scathless above the common tumult—those in whom nature has balanced the conflicting motives of selfishness and devotion in so rare and fitting a harmony that they seem never to be at variance, but one gives way to the other at the proper moment, as if by a delicate, divinely adjusted instinct. These are the beings who move among men like the gods—at ease, joyous and untroubled, receiving and conferring pleasure, universally loving and beloved. Joy comes to them with the fulness of health. Sorrow afflicts them but as a noble chastening.

Conscience does not prick them. Indeed, they have no need of it, for conscience is the monitor of the unbalanced.

To such of us as would not have the callous self-satisfaction of the egoist if we could—to whom the spiritual perfection of the altruist is impossible—the chance of happiness rests upon the development of the individual gift. Let each men find out what thing it is that nature specially intended him to do, and do it. Work is only toil when it is the performance of duties for which nature did not fit us, and a congenial occupation is only serious play. If a man has an overruling talent for music, let no force or persuasion, or trick or trend or circumstances, induce him to become a lawyer, or a physician, or a stock-broker, or anything but what he wants to be and nature distinctly indicates that he should be.

In a free and characteristic activity, though we may never fully attain the ends we seek, we shall easily annul and disregard all the secondary and feverish yearnings which harass and perplex the soul. What man is more happy than the retired student, who desires no better company than his beloved books, and to whom there is no keener pleasure than the possession of a new volume? The devoted artist who has made his canvas magical with some subtle effect of light and atmosphere, unaimed at or unconceived before? The poet who has succeeded in perpetuating in perfect verse some genuine sally of beautiful emotion? Or, to come down to modes of self-expression as honorable if less distinguished, the true carpenter, or iron-worker, or stone-cutter, whose spirit is eagerly occupied in the production of things excellent in their practical beauty and usefulness? Such spirits have it in them to flow lucidly and serenely, lapsing over all obstacles with the silent smoothness of deep and swift waters. They are happy not because they have no rebellious propensities, no faults or discords of temperament, but because they have shaped for themselves an adequate safety-valve. There is in every character that is worth anything a good deal of superfluous energy—energy over and above what is required for the discharge of the common duties of life. If a man has not some living occupation, born of the quality of his own soul, in which the superfluous energy may expend itself in creative activity, it gathers and ferments there as a bitter and destructive humor. If it is strictly suppressed, it breeds ennui, hypochondria, and despair. If it explodes, it goes far to ruin and wreck the frail tenement which it might have inhabited as a spirit of glowing and beneficent power. Unhappy is the soul which is possessed by an energy too wayward and too violent to be appeased by any normal activity, an energy driven to find vent in wild and tragic excesses. To those natures whose aptitudes and impulses are exceptionally quick and strong, one of the greatest dangers to happiness is in the refusal to accept genially the limitations which society has set to the undue expansion of the individual. The uncontrolled nature of genius has often dashed itself in youthful rebellion against the hosts of circumstance, and brought forth from the struggle only wretchedness and ruin. To each one of us there seems to be a barrier here and a barrier there, which we cannot but think that nature intended us to roughly overstep, since she planted in us exceptional forces. But it is not so. Nature's method is always that of development. Her violences are only incidental. It is our business to plant ourselves coolly within the narrow limits of practical life, and let the spirit shine there to its utmost intensity. It will shine if its quality is humanly sweet and genuine. At first the walls that close us in appear to be cold and massive; but if we watch and listen attentively, forgetful of ourselves, our ears become infinitely sharpened, our eyes are made clairvoyant. The sounds of life come to us from beyond the walls; their thickness fades away, and all the wealth and distance of the world lie open to us even as the heaven above. In the end the soul is rewarded with the humanest and most natural liberty. If we rebel and violently struggle, if we endeavor to force our ground, the barriers only loom the loftier and darker; our excursions beyond them are fruitless to ourselves and accompanied by infinite horror; finally they fall upon us and crush us.

To the vigorous and well-nurtured soul there is the finest of all joys in triumphing inwardly over the external pressure of circumstance, and thus displaying in the noblest and most human fashion the unconquerable lordship of the spirit. Thus the poet, when he might give to the impulse of expression the freest and wildest liberty, chooses for his own pride and pleasure to confine himself within the difficult bounds of the sonnet. The form is finite and severe, but it is his glory to prove that the spirit within may be gracious and infinite.

We should accept the limitations of life with this noble and pliant generosity of the poet; not with the austere spirit of the stoic, who plants himself in hostility to joy, gathers his skirts about him, and holds aloof. Stoicism is not happiness. It is simply armed peace, an attitude barren and comfortless. Happiness may almost be defined as the consciousness of adequate self-expression attained by the individual, within the limitations imposed by the social structure. A free expression of the individual, won by the transcending or violating of those limitations, may be accompanied by immense emotional gains, but the result is not happiness, for it is marred by the tragic sense of isolation and struggle. I do not mean to condemn those natures that are driven by the pressure of energies sometimes divine to overstep the bounds of custom and law —they are often the unhappy pioneers of better things—but I am speaking now of happiness, and such natures are not happy.

A quick sense of humor is surely one of the happiest of mortal possessions. It saves a man from many a bitter fall consequent upon his taking himself too seriously. He who has learned to laugh at himself is a near neighbor to happiness, for vanity never increases beyond the danger-point in the truly humorous man. A kindly feeling for the ludicrous easily smooths away the sharp edges of disappointment and humiliation, and the wise man draws back from many an act and many a speech which passion or even calculation dictates, but which humor instantly represents to him by an image as undignified and absurd. Humor also, which is inseparable from tenderness, illuminates for us the cranks and eccentricities of our neighbors, so that we are attracted by them rather than repelled. It is the source of that joyous spirit of tolerance which is a necessary condition of happy living. Through it we learn to find our delight in the mere sound and spectacle of life.

The season at which happiness is most fully within our reach is not, it seems to me, the season of youth, so much extolled, but rather that of early middle age. We have passed through our period of storm and stress. We are no longer torn by the deep agitations of youth. With the full capacity to enjoy, our mental and spiritual faculties are settled and matured. We are in a position to appreciate experience, to digest and make the most of it. Moreover, the soul is stored with memories, a possession of which few of us sufficiently avail ourselves, or realize the value. It is in memory, the recollection of things adventitious or episodical, that our deepest and secured pleasure consist. Let us illustrate this by a parable.

We paddled into a little lake—I and my friends—in our Indian birch canoe. We were hungry, and we wanted fish. We found a tanned and wrinkled trapper at the door of his cabin, and questioned him as to the waters. There had once, he said, been many grey trout there, but now they were all gone, and we must look for them in the next lake. We portaged and passed into the next lake. We found there another trapper, thin-lipped, and with deep-set furtive eyes, who told us that the grey trout had descended into the deep waters and could only with great difficulty be caught, but that there were many in the next lake. Into the next lake we portaged and passed, only to learn that the grey trout must be sought in a lake still farther beyond. On we went from lake to lake, till we had lost ourselves in the wilderness, but we never found the grey trout. Not the grey trout, indeed; but how many other things were conferred upon us, things vital and beautiful, a store of inextinguishable reminiscence! Years afterward we remembered the rare brown water, deep and dark, in the cool abysses of lakes, golden and glowing at midday over the rocks and shallows; the tingling forest air; the solemn and fanelike pine woods; the morning mists reeling before the sunrise into rosy shattered spirals; the cold and lonely nights, near and radiant with stars; the passing of the loons above us; voices of the Northern solitude, weird and disconsolate; the ringing of the axes of woodmen at dawn hewing a path in the unbroken wilderness. These and many other things we remembered afterward with luxurious joy, when the grey trout were no longer a care to us.

So is it with happiness.

Style

Written circa 1889–92. Undated, unsigned, National Archives of Canada (MG 29 D59 vol. 1, 532–84). Reprinted from *The Essays and Reviews of Archibald Lampman*, ed. D.M.R. Bentley, London: Canadian Poetry Press, 1996, 72–90. For valuable notes see: http://www.canadianpoetry.ca/confederation/Archibald%20Lampman/essays_reviews/editorial_notes.htm#style

Style I suppose might be defined as the habit or manner given to expression by the prevalence of a certain mental attitude peculiar to any individual or class of individuals or any age. A style therefore is the exact opposite of an affectation which is an assumed habit or manner of expression. Style as we know is not a quality peculiar to literature, but may be found in every sort of expression when carried to a certain point of culture, in action[,] in speech, in literature, and in all the arts[.] We know how noticeable the quality of style is in the conduct and bearing of many people who have a decided mental character and have mingled freely in the activities of the world. We observe in them a habitual manner of address[,] of speech, of bearing, a way they have of carrying off everything, which seems perfectly natural to them, but might seem quite unnatural in others. In its finest development this style or manner as we call it is a revelation of character but often in those whose contact with the world has been too full, or has perhaps been attended with bitterness[,] it comes to be in part a concealment. The most perfect development of style must be sought in those whose experience of the world has been full and at the same time in the main joyous and exhilarating. Have we not all of us known people of this kind—men and women whose almost invariable manner is the perfect expression of an exquisite indulgence and graciousness of disposition, and who exercise at all times a magical influence upon others. Have we not seen them moving about in a crowded room, putting everyone at his ease[,] delighting everyone, and diffusing an atmosphere of joyousness and friendly sympathy over the whole company yet remaining themselves perfectly calm[,] displaying not the slightest appearance of effort or embarrassment. This is the perfection of style as the expression of a certain poetic grace of nature, a happy attitude of mind, impulsive and yet controlled in the person possessing it. In others we notice a certain brusqueness of bearing which is the effect not of embarrassment, but of an inherent angularity of nature, in others whimsical and humorous or oddly deliberate and weighty forms of manner, which are all an unconscious expression of mental attitudes[.]

The distinction between a genuine style and a pure affectation is immediately noticeable in the bearing of men and women as it is in literature and art. Yet as in every kind of distinction the two things merge into one another so that it is sometimes not easy to ascertain how much of a manner is style, and how much of it is affectation[.] We often meet with people possessing a manner, undoubtedly to a great extent an expression of character, but heightened and consciously adorned so as to produce an effect of insincerity. It is the same conscious heightening of style which has injured the character for genuineness of many distinguished artists and writers.

There is also another sort of manner very common, perhaps the most common among men and women of the world, which can hardly be called either a style or an affectation. It is that artificial and customary manner which people who have no very decided character of their own adapt* in an unconscious spirit of self-defense in order that they may escape embarrassment in their contact with others. It is not a style, for it does not express any personal mental attitude; indeed it does not express anything unless it be the disposition to guard one's own dignity; and it is not an affectation exactly, for it is not consciously adopted. Nothing can be more effective in its way than this artificial manner of society. In the hands of a well practiced person it is an impenetrable shield, and to any straight-forward and simple-minded body who comes in contact with it, is utterly disconcerting. It is a valuable trick which, once learnt, enables a man to ascert [sic] and maintain his own personal majesty with the least expense of intelligence. In some of the common forms of literature too the same defensive manner is found; in the columns of the newspapers for instance. We know how empty a newspaper editorial may sometimes be, and yet how majestically

---

*   possibly "adopt"—see "adopted" below.

plausible in expression. In the more serious walks of literature this *modus vivendi* manner does not so often occur for people are not under the same necessity to write books as they are to associate with their neighbors or even to write newspaper paragraphs.

In fact true style in manners like true style in literature and the arts is exceedingly rare. For it is alway[s] in a certain sense the expression of genius[.] Genius like the varieties of style to which it gives rise is not confined to art or politics, or literature or music[.] There have been many people with a touch of genius who have never taken any part in politics, having never written anything, or expressed themselves in any of the arts. That woman for instance whose contact with life has resulted in the development of an exquisite manner peculiar to herself, which impresses one with the sense of the presence of something wonderfully gracious and noble; that woman has a touch of genius[.] We have sometimes met with men whose names have never become widely known to the world, but who possessed an unusual attractiveness of personality[,] who had the faculty of drawing people to them by reason of their extreme quickness of sympathy. Such men were touched with genius; for genius is simply the quickening of any mental faculty to point at which it begins to burn, so to speak, to the point at which it begins to find for itself passionate and stirring expression even though only in bearing and mode of life.

A style is liable to the same decay both in manners, literature and art. Its perfection is found in those whose gifts have been exercised freely and without compulsion and have not yet reached the period at which in so many expression has become incessant and too habitual. We know that many people who have acquired a very charming manner after long intercourse with the world, get to exercise it on occasion quite mechanically, although this may be only evident to observers of unusually acute penetration—just as some good writers to whom the practice of writing through long habit has become a necessity of life go on producing matter with exactly the old ring, but expressing little that the mind of the reader can apprehend as of any real moment[.]

It may be said that style[,] however honestly the peculiar development of the person possessing it, is a hindrance to absolute expression, and a concealment of actual truth. And this is of course true. Every mood of feeling and every attainment of thought may be imagined to be expressible in some absolute way altogether independent of every peculiar bent of the human mind. But he who should be able to give to all movements of the mind their absolute expression would be a genius of more than mortal compass. Some of the masters of art have made approaches to this supreme excellence, but of course have never reached and can never reach it. One of the great things to be said of Shakespeare is that he expressed many of the human passions, such as love, anger, pity, fear, remorse in a manner which as far as those passions are concerned may be called the universal style. That is to say he expressed them with such an impressiveness[,] such a glowing and overwhelming eloquence that nothing can be imagined nearer to the truth. Nevertheless some of the minor poets have carried expression into occult regions of feeling where their own peculiar gifts were better adapted to success than Shakespeare's more rapid hand and larger intelligence[.]

The formation of a style in fact is almost as necessary to the artist as the implements of his art. It is only by this means that he is enabled to proceed to each new undertaking with confidence and precision. Until he has developed some settled style of his own he is obliged at every new attempt to grope in a confused and laborious manner for the appropriate form of expression. In the end it happens to every power-ful and original artist that that peculiarity of thought or imagination which is uppermost in him, obtains an absorbing mastery and gives the tone to his creations, and this tone working itself out through the implements of his art is style.

So in every age of the world's life that peculiarity of thought or feel-ing which is uppermost in its aggregate of mind lends to the product of all its artists a broadly perceptible general character upon which the work of each individual is only a variation[.] The common tone of a picture with which the colour of each separate object is in harmony. In architecture as the art which expresses the mind of each age on the vastest scale, one most easily realizes the great distinctions of style. He who should accompany the traveller from Salisbury Cathedral or the Minster of Strasburg, to the old mosque at Cordova[,] from the Parthenon or the Temple of Apollo at Phigalia to the monstrous ruins of Medinet Aboo or Karnak or to the Taj Mahal by the stream of the Ganges would pass before five great attitudes of the human mind, and be overpowered by each in turn. If we turn to sculpture we find that the secrets of two ages of two civilizations and two almost antagonistic man-ifestations of mind and feeling inhabit the Aphrodite of Praxiletes [sic], and the Moses of Michel Angelo. Greece with its happy sense of the beauty of this earthly life, its mind occupied with subtle and untroubled thought, its life full of joyous energy—and modern Europe, half Gothic half Latin[,] with its melancholy, its restless searching after unattainable ideals, its vast imaginings, its passionate subjectivity. When we pass to literature we find the style of the Aphrodite of Praxiletes [sic] and the Parthenon translated into the verse of the *Oedipus Coloneus* [sic] and the prose of Plato—the style of the Strasburg Minster and the Moses of Buonarotti into the verse of the *Song of Roland* and the prose of the *Vita Nuova.*

In like manner we know that the lesser divisions in the ages of art are distinguished from one another by minor adaptations of style. If we consider the history of English poetry—and to that I propose to limit myself in the present paper—how many and how marked have been the changes in the general habit of expression since the middle of the 16th century. If we should meet anywhere with a passage from any of those great dramatists who wrote under Elizabeth and James; even though it should be new to us and unnamed would not the very manner of its utterance enable us immediately to refer it to its age[?] That was preeminently the age of the adventurous activity and sturdy manhood of England—an age of rough passions and rough enjoyments[,] of violent contrasts. The culture of the nation deep and solid as it was among the learned had not outgrown its rude animal vigor; consequently its art was characterized by immense force and magical tenderness. Such an age as that is the age of the dramatist. The strong ferment of its life is food and school and spur to his imagination[.] There were many dramatists then, more than there have ever been since. And in all of them—however Marlowe for instance may differ in bent of genius from Shakespeare or Ford from Johnson [sic] the same general character of utterance is marked. In a greater or less degree they all possessed the same euphuistic richness and boyancy [sic] of diction, the same inexhaustible fancy, the same daring magnitude of imagination, the same free and full-blooded sympathy with the movement of a full and strongly contrasted life. Milton also belongs intellectually to this age although he lived at a later time—like one of the elder Titan gods holding to his rocky fastness after all the lower lands about him had fallen under the dominion of deities of a meaner race.

In Shakespeare as we have already observed we sometimes find what may be called a universal style. In him there is no peculiarity, no eccentricity[,] no marked or special bias of thought or feeling. In his famous passages the method of expression is so spontaneous[,] so naturally forcible that it seems to be not the utterance of a single brain but the thought of all mankind. When we have read through for instance that most sweet and lofty passage in which King Henry IV apostrophises sleep; what can we say but that it is the very human heart that speaks. Again those terrible lines in which the Duchess of York addresses and describes her son Richard

> Tetchy and wayward was thy infancy
> Thy school-days frightful, desperate, wild and furious
> Thy prime of manhood daring bold and venturous
> Thy age confirmed, proud, subtle sly and bloody,
> More mild, and yet more harmful, kind in hatred:
> What comfortable hour canst thou name
> That ever graced me in thy company[?]

What other than the universal mind we think could have filled an evil character with such an array of faithful and fearful words. Shakespeare is the highest development of the common healthy human intelligence, and that is why he is so great, so universally beloved, so full of pleasure and exhilation [sic] for every sound mind. The one respect in which he deviates from this strong universal type of expression is in the humoring of an extraordinarily fertile fancy. He sometimes loads his phrases with an abundance of curious conceits which on the lips of another man would be the extinction of all force of thought. But even in such cases, so boyant [sic] and so vivacious is his movement, so touchingly apt is every part of that riotous flood of illustration that we hardly realize how far he has departed from the bound of actual simplicity. Let us instance that passage of *Richard II* in which the forlorn and vacillating king addresses his followers after their landing in Wales.

> Of comfort no man speak.
> Let's talk of graves, of worms, and epitaphs;
> Make dust our paper and with rainy eyes
> Write sorrow on the bosom of the earth.
> Let's choose executors and talk of wills:
> And yet not so—for what can we bequeath
> Save our deposèd bodies to the ground?
> Our lands, our lives and all are Bolingbroke's
> And nothing can we call our own but death
> And that small model of the barren earth
> Which serves as paste and cover to our bones.

For God's sake let us sit upon the ground,
And tell sad stories of the death of kings
How some have been deposed, some slain in war;
Some haunted by the ghosts they have deposed;
Some poisoned by their wives; some sleeping killed;
All murdered—for within the hollow crown
That rounds the mortal temples of a king
Keeps death his court; and there the antic sits
Scoffing his state and grinning at his pomp;
Allowing him a breath, a little scene,
To monarchize, be feared and kill with looks;
Infusing him with self and vain conceit—
As if this flesh which walls about our life
Were brass impregnable; and humoured thus
Comes at the last and with a little pin
Bores thro' his castle wall, and—farewell king!
Cover your heads and mock not flesh and blood
With solemn reverence; throw away respect,
Tradition, form, and ceremonious duty;
For you have but mistook me all this while;
I live with bread like you, feel want, taste grief
Need friends:—subjected thus,
How can you say to me, I am a king?

No poet perhaps would serve better than Milton as an illustration of the manner in which diction or the mode of utterance is moulded by character. Milton was a scholar, serious, able, intellectual, pure. His mental attitude was that of a stern self-trust, and a trust equally stern in the justice of the cause with which his life was linked. Every line in *Paradise Lost* bears the touch and impress of that proud austere and potent nature.

So spake the Son; and into terror changed
His countenance, too severe to be beheld
And full of wrath bent on his enemies.
At once the four spread out their starry wings
With dreadful shade contiguous, and the orbs
Of his fierce chariot rolled, as with the sound
Of torrent floods, or of a numerous host.
He on his impious foes right onward drove

Gloomy as night; under his burning wheels
The steadfast empyrean shook throughout
All but the throne, itself of God. Full soon
Among them he arrived; in his right hand
Grasping ten thousand thunders, which he sent
Before him, such as in their souls infixed
Plagues. They astonished all resistance lost
All courage; down their idle weapons dropped;
O'er shields and helms and helmed heads he rode
Of thrones and mighty seraphim prostrate
That wished the mountains now might be again
Thrown on them as a shelter from his ire[.]

That is what Matthew Arnold calls the grand manner. There is an austere pride in all the movement of the verse. Milton's isolation, his splendid power, his connection with great events and a strenuous cause combined to inure his soul to a severe and majestic attitude, and as we read him, in the very march and halt of his syllables we cannot but be reminded of his greatness[.]

How great a change do we find when we come to Dryden, Congreve[,] Pope—the sententious age—the age of the unvarying rounded verse, of neat sentiments, of the confinement of art to the portrayal of certain set artificial situations and the expression of a few set attitudes of mind. It was the age of the reaction, as we know, from the great Puritan rebellion, and the patronage of literature and art was in the hands of the leaders of that reaction, a set of people who wished to envelope [sic] everything in an atmosphere of artificial elegance, and to get as far away from the notions of the vulgar as possible[.] In their style we find a striving after a certain latin gracefulness and epigrammatic pointedness of expression and an almost entire absence of the real creative genius of those old Latin writers, who were the after fruit of the great deeds and the heroic mind of the republic. If we instance one specimen of the manner of this age we instance it all. The following lines from an "Epistle to Miss Blount," accompanying a copy of the works of Voiture, are by Pope in whom the wit of that age reached its perfection[:]

In these gay thoughts the loves and graces shine,
And all the writer lives in every line;
His easy art may happy nature seem,
Trifles themselves are elegant in him[.]

Sure to charm all was his peculiar fate
Who without flattery pleased the fair and great
Still with esteem no less conversed than read
With wit well natured and with books well bred
His heart his mistress and his friend did share
His time the muse, the witty and the fair
Thus wisely careless, innocently gay
Cheerful he played the trifle, life, away[:]
Even rival wits did Voiture's death deplore
And the gay mourned who never mourned before
The truest hearts for Voiture heaved with sighs
Voiture was wept by all the brightest eyes[....]
Let the strict life of graver mortals be
A long exact and serious comedy
In every scene some moral let it teach
And if it can at once both please and preach[:]
Let mine, an innocent gay farce appear
And more diverting still than regular,
Have humour, wit, a native ease and grace
Though not too strictly bound to time and place;
Critics in wit or life are hard to please,
Few write to those and none can live to these[.]

There is something pleasantly trim and natty about these lines. There is nothing in them to touch any emotion or prompt to any intensity of thought—there is never anything of that sort in the work of the age of Queen Anne, but nevertheless they are very pleasant reading and have a sort of charm. They are clever, witty, intelligent, perfectly poised, with a certain pointed grace.

Then we come to a transition age—the age of Johnson, Addison, Fielding and Sterne, of Thompson [sic], Grey [sic] and Cowper[.] The pendulum was swinging back. People were wearing of the nick-nack drawing room literature of the Restoration. The old sturdy English seriousness and vitality were beginning to reassert themselves, and perhaps England was already affected by the first faint vibration of that movement of Rousseau and Voltaire which had dawned in France. In the style of these men there was still lingering the well-bred sententious manner of the last generation, but there was also another note, indicating a determination toward a genuine criticism of life. They had begun to fasten upon nature as the only sourse [sic] of everything lasting in literature and art. In the prose of this transition age there was a good deal of humanity. It was easy[,] humourous, appreciative of character and touched with geniality; but lacking in force and without the higher qualities of the imagination.

The vast stir of revolutionary thought and feeling, that terminated the eighteenth century, brought on that great and impressive age, the last before our own, to which we owe so much. It was an age in which some full and immediate change in the destiny of mankind seemed so near and so possible, the dream of it so alluring that those among men who had anything of the prophetic gift of tongues spoke out in a new and world inspiring note. Theirs was the prophetic attitude, and in their style was the intonation of a high passionate earnestness and spiritual enthusiasm. Shelley was the representative of the time, and in him the note is strongest, but it is also clearly distinguishable in Byron, Coleridge, Southey and Wordsworth. Keats alone stands separated from his age, like a half completed palace of the Italian Renaissance, planted in nineteenth century England, absorbed in its own reminiscent dream of beauty and unconscious of all the spiritual fervour and social stir around it.

In Shelley let us repeat we find the representative of this age. In him an intense interest in the prospective moral and political emancipation of mankind had become an absorbing passion, a glowing enthusiasm, in which all the intellectual and imaginative faculties of his mind were fused. He was fortified with an intense confidence in the truth and beauty of his own limitless aspirations, and it was this attitude that lent to every wildest thing that he wrote that tone of burning sincerity and romantic prophesy which is the keynote of his style. The follow[ing] for example is a passage from *Alastor* purely descriptive but there is a voice in it of something wildly spiritual, the coloring of a certain habitual and irrepressible mood. In a word we find in it Shelley's style.

> On every side now rose
> Rocks which in unimaginable forms
> Lifted their black and barren pinnacles
> In the light of evening, and its precipice
> Obscuring the ravine, disclosed above,
> Mid toppling stones, black gulfs, and yawning caves
> Whose windings gave ten thousand various tongues
> To the loud stream. Lo! where the pass expands
> Its stony jaws, the abrupt mountain breaks

And seems with its accumulated crags
To overhang the world: for wide expand
Beneath the wan stars and descending moon
Islanded seas, blue mountains, mighty streams
Dim tracts and vast, robed in the lustrous gloom
Of leaden-coloured even, and fiery hills
Mingling their flames with twilight on the verge
Of the remote horizon. The near scene
In naked and severe simplicity
Made contrast with the universe. A pine,
Rock-rooted, stretched athwart the vacancy
Its swinging boughs, to each inconstant blast
Yielding one only response at each pause
In most familiar cadence, with the howl
The thunder and the hiss of homeless streams
Mingling its solemn song, whilst the broad river,
Foaming and hurrying o'er its rugged path,
Fell into that immeasurable void
Scattering its waters to the passing winds[.]

I should say that Byron's distinctive attitude of mind, when he was at his best, disposed him to a tragic review of the changes and desolations of time, and a sad or scornful contemplation of the crimes[,] weaknesses and miseries of human life. This was the mood that wrought out his style. It is the mood of the third Canto of *Childe Harold* in which some of his best work was done[.]

Wordsworth frequently touches the master note of his age. It is found in all the sonnets dedicated to liberty; as for instance in that most noble one on the "Extinction of the Venetian Republic"

Once did she hold the gorgeous East in fee;
And was the safe-guard of the West; the worth
Of Venice did not fall below her birth—
Venice, the eldest child of liberty!
She was a maiden city bright and free;
No guile seduced, no force could violate[;]
And[,] when she took unto herself a mate[,]
She must espouse the everlasting sea[.]

Again in that on the subjugation of Switzerland*

> Two voices are there—one is of the sea,
> One of the mountains—each a mighty voice;
> In each from age to age thou didst rejoice,
> They were thy chosen music, Liberty!
> There came a tyrant and with holy glee
> Thou fought'st against him; but hast vainly striven[:]
> Thou from thine Alpine holds at length art driven
> Where not a torrent murmurs heard by thee[.]
> Of one deep bliss thine ear hath been bereft[:]
> Then cleave[,] Oh cleave to that which still is left[;]
> For[,] high souled maid[,] what sorrow would it be
> That mountain floors should thunder as before[,]
> And ocean bellow from his rocky shore[,]
> And neither awful voice be heard by thee[!]

But the personal and distinctive attitude of Wordsworth's mind was that of a lofty contemplation of external nature, and a reverent interest in all the humble and laborious occupations of life. And this like every true prevailing instinct bred a peculiar manner in his verse, a manner exceedingly plain and simple and yet striking, unusual, distinctive[:]

> It is the first wild** day of March
>> Each minute sweeter than before
> The red breast sings from the tall larch
>> That stands beside our door
> There is a blessing in the air
>> Which seems a sense of joy to yield
> To the bare trees and mountains bare
>> And grass in the green field.

How every [sic] simple and apparently without distinction are these lines. Yet who with a practiced ear, though hearing them for the first time[,] could doubt that they were Wordsworth's. The same peculiarity

---

* Lampman quotes the sonnet "Thought of a Briton on the Subjugation of Switzerland," 1807.

** Wordsworth had written "mild." These are the opening lines of "To My Sister," 1798.

of touch is noticeable in many phrases and passages that readily occur to one.

> The Knight had ridden down from Wensley Moor[*]
> With the slow motion of a summer's cloud[.]

> All things that love the sun are out of doors[**]
> The sky rejoices in the morning's birth;
> The grass is bright with raindrops; on the moors
> The hare is running races in her mirth[.]

> Bees [that] soar for bloom[†]
> High as the highest peaks of Furness Fells
> Will murmur by the hour in foxglove bells[.]

> Calm is all nature as a resting wheel[.][††]
> The kine are couched upon the dewy grass[;]
> The horse alone[,] seen dimly as I pass[,]
> Is cropping audibly his later meal[.]

"Resolution and Independence" sometimes called "The Leach-Gatherer" [sic] is the most beautiful and original poem that Wordsworth wrote. It is one of those miracles that a true poet will perform in some moment of intellectual awakening and extraordinary imaginative insight, never perhaps repeated in a lifetime. The following stanzas are the most curiously vivid in all Wordsworth's work, and are an excellent illustration of his prevailing attitude of mind, an acute apprehension of the actual picturesque value of the common every day manifestations of life[:]

> Now[,] whether it were by a peculiar grace[,][‡]
> A leading from above, a something given,
> Yet it befell that[,] in this lonely place[,]
> Where up and down my fancy thus was driven
> And I with these untoward thoughts had striven,

---

[*]   These are the opening lines to "Hart-leap Well," 1800.
[**] The first four lines of stanza two from "The Leech-gatherer" or "Resolution and Independence," 1807.
[†]   These four lines occur in the sonnet "Nuns Fret Not at Their Convent's Narrow Room," 1806.
[††] These are the first four lines of the sonnet "Written in Very Early Youth," circa 1786.
[‡]   Stanza eight of "Resolution and Independence," 1807.

I saw a man before me unawares:
The oldest man he seemed that ever wore grey hairs.

My course I stopped as soon as I espied*
The old man in that naked wilderness:
Close by a pond upon the further side
He stood alone: a minute's space I guess
I watched him, he continued motionless:
To the pool's further margin then I drew
He being all the while before me in full view

As a huge stone is sometimes seen to lie **
Couched on the bald top of an eminence,
Wonder to all who do the same espy
By what means it could thither come[,] and whence[;]
So that it seems a thing endued with sense:
Like a sea beast crawled forth, which on a shelf[,]
Of rock or sand reposeth, there to sun itself.

Such seemed this man, not all alive, nor dead,
Nor all asleep, in his extreme old age:
His body was bent double, feet and head
Coming together in their† pilgrimage,
As if some dire constraint of pain, or rage
Of sickness felt by him in times long past,
A more than human weight upon his frame had cast.

Himself he propped his body, limbs and face,††
Upon a long grey staff of shaven wood[:]
And still, as I drew near with gentle pace,
Beside the little pond or moorish flood,‡
Motionless as a cloud the old man stood;
That heareth not the loud winds when they call
And moveth all together, if it move at all.

---

*   This stanza, while narratively in sequence, does not appear in a version of
      "Resolution and Independence" that I could locate.
**   Stanza nine of "Resolution and Independence."
†   Most texts read: "life's pilgrimage."
††   Should read: "Himself he propped, limbs, body and pale face."
‡   Should read: "Upon the margin of that moorish flood."

> At length himself unsettling, he the pond
> Stirred with his staff, and fixedly did look
> Upon the muddy water, which he conned
> As if he had been reading in a book.

In our own age the study of style becomes more interesting than in any other; for individual developements become more common, and any general or common quality of manner is hardly noticeable[.] The nearest we get to it is the similarity of method in the followers of certain schools[.] In poetry this is a lyrical and meditative age[.] The drama is almost impossible. It was the unconscious sympathy with the strong rush of a life in which all were passionately involved that produced the generalities in style noticeable in former ages. In our own[,] art is self-conscious and self-absorbed. Each individual mind is bent upon realizing and fixing its own mental attitude, and this must naturally result in the formation of many peculiar and dissimilar styles. Another natural result is that our poetry is characterised by great perfection of manner, great force of expression, great subtlety of thought, and feeling, but little real movement. A poem like Tennyson's "Revenge" for instance which is so picturesque and so stirring, if we examine into it, we find to have hardly any actual movement. It is after all just a piece of glorious rhetoric. But it is the perfection of style and a splendid expression of a heroic mood.

In the main Tennyson may be said to exemplify the English attitude of mind at its best. His attitude toward the problems of life is that of a brave and kindly common sense, warmed with all the fire and impulse of a most gifted poet. His painting of nature is less exquisitely happy and natural than Wordsworth's but it is more sumptuous, and the salient points of his picture thrown out with a more splendid touch.

Browning's genius seems to have been actuated by an intense and busy curiosity in regard to the inner working of human emotion, and the effect of imposing situations upon differing characters; this combined with an extraordinary appreciativeness of all kinds of force. A great deal of his verse is utterly wanting in that smootheness and rounded melody to which English ears had become too accustomed in Tennyson easily to endure its absence. Force and the truth of his presentment were what Browning aimed at, and melody had for the most part to be sacrificed. Yet not always even in the longer and subtler poems—for sometimes, out of the recklessly broken utterance of a discouraging page, the reader awakes to the power of some individual thought borne in upon him line upon line, a sudden tide of music irresistible and incomparable. In some of his magical short pieces he seems to unfetter the hands of the musician and set free the pure poetic sense in unequalled swing and splendor. Such a poem for instance as "Love among the Ruins." I dare say you all know it[.]

Browning was as we have said an enquirer and prober into the springs of human action, of great penetration, with the painter's sense largely developed and an intense vividness and inventiveness of imagi-nation, but his mind seldom reached those solemn and austere altitudes of feeling from which a few of our greatest lyric poets sang. We do not find in him any single poems or passages to compare with the broadest and weightiest utterances of Milton and Wordsworth or even of Keats[,] Shelley, Tennyson or Matthew Arnold. If we wish to instance a specimen of Browning's habitual style, we shall have to find it in such a passage as the following from a poem entitled "One Word More" addressed to Mrs. Browning.

> Dante once prepared to paint an Angel[:]*
> Whom to please? You whisper "Beatrice"
> While he mused and traced it and retraced it,
> (Peradvent[ture] with a pen corroded
> Still by drops of that hot ink he dipped for
> When, his left hand in the hair of the wicked,
> Back he held the brow and pricked its stigma,
> Bit into the live man's flesh for parchment,
> Loosed him, laughed to see the writing rankle
> Let the wretch go festering thro' Florence)—
> Dante who loved well because he hated
> Hated wickedness that hinders loving[,]
> Dante standing, studying his angel,—
> In there broke the folk of his ["]Inferno"
> Says he, "Certain people of importance"
> (Such he gave his daily dreadful line to)
> ["]Entered and would sieze, forsooth, the poet.["]
> Says the poet—"Then I stopped my painting[.]"
> You and I would rather see that angel

---

* From the fifth stanza of "One Word More" which Browning wrote for Elizabeth Barrett Browning, 1855.

Painted by the tenderness of Dante,
Would we not?—than read a fresh Inferno[.]

The mind of Matthew Arnold more than that of any other writer of these later times was impressed with a sense of the mystery of all life, the tragedy of human thought and effort, the power and lovelines of nature[,] this great external world. Over his soul there hung a vast and sceptical melancholy which lends to his utterance a turn and modulation strangely touching. He is the most modern of poets, and to men of our generation more interesting than any other. The following lines which are the ending of "Sohrab and Rustum" are exceedingly characteristic. Rustum, the aged Persian hero[,] has met his son Sohrab without knowing him in single combat between the assembled armies of the Tartars and Persians, and has wounded him to death. The armies draw off for the night to their camps by the Oxus and Rustum is left sitting by the corpse of his son on the solitary sands; and then the poet turns from the two tragic figures and finishes the poem.

But the majestic river floated on
Out of the mist and hum of that low land[,]
Into the frosty star-light, and there moved[,]
Rejoicing, through the hushed Chorasmian waste[,]
Under the solitary moon; he flowed
Right for the polar star, past Orgunjè[,]
Brimming and bright and large; then sands begin
To hem his watery march, and dam his streams,
And split his currents; that for many a league
The shorn and parcell'd Oxus strains along
Through beds of sand and matted rushy isles—
Oxus, forgetting the bright speed he had
In his high mountain-cradle in Pamere,
A foiled circuitous wanderer,—till at last
The longed-for dash of waves is heard, and wide
His luminous house[*] of waters opens, bright
And tranquil, from whose floor the new-bathed stars
Emerge[,] and shine upon the Aral sea.

What a breadth of vision and solemn simplicity of movement there are in these lines and there are many others in Matthew Arnold quite as fine.

[*] Arnold had written "home."

Dante Gabriel Ros[s]etti and Charles Algernon Swinburne are two poets who have exercised a large influence on the poetic style of the last fifteen or twenty years[.] They are usually classed together as forming with William Morris what is called the Preraphaelite school, though why nobody seems able satisfactorily to explain[.] They are writers of an extremely different genius, and nothing could be more different in many respects than their manner of workmanship. Ros[s]etti[']s attitude is that of a watcher for occult and subtle effects both in human emotions, and in external nature and these he siezes and realizes with a strange searching vividness of imagination. Swinburne on the [other] hand may claim more justly than any other English men [sic] that has ever lived to be possessed by what in the old phrase was called the poetic frenzy. He is utterly governed and carried away by the surge and glory of a most daring imagination, and the force of an unexampled sense of music. Ros[s]etti's movement is lingering, penetrating and bites into the imagination a most vivid conception of what he wishes to convey. Swinburne's movement is rushing[,] tumultuous, overpowering the imagination with a tide of chaotic splendor. The following stanzas are an excellent example of Ros[s]etti's far reaching subtl[et]y, and of the manner in which it has moulded his style. It is entitled

The Sea Limits

Consider the sea's listless chime:
    Time's self it is, made audible,—
    The murmur of the earth's own shell.
Secret continuance sublime
    Is the sea's end: our sight may pass
    No furlong further. Since time was[,]
This sound hath told the lapse of time.

No quiet, which is death's—it hath
    The mournfulness of ancient life,
    Enduring always at dull strife.
As the world's heart of rest and wrath,
    Its painful pulse is in the sands.
    Last utterly the whole sky stands,
Grey and not known, along its path[.]

Listen alone beside the sea,
    Listen alone among the woods;

Those voices of twin solitudes
Shall have one sound alike to thee:
    Hark where the murmurs of thronged men
    Surge and sink back and surge again,—
Still the one voice of wave and tree.

Gather a shell from the strown beach
    And listen at its lips: they sigh
    The same desire and mystery,
The echo of the whole sea's speech.
    And all mankind is thus at heart
    Not anything but what thou art:
And earth, sea, man are all in each.

As an example of Swinburne[']s power of melody, the following lines part of a chorus from the *Atalanta in Calydon** are often cited.

Before the beginning of years
    There came to the making of man
Time[,] with a gift of tears
    Grief[,] with a glass that ran[;]
Pleasure[,] with pain for leaven[;]
    Summer[,] with flowers that fel[;]l
Remembrance fallen from heaven[,]
    And madness risen from hell[;]
Strength without hands to smite[,]
    Love that endures for a breath[,]
Night[,] the shadow of light[,]
    And life[,] the shadow of death.

And the high gods took in hand
    Fire[,] and the falling of tears[,]
And a measure of sliding sand
    From under the feet of years[,]
And froth and drift of the sea[;]
    And dust of the laboring earth[;]
And bodies of things to be
    In the houses of death and of birth[;]
And wrought with weeping and laughter[,]

---

*   *Atalanta in Calydon—A Tragedy*, by Algernon Charles Swinburne, is a verse drama first published in 1865.

And fashioned with loathing and love[,]
With life before and after
And death beneath and above[,]
For a day and a night and a morrow[,]
That his strength might endure for a span
With travail and heavy sorrow[,]
The holy spirit of man[.]

These writers are both of them habituated to a mood so much the result of cultivation and so far removed from the mental habits of the most of men that they are sometimes in danger of straining style till it becomes affectation. It requires a peculiar twist of the imagination to enable one to entirely enter into the feeling of a poem like Ros[s]etti's "Wood-spurge," which I have not time to quote here, but which I dare say many of you know.

Amid all these varieties of style one might begin to think that I [sic] would be difficult to find anything new, and yet writers are rising into notice every day in whose work there is a voice and touch of something never heard before. The formation of a style is a most unconscious process. He who should set about premeditatedly to form a style would end most certainly in forming nothing but an affectation. But he who finds himself haunted persistently by certain peculiar ideas, certain peculiar images, certain tones of sound, colour and feeling and sets about expressing these simply in the manner most outright and clear and satisfactory to himself and continues to do so until his hand attains ease and certainty, will discover, or rather his readers will discover[,] that he has invented a style.

By way of concluding these ill-ordered remarks I would like to call attention to the work of one of our own younger poets, Professor Charles G.D. Roberts of Windsor, N.S., who in the last ten years has done some very fine writing, distinguished by marked peculiarities of style. It is on account of its very characteristic quality in regard to style, that I particularly mention Mr. Roberts in this connection[.] Mr. Roberts' feeling for nature is that of sensuous physical delight, the rapturous pleasure of contemplation, the joy of intellectual contact with life, and its manifold occupations. Sometimes his imagination touching upon the very commonest things invests them with an almost human significance and there are passages of description in his poems which for genuineness of vision and passionate stress of expression have been rarely, if at all, equalled, certainly in their way not surpassed, in America.

The following lines from "Tantramar Revisited" are, it seems to me, unsurpassably fine.

DUNCAN CAMPBELL SCOTT

DUNCAN CAMPBELL SCOTT (1862–1947)

Biographical Notes

Duncan Campbell Scott was born on 2 August 1862, in Ottawa, Ontario. He was educated in Smith's Falls, at various schools in Ontario and Quebec, and at Stanstead Wesleyan Academy in Stanstead, Quebec near the Vermont border. At seventeen he became a clerk in the Department of Indian Affairs, where he would remain for fifty-three years until his retirement in 1932. He was Deputy Superintendent from 1913 until 1923, when he became Deputy Superintendent General for the Federal Government. Scott's responsibilities included representing the Federal Government in intergovernmental negotiations with aboriginal peoples in landholding agreements and establishing treaty settlements. As Commissioner in the first of two Commissioners' visits in 1905–06 (the other in 1929–30) to Northern Ontario, Scott was instrumental in submitting Treaty No. 9 to the Governor General for ratification in January 1907. Scott was both a short story writer, and an amateur photographer, and during the Commissioners' visit in 1905–06 to the James Bay area, he photographed the native population and the local landscape. Much contemporary writing on Scott deals with Scott's sympathetic poetic treatment of native culture, in stark contrast to the severe policies of the department he headed. This sympathy is also evident in his book *The Administration of Indian Affairs in Canada* (1931). Many of his narrative poems, such as "The Forsaken," deal with Native American life. Recent

critical discussions of Scott's role with Indian Affairs have been con-
siderably less sympathetic.

Throughout his career in Ottawa, Scott actively corresponded with
the literary editor of the *Globe*, Melvin O. Hammond in Toronto, and
contributed many essays to the newspaper. Along with Wilfred Camp-
bell, and his close literary friend, Archibald Lampman, Scott published
a series of articles at the *Globe* under the byline "At the Mermaid Inn."
In 1893, at the age of thirty-one, Scott published his first book, *The Magic
House and Other Poems,* and in the Christmas *Globe* contest of 1908 won
a literary contest for the best poem with a Canadian historical theme
with his "The Battle of Lundy's Lane." The prize was, for the time, a siz-
able one hundred dollars. A staunch friend of Lampman, Scott assisted
in the publication of several of his books, and became his literary ex-
ecutor after Lampman's death.

Scott married Belle Warner Botsford, a well-known violinist, in 1894
and they had one daughter, who died prematurely in 1907. After his
wife's death in 1929, he married Elise Aylen in 1931. Scott earned
several distinctions during his career: in 1899, he was elected a fellow
of the Royal Society of Canada and served as president during 1921–22.
In 1903, he was elected Vice-President of the Canadian Society of
Authors, and in 1922, the University of Toronto conferred on him the
degree of D.Litt., while Queen's University awarded him an honorary
degree in 1939. He died in Ottawa in 1947 at the age of eighty-five.

Publications

The Magic House and Other Poems. Ottawa: J. Durie, 1893.

Labor and the Angel. Boston: Copeland and Day, 1898.

New World Lyrics and Ballads. Toronto: Morang, 1905.

Via Borealis. Toronto: W. Tyrrell, 1906.

Lundy's Lane and Other Poems. New York: G.H. Doran, 1916.

Beauty and Life. Toronto: McClelland and Stewart, 1921.

Poems. Toronto: McClelland and Stewart, 1926.

The Green Cloister: Later Poems. Toronto: McClelland and Stewart, 1935.

The Circle of Affection and Other Pieces in Prose and Verse. Toronto: McClelland and Stewart, 1947.

Selected Poems of Duncan Campbell Scott. Toronto: Ryerson, 1951.

Selected Poetry. Ed. Glenn Clever. Ottawa: Tecumseh, 1974.

Critical Materials

Book Length

At the Mermaid Inn, conducted by A. Lampman, W.W. Campbell, Duncan C. Scott. Being selections from essays on life and literature which appeared in the Toronto Globe, 1892–1893. Ed. Arthur S. Bourinot. Ottawa; privately printed, 1958.

Dragland, Stan, ed. *Duncan Campbell Scott: A Book of Criticism*. Ottawa: Tecumseh, 1974.

———. "Forms of imaginative perception in the poetry of Duncan Campbell Scott." Canadian Theses on Microfilm. Kingston, 1971.

Gerson, Carole. *The Piper's Forgotten Time: Notes on the Stories of D.C. Scott and A Bibliography*. Montreal: Bellrock P, 1976.

McDougall, Robert, ed. *The Poet and the Critic: A Literary Correspondence between D.C. Scott and E. K. Brown*. Ottawa: Carleton UP, 1983.

Articles

Bentley, D.M.R. "Duncan Campbell Scott and Maurice Maeterlinck." *Studies in Canadian Literature* 21.2 (1996): 104–19.

Dyer, Klay. "Passing Time and Present Absence: Looking to the Future in In the Village of Viger." *Canadian Literature* 141 (1994): 86–106.

Gerson, Carole. "The Piper's Forgotten Tune: Notes on the Stories of D.C. Scott and a Bibliography." *Journal of Canadian Fiction* 16 (1976): 138–43.

Harrison, Dick. "'So Deathly Silent': The Resolution of Pain and Fear in the Poetry of Lampman and D.C. Scott." *The Lampman Symposium.* Ed. Lorraine McMullen. Ottawa: U of Ottawa P, 1976. 63–74.

Lynch, Gerald. "In the Meantime: Duncan Campbell Scott's In the Village of Viger." *Studies in Canadian Literature* 17.2 (1992): 70–91.

MacSween, R.J. "Three poetic landmarks in Canadian cultural history." *Antigonish Review* 87–88 (1991–92): 138–45.

McDougall, Robert L. "D.C. Scott: The Dating of the Poems." *Canadian Poetry* 2 (1978): 13–27.

Normey, Rob. "Warring Elements of a Confederation Poet." *Law Now* 23.3 (1998–99): 36–37.

Salem, Lisa. "'Her Blood Is Mingled with Her Ancient Foes': The Concepts of Blood, Race and 'Miscegenation' in the Poetry and Short Fiction of Duncan Campbell Scott." *Studies in Canadian Literature* 18.1 (1993): 99–117.

———. "'Verily, the White Man's Ways Were the Best': Duncan Campbell Scott, Native Culture, and Assimilation." *Studies in Canadian Literature* 21.2 (1996): 120–42.

Slonim, Leon. "D.C. Scott's 'At Gull Lake: August, 1810.'" *Canadian Literature* 81 (1979): 142–43.

Titley, Brian. "Narrow Vision: Duncan Campbell Scott and the Administration of Indian Affairs in Canada." *Canadian Literature* 116 (1988): 187–89.

Ware, Tracy. "The Beginnings of Duncan Campbell Scott's Poetic Career." *English Studies in Canada* 26.2 (1990): 215–31.

Ware, Tracy. "Notes on D.C. Scott's 'Ode for the Keats Centenary.'" *Canadian Literature* 126 (1990): 176–79.

Woodard, Joseph. "Tragic and Prophetic Voice: A NFB Documentary Criticizes Canada's Poetic Indian Agent for Being Right." *Western Report* 10.6 (March 6 1996): 44.

Online Resources

http://www.ucalgary.ca/UofC/faculties/HUM/ENGL/canada/poet/d_scott.htm

http://rpo.library.utoronto.ca/poet/288.html

http://digital.library.upenn.edu/women/garvin/poets/scottdc.html

From the Globe
29 October 1892

Reprinted from *At The Mermaid Inn: Wilfred Campbell, Archibald Lampman, Duncan Campbell Scott in The Globe 1892–93*, intro. by Barrie Davies, Toronto: U of Toronto P, 1979, 182–83.

A lyric to be perfectly successful should not need any special interpretation. It should not be so involved with personal feeling that it would need a commentary upon the event or upon the special mood which called it forth. All the great lyrics which have been preserved by the common decree of the people have some expression of general experience which renders them capable of proof, as it were, by any human soul. Thus it has often happened that a writer who toiled to win fame by some creation of great length, filled with imagination, accomplished his object by some fragment wherein he gave voice to some common experience of the race. There are too many of the lyrics in Mr. W.E. Henley's new book of which it can be said that they require a special interpretation; that they are not self-evident. Although the mass of the work leaves an impression of extreme cleverness, the effect is not one either of pleasure or profit. Mr. Henley seems to have looked at everything which he attempts to portray with the eye of a painter, and a painter of the impressionist school. The poem dedicated to Mr. Whistler is an attempt to reproduce the effect of one of the painter's harmonies. But it is far from being a success. The choice of words and imagery gives no effect of beauty, which must be the basis for every work of art, however small in dimension. And this principle of beauty would be present in the scene which inspired the picture or the poem, no matter to what thoughts the associations which accompany the scene might give rise. Now these associations are specially the material of poetry; painting cannot reproduce them and it is fatuous for poetry to attempt to give by the choice of special words the exact value of tone and colour in painting. The beauty of a scene is ever present, and although it may influence the mind in many different ways the effect can never be immoral, no matter how terrible the associations may be. And in such work as the third of the "London Voluntaries" the feeling of beauty is entirely absent, and we have the sense of actual immorality forced upon the material picture. The wind "comes sullen and obscene, in a cloud unclean of excremental humours," and every natural appearance wears a sort of lewdness, an abject awfulness of shape and purpose. There is present neither the element of beauty nor the element of human interest, but the landscape exists by itself and for itself in this unreal and grotesque masque as if it had a separate, conscious, and rather immoral personality. An example of the legitimate treatment of a weird and terrible landscape is Browning's "Childe Roland to the Dark Tower Came," where we have a human interest informing the whole poem, accompanied by a sense of strange wild beauty. In his actual choice of word and phrase Mr. Henley has been undoubtedly influenced by Rudyard Kipling, and, although in some instances the result of this insolent realism of expression is fine, in the majority of cases the striving after an effect is too apparent. Mr. Henley's philosophy is not deep. When he leaves life he but leaves "books and women and talk and drink and art," and he goes into the ways of death stoically with a sense of relief and release.

Poetry and Progress

Presidential Address delivered before the Royal Society of Canada, 17 May 1922. Reprinted from Duncan Campbell Scott, *The Circle of Affection and Other Pieces in Prose and Verse*, Toronto: McClelland and Stewart, 1947, 123–47.

I have the honour to deliver this evening the forty-first presidential address of the Royal Society of Canada. It is the custom of our Society that the presidency shall devolve in turn upon each of our Sections, and the Section Literature last year claimed the privilege of nominating the president of the Society.

I have thought to speak on this occasion of ideals and progress: first, and briefly, on the ideals of the Society,—those who formed it and gave it body and constitution, and then, in a more discursive fashion, about ideals in poetry and the literary life, and their relation to progress. There is, I claim, something unique in the constitution of a society that comprises Literature and Science, that makes room for the Mathematician and the Chemist, the Historian and the Biologist, the Poet and the Astronomer. Every intellectual type can be accommodated under the cloak of our charter, and we have survived forty-one years of varied activity with a degree of harmony and a persistence of effort towards the end and purpose of our creation that is worthy of comment. We are unique also in this, that two languages have equal recognition and authority in our literature sections, and that the premier place is occupied by the first civilized language heard by the natives of this country, which is ever the pioneer language of ideals in freedom and beauty and in the realm of clear logic, criticism and daring speculation. It here represents not a division of race, but a union of nationality, and joins the company of intellectuals by the dual interests of the two great sections of our people. We find our scientific sections welcoming essays in the French language and our literary sections interchanging papers and holding joint sessions on folklore and history. The ideal which possessed the founder of this Society and its charter members was undoubtedly that such an organism could live and flourish, that it could become a useful institution in Canadian life. We have progressively proved that, we prove it tonight, and we shall, I am confident, continue our demonstration in the future. Is it too fanciful to think or say that the element of cohesion which made this possible is idealism, or that gift of ideality which all workers who use Mind as an instrument possess in varying degree? The mental process by which a poet develops the germ of his poem and perfects it is analogous to the process by which a mathematician develops his problem from vagueness to a complete demonstration, or to the mental process whereby the shadow of truth apprehended by the biologist becomes proven fact. The scientist and mathematician may proceed in diverse ways to give scope to the creative imagination, and their methods are inherent in their problems. They proceed by experiment and by the logical faculty to a point of rest, of completion. The poet is unsatisfied until his idea is cleared of ambiguity and becomes embodied in a perfect form. The art of the poet is to clothe his idea with beauty and to state it in terms of loveliness but the art of fine writing—style—need not be absent from the record of scientific achievement: it is, in fact, often present in marked degree. I doubt whether the satisfaction of the poet in finishing his work and perfecting it is essentially different or greater than the satisfaction of the scientist who rounds out his experiment and proves his theory. Such delights cannot be weighed or measured, but they are real and are enjoyed in common by all workers who seek perfection. I now boldly make the statement, which I at first put hesitatingly, in the form of a question, that it is ideality that holds our Society together, and that it was founded truly in the imagination of those who thought that such an institution could flourish in our national life.

During the past forty years many distinguished men have joined in this Fellowship—some have passed from this to greater honours, and others have passed away, but our methods of election and the keenness which our Fellows show in choosing their future colleagues ensure a steady stream of vigorous thought.

The subjects comprised in Section II, to which I have the honour to belong, are certainly varied,—English Literature, History, Archaeology, Sociology, Political Economy and allied subjects; and some of the allied subjects are most important, such as Philosophy and Psychology. While we have this wealth of subject matter, the scientific sections have an advantage over us in that they have greater solidarity of aim, that their groups have clearly-defined objects of study and investigation, and their results are more tangible We must envy the scientists the excitement of the intellectual world in which they live. Consider for a moment the changes in scientific theory, method, and outlook since the charter members of this Society met together in 1882. It would not become me to endeavour to mention even the most important, but the realm of science appears to an outsider to be a wonderland. By comparison, literature seems to be divorced from life, and we would need to point to some book that had altered definitely the course of the world's thought to match some of the discoveries of Science which have changed our conceptions of the nature of life and of the universe. Perhaps, in making this remark, I am confusing for a moment the function of pure litera-ture with the functions of Science. Literature in its purest form is vowed the service of the imagination; its ethical powers are secondary, though important; and it cannot be forced to prove its utility. Literature engaged with the creation of beauty is ageless. The biological notions of Elizabeth's day are merely objects of curiosity, but Marlowe, Webster and Shakespeare are living forces. Sir Thomas Browne's medical knowledge is useless, but his "Urn Burial" is a wonder and a delight. Created, beauty persists; it has the eternal element in its composition, and seems to tell us more of the secret of the universe than philosophy or logic. But Letters will always envy Science its busyness with material things, and its glowing results which have rendered possible many of the imaginative excursions which poetry, for example, has made into the unknown.

It would be difficult, nay, impossible, to change radically the methods of pure literature working in the stuff of the imagination. New ideas can be absorbed, new analogies can be drawn, new imagery can be invented, but the age-old methods of artistic expression will never be superseded. Apart from pure literature, or Belles Lettres, those subjects allotted to our section which are capable of scientific treatment, for in-stance, History, show a remarkable development. The former story-telling function of History and the endless reweaving of that tissue of tradition which surrounded and obscured the life of a people has given place to a higher conception of the duty of the Historian and the obligation to accept no statement without the support of documentary evidence. The exploration and study of archives and the collation of original contemporaneous documents are now held to be essential, and the partisan historian fortified with bigotry and blind to all evidence uncongenial to his preconceptions is an extinct being. International effort and co-operation have taken the place of jealous sectionalism and the desire to unfold the truth has displaced the craze to prove a theory. The new Science of History has its material in archives and collections of original documents, and one must here refer to the growth of our own Dominion collections under the guidance of an Archivist who is one of us, and who is aided by other distinguished Fellows of the Society. It should be remarked that one of the objects set forth by our charter was to assist in the collection of archives and to aid in the formation of a National Museum of Ethnology, Archaeology and Natural History. Let us not weaken for a moment in the discharge of this obligation. The Archives and the Museum exist largely owing to the influence of our Society, exerted constantly with great pressure, and, in times of necessity, with grave insistence. The Museum needs we consider highly important, and, as you are all aware, we intend to assist the Government to come to wise conclusions in these matters, and to keep alive and vigorous all projects that aim at conserving and developing our intellectual resources.

We talk too often and too lengthily about Canadian poetry and Canadian literature as if it was, or ought to be, a special and peculiar brand, but it is simply poetry, or not poetry; literature or not literature; it must be judged by established standards, and cannot escape criticism by special pleading. A critic may accompany his blame or praise by describing the difficulties of the Canadian literary life, but that cannot be allowed to prejudice our claim to be members of the general guild. We must insist upon it. If there be criticism by our countrymen, all that we ask is that it should be informed and able criticism, and that it too should be judged by universal standards. Future critics will recognize the difficulties which oppress all artistic effort in new countries, as do the best of contemporary critics. As Matthew Arnold wrote, in countries and times of splendid poetical achievement: "The poet lived in a current of ideas in the highest degree animating and nourishing to the creative power; society was, in the fullest measure, permeated by fresh thought, intelligent and alive; and this state of things is the true basis for the creative power's exercise." When we seek in our contemporary society for the full permeation of fresh thought, intelligent and alive, we do not find it; we do not find it in America or elsewhere, and if the premise is sound we can say, therefore, we do not find an ample and glorious stream of creative power. It is casual, intermittent, fragmentary, because society is in like state. But we may be thankful that in our country there has been and is now a body of thought, intelligent and alive, that gives tangible support to the artist and that has assisted him in his creative work.

You will note that I am taking high ground, in fact, the highest, in dealing with literature and the highest form of literature—poetry. I am well aware that there is a great increase in our written word during the last twenty-five years, and our writers are now competently meeting the varied demand of readers whose taste does not require anything too finely wrought nor too greatly imagined. I heard one of our successful writers declare the other day that what we should do now is to get the "stuff" down somehow or other and never to mind how it was done so long as it was done. Well, that would give us all the rewards of haste, but would hardly assist in building a literature. There must ever be this contrast between the worker for instant results and the worker who toils for the last perfection. One class is not without honour, the other is precious beyond valuation. As time passes we shall find in this country, no doubt, a growing corpus of stimulating thought that will still more tend to the nourishing and support of creative genius.

While we do not wish to part Canadian Literature from the main body of Literature written in English, we may lay claim to the possession of something unique in the Canadian literary life,—that may be distinguishable to even casual perception by a peculiar blend of courage and discouragement. In truth, there is such lack of the concentration that makes for the drama of literary life that it is almost non-existent. But, nevertheless, our resident authors, those who have not attempted to escape from this environment, have done and are doing important work in imaginative literature. I have thought to touch briefly upon two such lives typical of the struggle for self-expression in a new country.

If there had existed in our Society a rule that is observed in the French Academy, it would have been my duty to have pronounced, upon taking my chair, a eulogy on Archibald Lampman, who had died the year previous to my election, and to whose chair I succeeded. I would hardly have been as competent then to speak of him and his work as I am now, for both were too near to me then, and now I have the advantage of added experience, and, after a lapse of twenty odd years, poetic values shift. But what is poetic truth does not change, and it is a high satisfaction to find that there was so much of poetic truth in the work of my friend, our colleague, truth that fortifies, and beauty that sweetens life. He felt the oppression of the dullness of the life about us more keenly than I did, for he had fewer channels of escape, and his responsibilities were heavier; he had little if any enjoyment in the task-round of every day, and however much we miss the sense of tedium in his best work, most assuredly it was with him present in the days of his week and the weeks of his year. He had real capacity for gaiety and for the width and atmosphere of a varied and complex life, not as an actor in it perhaps, but as a keen observer and as a drifter upon its surface, one in whom the colour and movement of life would have created many beautiful and enchanting forms. But he was compelled to work without that stimulus, in a dull environment and the absence also of any feeling of nationality, a strong aid and incitement to a poet, no matter how much we may talk nowadays about the danger of national feeling. This lack made sterile a broad tract of his mind; it was a discouragement that he could not know that he was interpreting the aspirations and ideals of a national life. We still feel that lack of national consciousness, but perhaps it is a trifle less evident now. His love of country was very strong and took form in his praise of nature, that unsoiled and untrammelled nature that we think of as Canada, and his work in this kind has a verity and vigour that is unmatched. He filled the rigid form of the sonnet with comments on the life of the fields and woods and waters that ring as true as the notes of birds. A single half-hundred of these sonnets of his may be placed in any poetic company and they will neither wilt nor tarnish. Towards the end of his life he chose by sympathy to write more imaginatively about stirrings in the mind and heart of man and there is a deep and troubled note in these things that gave portent of a new development. His career was closed too soon, and we have but to cherish what is left and rejoice over it as a treasure of our literary inheritance.

It is twenty-three years since Lampman died, and the period is marked by the death of Marjorie Pickthall, which occurred during April of this year at Vancouver. Her's was a literary life of another and contrasted kind. She was of English parentage, born in England, but educated in Canada, and she was in training and sentiment a good Canadian.

If one were looking for evidence of progress in Canadian literature during the period just referred to, one positive item would be the difference in the reception of the first books published by these two authors. Until the generous review by William Dean Howells of Lampman's book had been published in *Harper's Magazine*, it was here considered, when any consideration whatever was given to the subject, a matter of local importance. But the warm-hearted welcome of Howells led to sudden recognition of the fact that the book was an acquisition to general literature, and was not merely parochial. After that incident, and others like it, we find that recognition of Miss Pickthall's first book took place at once, and from our independent judgment, as an important addition to poetical literature. Advance is clearly shown by this fact; for until we have faith in the power of our writers we can have no literature worth speaking about; our position, in arts and letters will be secured when we find foreign critics accepting a clear lead from us. We accepted Miss Pickthall, and our opinion was confirmed very generally afterwards.

It is to be deeply regretted that her career is closed and that we shall not again hear, or overhear, that strain of melody, so firm, so sure, floating towards us, to use a phrase of Lampman's, "as if from the closing door of another world and another lovelier mood." "Overhear" is, I think, the right word, for there was a tone of privacy, of seclusion, in her most individual poems, not the seclusion of a cloister, but the seclusion of a walled garden with an outlook towards the sea and the mountains. Life was beyond the garden somewhere, and murmurously, rumours of it came between the walls and caused longing and disquiet. The voice could be heard mingling the real appearance of the garden with the imagined forms of life beyond it and with remembrances from dim legends and from the untarnished old romances of the world. Her work was built on a ground bass of folk melody, and wreathed about it were Greek phrases and glamours from the "Song of Songs." But composite of all these influences, it was yet original and reached the heart with a wistfulness of comfort. She had a feeling for our little brothers of the air and the woods that was sometimes classical, sometimes mediaeval. Fauns and hamadryads peopled her moods, and our familiar birds and flowers took on quaint forms like the conventional shapes and mellow colours of tapestries woven long ago. "Bind above your breaking heart the echo of a Song"—that was her cadence, the peculiar touch that gives a feeling of loneliness and then heals it, and if one might have said to her any words at parting, they would have been her own words—"Take, ere yet you say good-bye, the love of all the earth."

These two lives are typical of the struggle of those who attempt the literary life in Canada. Lampman existed in the Civil Service, and was paid as any other clerk for the official work he did. Neither his position nor his advances in that position were given in recognition of his literary gifts. From this bleak vantage ground he sent out his version of the beauty of the world. Miss Pickthall was more definitely in the stream of letters, and her contributions to the periodical press in prose and verse gave her an assured standing and due rewards.

There is no necessity here and now for an apology for poetry nor for a defence of anyone who in Sir Philip Sydney's words "showeth himself a passionate lover of that unspeakable and everlasting beauty to be seen by the eyes of the mind." I admire that ideal, set up by the Welsh saying for the perfect man, the man who could "build a boat and sail it, tame a horse and ride it, make an ode and set it to music." None of us could qualify for perfection under this hard and inclusive test. It covers, you will observe, mastery of several kinds—mastery of craftsmanship, and fearless daring; mastery of a difficult and most noble animal; and, finally, the crowning mastery of poetry and music. We find it true of all peoples that these two arts are the cap stones of their civilizations. We are as far as ever from an understanding of what poetry really is, although we are at one in giving it supremacy in the arts and we are as far as ever from a perfect definition of poetry. Perhaps the best, the only definition of poetry is a true poem, for poetry and the poetic is a quality or state of mind and cannot be described, it is apprehended by sensation, not comprehended by reason. This renders ineffectual all attempts to answer the question "What is poetry?," and makes futile the approved definitions.

These efforts to define what is undefinable inevitably tend to become creative attempts, approximate to poetic utterance, and endeavour to capture the fugitive spirit of poetry by luring it with a semblance of itself. But the question is answered perfectly by even the fragment of a true poem. We know instinctively and say, "This is poetry," and the need for definition ceases.

The finest criticism of poetry plays about this central quality like lightning about a lovely statue in a midnight garden. The beauty is flashed upon the eye and withdrawn. It is remembered in darkness and is verified by the merest flutter or flash of illumination, but the secret of the beauty is shrouded in mystery. I refer to such sayings as this of Coleridge: "It is the blending of passion with order that constitutes perfection" in poetry; that of Keats, "The excellence of every art is its intensity"; that of Rossetti, "Moderation is the highest law of poetry." There are numerous like apothegms written by poets and critics about the art of poetry that accomplish perfectly the necessary separation between the art and the spirit of the art, between the means and the effect. They are flashed upon the mystery and isolate it so that it may be apprehended by its aloofness and separation from things and appearances. We can apply Coleridge's words to any chosen passage of Keats, for example, the familiar "magic casements opening on the foam of perilous seas in faery lands forlorn." We acknowledge that the perfection of the passage lies in the romantic passion blended with the order that is the sense of balance and completion, but the poetic quality escapes, it is defined, by the effect of the passage and by that alone.

We quote the words that Shakespeare puts into Anthony's mouth—

> "I am dying, Egypt, dying; only
> I here importune death awhile, until
> Of many thousand kisses the poor last
> I lay upon thy lips."

We recognize that the excellence of this passage comes from its intensity. And even such an outcry, poignant to the verge of agony, is not inconsistent with the saying of Rossetti; for moderation is a question of scale. The high law of moderation is followed in such an utterance of Anthony's as competently as when Hamlet says simply "The rest is silence," because it is true in the scale of emotion.

Of a truth the ideals of our contemporary poets are not those of the masters of the past,—neither their ideals of matter, of manner, of content or of form. Tennyson's thought "of one far off divine event to which the whole creation moves" is not only inadequate to express what a poet of the present day feels about the destiny of man and about the universe; it fails in appeal, it is merely uninteresting to him; and no modern poet would say as Matthew Arnold said: "Weary of myself, and sick of asking what I am and what I ought to be." Tennyson and Arnold are comparatively recent leaders of thought, and we are more akin to the Elizabethans with their spirit of quest than we are to Wordsworth and Arnold. In our ideals of technique we are farther removed from the eighteenth century, from Pope and Gray, than from Donne and Herrick and Vaughan. Our blank verse at its best shuns all reference to Milton and has escaped once again into the freedom of Shakespeare and the wilderness of natural accent. The best of the work shows it, and from the mouths of the poets themselves we sometimes gather their perception of kinship with masters whose influence was unfelt by the Victorians. I remember well an observation Rupert Brooke made to me one evening during his visit to Ottawa in July, 1913, as we strolled over the golf links. There was a heavy dew on the grass, I remember, one could feel it in the air, and the sky was crowded full of stars; the night, and peculiarly the coolness of the dew-saturated air recalled some line of Matthew Arnold. "How far away that seems," Brooke said, "far away from what we are trying to do now; John Donne seems much nearer to us." It is the intensity of Donne that fascinated Brooke. It was that intensity that he was endeavouring to reach in his poem "The Blue Room," or in the stillness of arrested time portrayed in "Afternoon Tea." The diffuseness in Wordsworth and Arnold was the quality that made them remote. Brooke was fated for other things than to pursue the cult of intensity. Now we think of him as the interpreter of certain emotional states that arose from the war, and we may select Wilfred Owen as the exponent of certain other sharply hostile states.

The contrast between these typical natures is the contrast between the traditional feeling for glory and the personal feeling of loss and defeat to be laid to the national debit. Brooke identifies himself with the magnificence of all the endeavour that has gone to create national pride; his offering is one of joy, all is lost in the knowledge that he continues the tradition of sacrifice for the national ideal. Wilfred Owen feels only the desperate personal loss, loss of the sensation of high living, the denial by the present of the right of youth to the future. The contrast is known when we place Brooke's sonnet "Blow Out Ye Bugle Over the Rich Dead," beside Owen's "Apologia." The first glows with a sort of mediaeval ecstasy, the second throbs with immediate sincerity and ironic truth. It is the voice of a tortured human soul. There has been agony before in English poetry, but none like unto this agony. How far removed is it from echoes of the drums and trumpets of old time valour, how far away from such a classic as "The Burial of Sir John Moore"? Here is an accent new to English poetry. There is the old power of courage, the indomitable spirit of the forlorn hope, but the anaesthetic of glory is absent, and the pain of all this futile sacrifice based on human error and perversity is suffered by the bare nerve without mitigation.

Rupert Brooke's admiration of that bare technique, fitted to that strange and candescent intellect of Donne's was forgotten when he touched those incomparable sonnets of his. In them the intensity of feeling takes on a breath and movement which is an amalgam of many traditions in English poetry, traditions of the best with the informing sense of a new genius added, the genius of Rupert Brooke. In his case, as in the case of all careers prematurely closed, it is idle to speculate upon the future course of his genius. It may be said, however, that his prose criticism, his study of Webster and his letters show that his mind was philosophic and that his poetic faculty was firmly rooted in that subsoil and had no mere surface contact with life. Our faith that Keats would have developed had he lived, takes rise from our knowledge of the quality of his mind, as shown in his criticism and in his wonderful letters. We can say confidently that a poetic faculty based on such strong masculine foundation, with such breadth of sympathy, would have continued to produce poetry of the highest, informed with new beauty and with a constant reference to human life and aspirations. With due qualifications the same confidence may be felt in the potential power of Rupert Brooke. He had not Keats' exquisite gift, but he was even more a creature of his time, bathed in the current of youthful feeling that was freshening the life of those days, and he would have been able to lead that freshet of feeling into new and deep channels of expression. Close association for a week with so eager a mind served to create and enforce such opinions. He seemed, so far as his talk went, more interested in life than art, and there was a total absence of the kind of literary gossip that so often annoys. His loyalty to his friends and confrères was admirable, and he had greater pleasure in telling what they had done than in recounting his own achievements,—what their hopes were rather than his own. I remember his saying that he intended to write drama in the future and put himself to the supreme test in this form of art. One cannot think of his figure now except in the light of tragic events that were hidden then, when there was no shadow, only the eagerness of youth and the desire of life.

Wilfred Owen too, and others of his group, inherited that touch of intensity, but there was bitterness added and he had to bear the shock of actual war which Brooke did not experience,—the horrors of it and the futility. It is to be doubted whether such writers as Owen or Sorley could have assumed or continued a position in post war literature, whether they could have found subjects for the exercise of such mordant talents.

There was a tremendous activity of verse-writing during the war, and the hope was often expressed that there was to be a renaissance of poetry and our age was to be nobly expressed. But the war ceased; the multitude of war poets ceased to write; the artificial stimulus had departed and they one and all found themselves without a subject.

Whatever technique they had acquired for the especial purpose of creating horror or pity was unfitted for less violent matter. The ideals which they had passionately upheld received the cold shoulder of disillusionment. The millennium had not arrived, in very truth it seemed farther off than ever, and the source of special inspiration had dried up. But the elimination of these poets of the moment did not affect the main development of poetry. Those poets, who had been in the stream of tendency, and who were diverted by the violent flood of war feelings and impressions settled back upon the normal. They had not required subjects more stimulating than those ordinary problems or appearances of life and nature which are always present. Their technical acquirements were as adequate as ever and they took up the task of expression where it had been interrupted.

There are many mansions in the house of poetry; the art is most varied and adaptable; we must acknowledge its adequacy for all forms and purposes of expression, from the lampoon, through the satire, through mere description and narrative, through the epic, to the higher forms of the lyric and the drama. Rhythm, being the very breath and blood of all art, here lends itself dispassionately and without revolt to the lowest drudgery as well as the highest inspiration. But when so often calling on the name of poetry, I am thinking of that element in the art which is essential, in which the power of growth resides, which is the winged and restless spirit keeping pace with knowledge and often beating into the void in advance of speculation; the spirit which Shakespeare called "the prophetic soul of the wide world dreaming on things to come." This spirit endeavours to interpret the world in new terms of beauty, to find unique symbols, images and analogies for the varied forms of life. It absorbs science and philosophy, and anticipates social progress in terms of ideality. It is rare, but it is ever present, for what is it but the flickering and pulsation of the force that created the world.

I remarked a moment ago upon the remoteness of that mood of Matthew Arnold in which he expresses soul weariness and the need of self-dependence. Arnold advises the soul to learn this self-poise from nature pursuing her tasks, to live as the sea and the mountains live. But our modern mood does not seek self-dependence, having no knowledge of that lack, nor does it refer to the unconscious for comfort or example. It asks for deeper experience, for more intense feeling and for expression through action. Science has taught the modern that nature lives and breathes, and in looking at the mountains and the sea, he is moved to feelings based on growing knowledge, unutterable as yet in thought. The modern feels no sickness of soul which requires a panacea of quiescence; he is aware of imperfections and of vast physical and social problems, but life does not therefore interest him less but more. He has the will to live and persistence to grapple with the universal complexities. This becomes evident in the revolt against established forms and in the intellectual daring that forces received opinion before a new jurisdiction.

This is a critical age and has its peculiar tone of criticism. Compared with other times it more loudly and insistently questions and mocks at the past—the past exists merely "to be the snuff of younger spirits whose apprehensive senses all but new things disdain." Art that takes on new forms has more than ever a critical outlook, and the criticism seems to be based on irritation. The purpose of the effort is not so much, if at all, to create beauty, as to insult older ideas of beauty, to *épater le bourgeois*, to shock with unwholesome audacities, to insert a grain of sand into each individual oyster shell and set up an irritation, seemingly without any hope of ultimately producing pearls thereby, but with the mere malicious design of awakening protest, the more violent the better. I might continue my quotation of Shakespeare, and say of these ultra modern minds that their "Judgments are mere fathers of their garments, whose constancies expire before their fashions"; but no matter how long the present fashion lasts, it may be treated in retrospect as a moment of irony.

A virus has infected all the arts; the desire for rebellious, violent and discordant expression has invaded even the serene province of Music. The extremists in this art invoke satire as their principal divinity. They set out to describe, for example, the feelings of the heir of a maiden aunt who has left him her pet dog instead of fifty thousand pounds. They write waltzes for the piano with the right-hand part in one key, and the left-hand part in another. Masses of orchestral sound move across each other careless of what happens in the passing.

Perhaps I might be pardoned a short digression here on the subject of Music, its true progress in the path of perfection; for Music is the art of perfection, and, as Walter Pater declared, all other arts strive towards the condition of Music. The rise and development of modern Music is a matter of barely five hundred years and parallels the growth of modern Science. The developments of both in the future cannot be limited. They may progress side by side; Science expanding and solving the problems of the universe, and Music fulfilling the definition that Wagner made for it as "the innermost dream-image of the essential nature of the world." Wagner's music was once satirically called the "Music of the Future." It is now firmly and gloriously fixed in the past. But Music is truly the art of the future. Men will come to it more and more as the art which can express the complex emotions of life in terms of purest beauty. It is the art most fitted to give comfort and release to the spirit and to resolve scepticism as it resolves discords. Side by side with a tone of supersensualism that runs through modern Music we have intellectual developments and also a straining towards spiritual thoughts which restore the balance. It is gratifying to note that Britain is taking the place she once occupied as a leader in musical creation. The obstacle to the understanding of Music has not been the absence of natural correspondences in the mind. Music has universal appeal, but because of the fact that it must reach the understanding through the ear, it must be twice created, and the written stuff is dumb until awakened into vibrating life. The invention of mechanical means for the reproduction of Music and their gradual improvement has made Music as accessible as the reproductions of fine paintings. The widespread use of these music machines proves the desire of the people to hear and to understand, and the effect upon the public taste will be appreciable. The style of amateur performances will be improved, and it may not be too much to claim for this wide distribution of beautiful and deeply felt music an influence on the creative side and a stimulation to eager youthful spirits to translate their emotions into sound. Music is the great nourisher of the imagination, and the prevalence of great music means the production of great verse. Over and against the poets who have been deaf to the stimulation of Music we can quote some of the greatest who have been sensitive to it,—Shakespeare, Milton, Keats, and I may quote the remark of Coleridge, made in 1833: "I could write as good verses as ever I did if I were perfectly free from vexations and were in the *ad libitum* hearing of fine music, which has a sensible effect in harmonizing my thoughts, and in animating and, as it were, lubricating my inventive faculties." The leaders of what is called the 'New Movement in Poetry' have some ground for argument, but make unconvincing uses of it. The most voluble centres of the New Movement are in the United States, and the subject is pursued with all the energy and conviction that we have learned to expect from the adoption of any cause to the south of us. We must willingly confess that Americans are an art-loving people, and that now they are immensely interested in all the arts. From the first they were hospitable to foreign production and absorbed all that was best in the work of other nationalities, and lately they have grown confident of their native artists and reward them with patronage and praise.

The protagonists of the Modern Movement in Poetry are most hospitable to the old poets; they are orthodox in their inclusions and throw a net wide enough to catch all the masters of the art from the earliest to the latest times. They approve of poets of our own day who use the established verse-forms as well as the writers of vers-libre and the innovators. Their quarrel, therefore, must be with the poetasters, with the slavish imitators, with the purveyors of conventional ideas and the innumerable composers of dead sonnets. But these people have always been among us and have always been intolerable to the children of light. The weariness they occasion is no new experience. They at once fastened themselves on the New Movement and welcomed vers-libre as the medium which would prove them poets. In proclaiming freedom as the war cry of the New Movement, the leaders admitted all the rebels against forms which they had never succeeded in mastering, and while they poured into vers-libre a vast amount of loose thinking and loose chatter, as if freedom were to include licence of all kinds, they were still unable to master the form or prevail in any way except to bring it into contempt. The avowed object of the Movement is "a heroic effort to get rid of obstacles that have hampered the poet and separated him from his audience," and "to make the modern manifestations of poetry less a matter of rules and formulae and more a thing of the spirit and of organic as against imposed rhythm." A praiseworthy ideal! But has the poet ever been separated from his audience? Can poetry be made more than it ever was, a thing of the spirit? Did Browning separate himself from his audience when he cast his poem "Home Thoughts from Abroad" into its irregular form? Can one create a poem of greater spirituality than Vaughan's "I Saw Eternity the Other Night"? To exorcise this senseless irritation against rhyme and form, those possessed should intone the phrases of that great iconoclast, Walt Whitman, written in the noble preface to the 1855 edition of "Leaves of Grass." "The profit of rhyme is that it drops seeds of a sweeter and more luxuriant rhyme, and of uniformity that it conveys itself into its own roots in the ground out of sight. The rhyme and uniformity of perfect poems show the free growth of metrical laws, and bud from them as unerringly and loosely as lilacs and roses on a bush, and take shapes as compact as the shapes of chestnuts and oranges, and melons and pears, and shed the perfume impalpable to form."

All that I intend to inveigh against in these sentences is the cult that seeks to establish itself upon a false freedom in the realm of art. Sincerity, or, if you will, freedom, is the touchstone of poetry of any and all art work in fact. Originality is the proof of genius, but all geniuses have imitated. Poetry is an endless chain of imitation, but genius comes dropping in, adding its own peculiar flavour in degree. Sainte Beuve has written it down: "The end and object of every original writer is to express what nobody has yet expressed, to render what nobody else is able to render .... " This may be accepted as axiomatic, it governs production here and elsewhere, present and future, and any literary movement is doomed to failure if it attempts to pre-empt the conception that poetry should be original, should be freshened constantly by the inventions of new and audacious spirits.

The desire of creative minds everywhere is to express the age in terms of the age, and by intuition to flash light into the future. Revolt is essential to progress, not necessarily the revolt of violence, but always the revolt that questions the established past and puts it to the proof, that finds the old forms outworn and invents new forms for new matters.

It is the mission of new theories in the arts, and particularly of new theories that come to us illustrated by practice, to force us to re-examine the grounds of our preferences, and to retest our accepted dogmas. Sometimes the preferences are found to be prejudices and the dogmas hollow formulae. There is even a negative use in ugliness that throws into relief upon a dark and inchoate background the shining lines and melting curves of true beauty. The latest mission of revolt has been performed inadequately, but it has served to show us that our poetic utterance was becoming formalized. We require more rage of our poets. We should like them to put to the proof that saying of William Blake: "The tigers of wrath are wiser than the horses of instruction."

I may possibly have taken up too much time in referring to modern tendencies in poetry, which are only ephemeral, and in combating the claim, put forward with all gravity, to distinction that flows from a new discovery. Already many of these fads have faded or disappeared. The constancies of these bright spirits have expired before their fashions. They are already absorbed with a new fad. But let it pass,—modernity is not a fad, it is the feeling for actuality.

If I am ever to make good the title imposed on this address, I must soon do so, and trace a connection between Poetry and Progress, if there be any. Maybe we shall find that there is no connection, and that they are independent, perhaps hostile. It is certain that Poetry has no connection with material progress and with those advances which we think of as specialties of modern life—the utilization of electricity for example. Euripides living in his cave by the seashore, nourished and clothed in the frugalist and simplest fashion, has told us things about the human spirit and about our relation to the gods which are still piercingly true. Dante's imagination was brooding and intense within the mediaeval walls of Tuscany. Shakespeare, when he lodged in Silver Street with the Mountjoys, was discomfortably treated, judged by our standards, and yet he lives forever in the minds of men. It is useless to elaborate this trite assertion; if material progress, convenience, comfort, had any connection with poetry, with expression, our poets would be as much superior to the old poets as a nitrogen electric bulb is to a rush light. Poetry has commerce with feeling and emotion, and the delight of Nausicaa as she drove the mules in the high wain heaped with linen to the river shore, was not less than the joy which the modern girl feels in rushing her motor car along a stretch of tar-macadam. Nausicaa also was free of her family for a while and felt akin to the gull that turned on silver wing over the bay; felt the joy of control over the headstrong mules, and the clean limbed maidens who tossed the ball by the wine-dark sea.

The feeling of delight is the thing, not its cause, and if there be any progress in the art of poetry, it must be proved in the keenness with which we feel the expression of the emotion. But the emotion gives rise to correspondences. What were the trains of thought set up in the Greek hearers who listened to the recital of that little journey of Nausicaa to the swift running river with the family washing? We can imagine they were simple enough, and we can compare them with the collateral ideas set up by the description of a journey in a high-power car set forth in that profane poem on Heaven by one of the moderns. The power of poetry has here expanded to include a world unknown to Greek expression. Here is progress of a sort. The poetry of the aeroplane has yet to be written, but, when it comes, it will pass beyond the expressions of bird-flight in the older poets and will awaken images foreign to their states of feeling. Shakespeare wrote of "daffodils, that come before the swallow dares, and take the winds of March with beauty." The aeroplane has a beauty and daring all its own, and the future poet may associate that daring with some transcendent flower to heighten its world-taking beauty. Here may be found a claim for progress in poetry, that it has proved adequate to its eternal task and gathers up the analogies and implications, the movement and colour of modern life—not as yet in any supreme way, but in a groping fashion. It is far-fetched to compare the work of Homer to that of a lively modern—an immortal to one of those who perish—but how many poets perished in the broad flood of Homer? Immortal! The idea becomes vague and relative when we think of the vestiges of great peoples, confused with the innumerable blown sand of deserts, or dissolved in the brine of oblivious oceans, lost and irretrievable. Art is immortal, not the work of its votaries, and the poets pass from hand to hand the torch of the spirit, now a mere sparkling of light, now flaming gloriously, ever deathless.

If this be one contact between Poetry and Progress there may be another in the spread of idealism, in the increase in the poetic outlook on life, which is, I think, apparent. The appeal of poetry has increased and the number of those seeking self-expression has increased. The technique of the art is understood by many and widely practised with varying success, but with an astonishing control of form. This may be regretted in some quarters. One of our distinguished poets was saying the other day that there are too many of us, too many verse writers crowding one another to death. My own complaint, if I have any, is not that we are too many, but that we do not know enough. Our knowledge of ourselves and the world about us and of the spirit of the age, the true spring of all deep and noble and beautiful work, is inadequate.

There is evidence of Progress in the growing freedom in the commerce and exchange of ideas the world over. Poetic minds take fire from one another, and there never was a time when international influences were so strong in poetry as they are to-day. France and Italy have, from the time of Chaucer, exerted an influence on the literature of England. The influence is still evident, and to it is added that of the Norse countries, of Russia and of Central Europe. Oriental thought has touched English minds, and in one instance gave to an English poet the groundwork for an expression in terms of final beauty of the fatalistic view of life. Of late, mainly through the work of French savants, the innumerable treasures of Chinese and Japanese poetry have been disclosed and have led poets writing in English to envy them the delicate touch, light as "airy air," and to try to distil into our smaller verse forms that fugitive and breath-like beauty. English poetry has due influence on the Continent, and there is the constant inter-play of the truest internationalism, the internationalism of ideals and of the ever-changing, ever-advancing laws of the republic of beauty. National relations will be duly influenced by this free interchange of poetic ideals, and the ready accessibility of new and stimulating thought must eventually prevail in mutual understanding. We can resolutely claim for Poetry a vital connection with this Progress.

In these relationships between Poetry and Progress, Poetry is working in its natural medium as the servant of the imagination, not as the servant of Progress. The imagination has always been concerned with endeavours to harmonize life and to set up nobler conditions of living; to picture perfect social states and to commend them to the reason. The poet is the voice of the imagination, and the art in which he works, apart from the conveyed message, is an aid to the cause, for it is ever striving for perfection, so that the most fragile lyric is a factor in human progress as well as the most profound drama. The poets have felt their obligation to aid in this progress and many of them have expressed it. The "miseries of the world are misery and will not let them rest," and while it is only given to the few in every age to crystallize the immortal truths, all poets are engaged with the expression of truth. Working without conscious plan and merely repeating to themselves, as it were, what they have learnt of life from experience or convey the hints that intuition has whispered to them, they awaken in countless souls sympathetic vibrations of beauty and ideality: the hearer is charmed out of himself, his personality dissolves in the ocean of feeling, his spirit is consoled for sorrows which he cannot understand and fortified for trials which he cannot foretell. This influence is the reward of the poet and his beneficiaries have ever been generous in acknowledging their debt. The voices are legion, but let me choose from the multitude as a witness one who was not a dreamer, one who was a child of his age and that not a poetical age, one who loved the excitement of an aristocratic society, insolent with the feeling of class, dissolute and irresponsible, one whose genius exerted itself in a political life, soiled with corruption and intrigue but dealing with events of incomparable gravity. Charles James Fox said of poetry: "It is the great refreshment of the human mind" ... "The greatest thing after all." To quote the words of his biographer, the Poets "consoled him for having missed everything upon which his heart was set; for the loss of power and fortune; for his all but permanent exclusion from the privilege of serving his country and the opportunity of benefiting his friends."

I should like to close this address upon that tone, upon the idea of the supremacy of poetry in life—not a supremacy of detachment, but a supremacy of animating influence—the very inner spirit of life. Fox felt it in his day, when the conditions in the world during and after the French Revolution were not very different from the confused and terrifying conditions we find around us now. He took refreshment in that stream of poetry, lingering by ancient sources of the stream, the crystal pools of Greece and Rome. The poetry of his day did not interest him as greatly as classical poetry, but it did interest him. The poetry of the 18th century was a poetry with the ideals of prose: compared with the Classics and the Elizabethans, it lacked poetic substance. The poetry of our day may not satisfy us, but we have, as Fox had, possession of the Classics and the Elizabethans, and we have, moreover, the poetry of a later day than his that is filled with some of the qualities that he cherished.

If the poetry of our generation is wayward and discomforting, full of experiment that seems to lead nowhither, bitter with the turbulence of an uncertain and ominous time, we may turn from it for refreshment to those earlier days when society appears to us to have been simpler, when there were seers who made clear the paths of life and adorned them with beauty.